Advanced
Apple
Debugging

& Reverse Engineering

By Derek Selander

Advanced Apple Debugging & Reverse Engineering

Derek Selander

Copyright ©2017 Razeware LLC.

Notice of Rights

Notice of Liability

Trademarks

ISBN: 978-1-942878-33-9

Dedications

"I would like to thank my wife, Brittany, for all her love and
support while I silently wept in the fetal position trying to get
this book out the door"

— *Derek Selander*

About the author

Derek Selander is the author of this book. His interest with debugging grew when he started exploring how to make (the now somewhat obsolete) Xcode plugins and iOS tweaks on his jailbroken phone, both of which required exploring and augmenting programs with no source available. In his free time, he enjoys pickup soccer, guitar, and playing with his two doggies, Jake & Squid.

About the editors

Chris Belanger is the editor of this book. Chris Belanger is the Book Team Lead and Lead Editor for raywenderlich.com. If there are words to wrangle or a paragraph to ponder, he's on the case. When he kicks back, you can usually find Chris with guitar in hand, looking for the nearest beach, or exploring the lakes and rivers in his part of the world in a canoe.

Matt Galloway is a software engineer with a passion for excellence. He stumbled into iOS programming when it first was a thing, and has never looked back. When not coding, he likes to brew his own beer.

Darren Ferguson is the final pass editor of this book. He is a Software Developer, with a passion for mobile development, for a leading systems integration provider based out of Northern Virginia in the D.C. metro area. When he's not coding, you can find him enjoying life with his wife and daughter trying to travel as much as possible.

Table of Contents:

Chapter 15: Hooking & Executing Code with dlopen & dlsym 199

Chapter 16: Exploring and Method Swizzling Objective-C Frameworks 217

Section IV: Custom LLDB Commands 237

Chapter 17: Hello Script Bridging 239

Chapter 18: Debugging Script Bridging 249

Introduction

Debugging has a rather bad reputation. I mean, if the developer had a complete understanding of the program, there wouldn't be any bugs and they wouldn't be debugging in the first place, right?

Don't think like that.

There's always going to be bugs in your software — or any software, for that matter. No amount of test coverage imposed by your product manager is going to fix that. In fact, viewing debugging as *just* a process of fixing something that's broken is actually a poisonous way of thinking that will mentally hinder your analytical abilities.

Instead, you should view debugging as simply **a process to better understand a program**. It's a subtle difference, but if you truly believe it, any previous drudgery of debugging simply disappears.

The same negative connotation can also be applied to reverse engineering software. Images of masked hackers stealing bank accounts and credit cards may come to mind, but for this book, reverse engineering really is just debugging without source code — which in turn helps you gain a better understanding of a program or system.

There's nothing wrong with reverse engineering in itself. In fact if debugging was a game, then reverse engineering is simply debugging on the "difficult" setting — which is quite a fun setting if you've been playing the game for a while. :]

In this book, you'll come to realize debugging is an enjoyable process to help you better understand software. Not only will you learn to find bugs faster, but you'll also learn how other developers have solved problems similar to yours. You'll also learn how to create custom, powerful debugging scripts that will help you quickly find answers to any item that piques your interest, whether it's in your code — or someone else's.

Early access

By purchasing this "early access" book, you have advance, exclusive access to this book while it is in development. This release has the following chapters ready:

- Chapter 1: Getting Started

- Chapter 2: Help & Apropos

- Chapter 3: Attaching with LLDB

- Chapter 4: Stopping in Code

- Chapter 5: Expression

- Chapter 6: Thread, Frame and Stepping Around

- Chapter 7: Image

- Chapter 8: Persisting & Customizing Commands

- Chapter 9: Regex Commands

- Chapter 10: Assembly Register Calling Convention

- Chapter 11: Assembly & Memory

- Chapter 12: Assembly and the Stack

- Chapter 13: Hello, Ptrace

- Chapter 14: Dynamic Frameworks

- Chapter 15: Hooking & Executing Code with dlopen & dlsym

- Chapter 16: Exploring and Method Swizzling Objective-C Frameworks

- Chapter 17: Hello Script Bridging

- Chapter 18: Debugging Script Bridging

- Chapter 19: Script Bridging Classes and Hierarchy

- Appendix A: LLDB Cheatsheet

- Appendix B: Python Environment Setup

You may wish to wait until all chapters are ready before reading the book. But if you want a head start or a sneak peek of what's coming, that's what this early access release is for. Send any suggestions, comments, or ideas to support@razeware.com. Your input will actively shape the final version of this book. Thanks!

What you need

To follow along with the tutorials in this book, you'll need the following:

- A **macOS** running **El Capitan** (10.11.6) or later. Earlier versions might work, but they're untested.

- **Xcode 8.2 or later.** Packaged with Xcode is the latest and greatest version of **LLDB**, the debugger you'll use extensively throughout this book. At the time of this writing, the version of LLDB packaged with Xcode is **lldb-360.1.70**.

- **Python 2.7**. LLDB uses Python 2.7 to run its Python scripts. Fortunately, Python 2.7 automatically ships with macOS, as well as with Xcode. You can verify you have the correct version installed by typing `python --version` in `Terminal`.

- **A 64 bit iOS device running iOS 10 or later, and a paid membership to the iOS development program [optional]**. For most chapters in the book, you can run any iOS programs in the Simulator. However, you'll get more out of this book by using a 64-bit iOS device to test out certain ideas or suggestions littered throughout the book.

Once you have these items in place, you'll be able to follow along with almost every chapter in this book. For certain sections, you'll need to disable the **Rootless** security feature in order to use some of the tools (i.e. **DTrace**). This is discussed in Chapter 1.

Who this book is for

The art of debugging code should really be studied by every developer. However, there will be some of you that will get more out of this book. This book is written for:

- Developers who want to become better at debugging with LLDB

- Developers who want to build complex debugging commands with LLDB

- Developers who want to take a deeper dive into the internals of Swift and Objective-C

- Developers who are interested in understanding what they can do to their program through reverse engineering

- Developers who are interested in modern, proactive reverse engineering strategies

- Developers who want to be confident in finding answers to questions they have about their computer or software

This book is for intermediate to advanced developers who want to take their debugging and code exploration game to the next level.

Book source code and forums

You can get the source code for the book here:

www.raywenderlich.com/store/advanced-apple-debugging/source-code

You'll find all the code from the chapters, as well as the solutions to the challenges for your reference.

We've also set up an official forum for the book at raywenderlich.com/forums. This is a great place to ask questions about the book, discuss debugging strategies or to submit any errors you may find.

Custom LLDB scripts repo

Finally, you can find a repo of interesting LLDB Python scripts here:

https://github.com/DerekSelander/LLDB

These scripts will help aid in your debugging/reverse engineering sessions and provide novel ideas for your own LLDB scripts.

PDF Version

We also have a PDF version of this book available, which can be handy if you want a soft copy to take with you, or you want to quickly search for a specific term within the book.

Buying the PDF version of the book also has a few extra benefits: free PDF updates each time we update the book, access to older PDF versions of the book, and you can download the PDF from anywhere, at anytime.

Visit the book store page here: store.raywenderlich.com/products/store/advanced-apple-debugging.

License

By purchasing *Advanced Apple Debugging & Reverse Engineering*, you have the following license:

- You're allowed to use and/or modify the source code in *Advanced Apple Debugging & Reverse Engineering* in as many applications as you want, with no attribution required.

- You're allowed to use and/or modify all art, images, or designs that are included in *Advanced Apple Debugging & Reverse Engineering* in as many applications as you want, but must include this attribution line somewhere inside your game: "Artwork/images/ designs: from the *Advanced Apple Debugging & Reverse Engineering* book, available at www.raywenderlich.com".

- The source code included in *Advanced Apple Debugging & Reverse Engineering* is for your own personal use only. You're **NOT** allowed to distribute or sell the source code in *Advanced Apple Debugging & Reverse Engineering* without prior authorization.

- This book is for your own personal use only. You're **NOT** allowed to sell this book without prior authorization, or distribute it to friends, co-workers, or students; they must to purchase their own copy instead.

All materials provided with this book are provided on an "as is" basis, without warranty of any kind, express or implied, including but not limited to the warranties of merchantability, fitness for a particular purpose and noninfringement. In no event shall the authors or copyright holders be liable for any claim, damages or other liability, whether in an action of contract, tort or otherwise, arising from, out of or in connection with the software or the use or other dealings in the software.

All trademarks and registered trademarks appearing in this guide are the property of their respective owners.

Acknowledgments

We would like to thank many people for their assistance in making this possible:

- **Our families:** For bearing with us in this crazy time as we worked all hours of the night to get this book ready for publication!

- **Everyone at Apple:** For developing an amazing platform, for constantly inspiring us to improve our games and skill sets and for making it possible for many developers to make a living doing what they love!

- **And most importantly, the readers of raywenderlich.com — especially you!** Thank you so much for reading our site and purchasing this book. Your continued readership and support is what makes all of this possible!

About the cover

The Wana (pronounced "vah-na") is a sea urchin native to the Indo-West Pacific region. This sea urchin has two types of spines: a longer hollow spine and a shorter, toxin producing spine. The Wana contains light-sensitive nerves on its skin which can detect potential threats and can move its spines accordingly towards the threat.

Much like finding bugs in a program, stepping on one of these creatures really, really sucks. Pain settles in (inflicted by either your product manager or the sea urchin) and can last up to several hours, even though the issue may remain for an extended period of time. In addition, just like bugs in a program, if you find one of these lovely creatures, there are usually many more in close proximity!

Section I: Beginning LLDB Commands

This section will cover the basics of using LLDB, Apple's software debugger. You'll explore an application named **Signals**, an Objective-C/Swift application that illustrates how Unix signals can be processed within an application. You'll learn some strategies to find and create Swift syntax-style breakpoints as well as Objective-C style breakpoints.

By the end of this section, you'll be able to wield the debugger to perform most of the basic tasks needed for debugging, as well as create your own simple custom commands.

Chapter 1: Getting Started

Chapter 2: Help & Apropos

Chapter 3: Attaching with LLDB

Chapter 4: Stopping in Code

Chapter 5: Expression

Chapter 6: Thread, Frame and Stepping Around

Chapter 7: Image

Chapter 8: Persisting & Customizing Commands

Chapter 9: Regex Commands

Chapter 1: Getting Started

In this chapter, you're going to get acquainted with LLDB and investigate the process of introspecting and debugging a program. You'll start off by introspecting a program you didn't even write — Xcode!

You'll take a whirlwind tour of a debugging session using LLDB and discover the amazing changes you can make to a program you've absolutely zero source code for. This first chapter heavily favors doing over learning, so a lot of the concepts and deep dives into certain LLDB functionality will be saved for later chapters.

Let's get started.

Getting around Rootless

Before you can start working with LLDB, you need to learn about a feature introduced by Apple to thwart malware. Unfortunately, this feature will *also* thwart your attempts to introspect and debug using LLDB and other tools like DTrace. Never fear though, because Apple included a way to turn this feature off — for those who know what they're doing. And you're going to become one of these people who knows what they're doing!

The feature blocking your introspection and debugging attempts is **System Integrity Protection**, also known as **Rootless**. This system restricts what programs can do — even if they have root access — to stop malware from planting itself deep inside your system.

Although Rootless is a substantial leap forward in security, it introduces some annoyances as it makes programs harder to debug. Specifically, it prevents other processes from attaching a debugger to programs Apple signs.

Since this book involves debugging not only your own applications, but any application you're curious about, it's important that you to remove this feature while you learn about debugging so you can inspect any application of your choosing.

If you currently have Rootless enabled, you'll be unable to attach to the majority of Apple's programs. There are exceptions however, such as any apps shipped on the iOS Simulator.

For example, try attaching LLDB to the `Finder` application.

Open up a Terminal window and look for the Finder process, like so:

```
lldb -n Finder
```

You'll notice the following error:

```
error: attach failed: cannot attach to process due to System
Integrity Protection
```

> **Note**: There are many ways to attach to a process, as well as specific configurations when LLDB attaches successfully. To learn more about attaching to a process check out Chapter 3, "Attaching with LLDB".

Disabling Rootless

To disable Rootless, perform the following steps:

1. Restart your macOS machine.

2. When the screen turns blank, hold down **Command + R** until the Apple boot logo appears. This will put your computer into **Recovery Mode**.

3. Now, find the **Utilities** menu from the top and then select **Terminal**.

4. With the Terminal window open, type:

```
csrutil disable; reboot
```

5. Your computer will restart with Rootless disabled.

> **Note**: A safer way to follow along with this book would be to create a dedicated virtual machine using **VMWare** or **VirtualBox** and only disable Rootless on this.

You can verify if you successfully disabled Rootless by trying the same command in Terminal again once you log into your account.

```
lldb -n Finder
```

LLDB should now attach itself to the current Finder process. The output of a successful attach should look like this:

After verifying a successful attach; detach LLDB by either killing the Terminal window, or typing quit and confirming in the LLDB console.

Attaching LLDB to Xcode

Now you've disabled Rootless, and you can attach LLDB to processes, it's time to start your whirlwind tour in debugging. You're first going to look into an application you frequently use in your day-to-day development: Xcode!

Open a new Terminal window. Next, edit the Terminal tab's title by pressing ⌘ + Shift + I. A new popup window will appear. Edit the **Tab Title** to be **LLDB**.

Next, make sure Xcode isn't running, or you'll end up with multiple running instances of Xcode, which could cause confusion.

In the Terminal, type the following:

```
lldb
```

This launches LLDB.

Now, create a new Terminal tab by pressing ⌘ + T. Edit the tab's title again using ⌘ + Shift + I and name the tab **Xcode stderr**. This Terminal tab will contain all output when you print content from the debugger.

Make sure you are on the **Xcode stderr** Terminal tab and type the following:

```
~ $ tty
```

You should see something similar to below:

```
/dev/ttys027
```

Don't worry if yours is different; I'd be surprised if it wasn't. Think of this as the address to your Terminal session.

To illustrate what you'll do with the Xcode stderr tab, create yet another tab and type the following into it:

```
echo "hello debugger" 1>/dev/ttys027
```

Be sure to replace your Terminal path with your unique one obtained from the `tty` command.

Now switch back to the **Xcode stderr** tab. The words `hello debugger` should have popped up. You'll use the same trick to pipe the output of Xcode's stderr to this tab.

Finally, close the third, unnamed tab and navigate back to the LLDB tab.

From there, enter the following into LLDB:

```
(lldb) file /Applications/Xcode.app/Contents/MacOS/Xcode
```

This will set the executable target to Xcode.

> **Note**: If you are using a prerelease version of Xcode then the name and path of Xcode could be different.
>
> You can check the path of the Xcode you are currently running by launching Xcode and typing the following in Terminal:
>
> ```
> $ ps -ef `pgrep -x Xcode`
> ```
>
> Once you have the path of Xcode, use that new path instead.

Now launch the Xcode process from LLDB, replacing `/dev/ttys027` with your Xcode stderr tab's tty address again:

```
(lldb) process launch -e /dev/ttys027 --
```

The launch argument `e` specifies the location of `stderr`. Common logging functionality, such as Objective-C's `NSLog` or Swift's `print` function, outputs to stderr — yes, not stdout! You will print your own logging to stderr later.

Xcode will launch after a moment. Switch over to Xcode and click **File\New\Project...**. Next, select **iOS\Application\Single View Application** and click **Next**. Name the product **Hello Debugger**. Make sure to select **Swift** as the programming language and deselect any options for Unit or UI tests. Click **Next** and save the project wherever you wish.

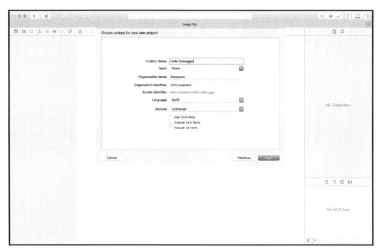

You now have a new Xcode project. Arrange the windows so you can see both Terminal and Xcode.

Navigate to Xcode and open **ViewController.swift**.

> **Note:** You might notice some output on the Xcode stderr Terminal window; this is due to content logged by the authors of Xcode via NSLog or another stderr console printing function.

Finding a class with a click

Now that Xcode is set up and your Terminal debugging windows are correctly created and positioned, it's time to start exploring Xcode using the help of the debugger.

While debugging, knowledge of the Cocoa SDK can be extremely helpful. For example, −[NSView hitTest:] is a useful method that returns the class responsible for the handled click or gesture for an event in the run loop. This method will first get triggered on the containing NSView and recursively drill into the furtherst subview that handles this touch. You can use this knowledge of the Cocoa SDK to help determine the class of the view you've clicked on.

In your LLDB tab, type Ctrl + C to pause the debugger. From there, type:

```
(lldb) breakpoint set -n "-[NSView hitTest:]"
Breakpoint 1: where = AppKit`-[NSView hitTest:], address =
0x000000010338277b
```

This is your first breakpoint of many to come. You'll learn the details of how to create, modify, and delete breakpoints in Chapter 4, "Stopping in Code", but for now simply know you've created a breakpoint on -[NSView hitTest:].

Xcode is now paused thanks to the debugger. Resume the program:

```
(lldb) continue
```

Click anywhere in the Xcode window (or in some cases even moving your cursor over Xcode will do the same); Xcode will instantly pause and LLDB will indicate a breakpoint has been hit.

The hitTest: breakpoint has fired. You can inspect which view was hit by inspecting the **RDI** CPU register. Print it out in LLDB:

```
(lldb) po $rdi
```

This command instructs LLDB to print out the contents of the object at the memory address referenced by what's stored in the RDI assembly register.

Wondering why the command is po? po stands for *print object*. There's also p, which simply prints the contents of RDI. po is usually more useful as it gives the NSObject's description or debugDescription, if available.

Assembly is an important skill to learn if you want to take your debugging to the next level. It will give you insight into Apple's code — even when you don't have any source code to read from. It will give you a greater appreciation of how the Swift compiler team danced in and out of Objective-C with Swift, and it will give you a greater appreciation of how everything works on your Apple devices. You will learn more about registers and assembly in Chapter 10: "Assembly Register Calling Convention".

For now, simply know the $rdi register contains the instance of NSView or subclass the hitTest: method was called upon.

Note the output will produce different results depending on where you clicked and what version of Xcode you're using. It could give a private class specific to Xcode, or it could give you a public class belonging to Cocoa.

In LLDB, type the following to resume the program:

```
(lldb) continue
```

Instead of continuing, Xcode will likely hit another breakpoint for hitTest: and pause exection. This is due to the fact that the hitTest: method is recursively calling this method for all subviews contained within the parent view that was clicked. You can inspect the contents of this breakpoint, but this will soon become tedious since there are so many views that make up Xcode.

Filter breakpoints for important content

Since there are so many NSViews that make up Xcode, you need a way to filter out some of the noise and only stop on the NSView relevant to what you're looking for. This is an example of debugging a frequently-called method, in which you want to find a unique case that helps pinpoint what you're really looking for.

As of Xcode 8, the class responsible for editing your code in the Xcode IDE is a private subclass of NSTextView. If you're from a UIKit background, it's like UITextView, except for macOS. This class acts as the visual coordinator to hand off all your code to other private classes to help compile and create your applications.

Say you want to break only when you click an instance of NSTextView. You can modify the existing breakpoint to stop only on a NSTextView click by using **breakpoint conditions**.

Provided you still have your -[NSView hitTest:] breakpoint set, and it's the only active breakpoint in your LLDB session, you can modify that breakpoint with the following LLDB command:

```
(lldb) breakpoint modify 1 -c "(BOOL)[$rdi isKindOfClass:
[NSTextView class]]"
```

This command modifies breakpoint 1 and sets a condition so the breakpoint only hits if the supplied Boolean is evaluated as true. You've only one breakpoint so far, that's why it's breakpoint number 1.

The Boolean expression is the output of isKindOfClass: to check if the class is a subclass of NSTextView.

After modifying your breakpoint as above, click on the code area in Xcode. LLDB should stop on hitTest:. Print out the instance of the class this method was called on:

```
(lldb) po $rdi
```

Your output should look something like this:

```
<NSTextViewSubclass: 0x14b7a65c0>
    Frame = {{0.00, 0.00}, {1089.00, 1729.00}}, Bounds = {{0.00,
0.00}, {1089.00, 1729.00}}
    Horizontally resizable: NO, Vertically resizable: YES
    MinSize = {1089.00, 259.00}, MaxSize = {10000000.00,
10000000.00}
```

The NSTextViewSubclass above is a placeholder for the private class' name. Take note of it, since you'll need this throughout the rest of the chapter. You'll also have a unique reference in your own output. For this example, the reference to this memory address is 0x14b7a65c0, but your memory address will be different.

Since this isn't immediately apparent as an NSTextView subclass, you can check if this instance is an NSTextViewsubclass by repeatedly figuring out the class's superclass.

```
(lldb) po [$rdi superclass]
```

... Keep on going until you find it.

```
(lldb) po [[$rdi superclass] superclass]
```

Wait — that's Objective-C. You should confirm this is the case in Swift. To do this, first enter the following:

```
(lldb) ex -l swift -- import Foundation
(lldb) ex -l swift -- import AppKit
```

The ex command (short for expression) lets you evaluate code. -l swift tells LLDB this is Swift code. These commands tell LLDB all it needs to know about Foundation and AppKit. You'll need these in the next two commands.

Enter the following, replacing 0x14bdd9b50 with the memory address of your NSTextView subclass you found previously:

```
(lldb) ex -l swift -o -- unsafeBitCast(0x14bdd9b50, to:
NSObject.self)
(lldb) ex -l swift -o -- unsafeBitCast(0x14bdd9b50, to:
NSObject.self) is NSTextView
```

These commands print out the NSTextView subclass, and then check if it's an NSTextView subclass — but this time using Swift! You'll see something similar to below:

```
(lldb) ex -l swift -o -- unsafeBitCast(0x14bdd9b50,
NSObject.self)
<NSTextViewSubclass: 0x14b7a65c0>
    Frame = {{0.00, 0.00}, {1089.00, 1729.00}}, Bounds = {{0.00,
0.00}, {1089.00, 1729.00}}
    Horizontally resizable: NO, Vertically resizable: YES
    MinSize = {1089.00, 259.00}, MaxSize = {10000000.00,
10000000.00}

(lldb) ex -l swift -o -- unsafeBitCast(0x14bdd9b50,
NSObject.self) is NSTextView
true
```

Using Swift requires much more typing. In addition, when stopping the debugger out of the blue, or on Objective-C code, LLDB will default to Objective-C. It's possible to alter this, but this book prefers to use Objective-C since the Swift REPL can be brutal for error checking in the debugger.

For now, you'll use the Objective-C debugging context to aid in manipulating this NSTextView.

Since this is a subclass of NSTextView, all the methods of NSTextView apply. Enter the following:

```
(lldb) po [$rdi string]
```

This should print out the contents of whatever file you have open in Xcode.

It's even possible to set the contents of the text view:

```
(lldb) po [$rdi setString:@"// Yay! Debugging!"]
(lldb) po [CATransaction flush]
```

Notice the text in your Xcode window has changed. Neat! :]

Hunting for private classes and methods in modules

Going back to the NSTextView subclass — from here on in, referred to as NSTextViewSubclass — there are likely some additional or overridden methods in there. But how do you go about finding them? It's not likely Apple would publish documentation about the private classes in Xcode.

Enter the following, replacing NSTextViewSubclass with the class you found your text view to be:

```
(lldb) image lookup -rn 'NSTextViewSubclass\ '
```

This command lets you introspect the running binary and all loaded dynamic libraries. The r option instructs it to use a regular expression search. The n option instructs it to search functions or symbols by name.

You'll see a list of methods your NSTextView subclass implements! How cool is that?

If you want to learn about querying code using the image lookup commands, check out Chapter 7, "Image".

Swizzling with block injection

The Objective-C runtime can be a truly useful aid when reverse engineering binaries. You're now going to experience the power of the Objective-C runtime and get a glimpse of what you can do with it inside LLDB.

First, import the Objective-C runtime information using the headers linked in the Foundation library:

```
(lldb) po @import Foundation
```

Although the code compiled into Xcode knows about certain methods, the LLDB process doesn't know about them. Importing Foundation lets you access all parts of the Objective-C runtime from within LLDB.

Now type po into the LLDB console without entering anything else, like so:

```
(lldb) po
```

LLDB will go into the multi-line form. You'll see the following:

```
(lldb) po
Enter expressions, then terminate with an empty line to
evaluate:
  1:
```

From here, you can enter multiple expressions for evaluation. Add the following:

```
@import Cocoa;
id $class = [NSObject class];
SEL $sel = @selector(init);
void *$method = (void *)class_getInstanceMethod($class, $sel);
IMP $oldImp = (IMP)method_getImplementation($method);
```

Press Return again to enter a blank line. LLDB will then execute all of your expressions in order.

> **Note:** Be *very* careful when typing in this code since it's only verified after you press Return. If you make a mistake you'll have to start all over, although you do have the up arrow to use for history recall. Make sure you remember those semicolons!

You've created several variables in memory through LLDB: $class, $sel, and $oldImp. Variables in LLDB need to be prefixed with dollar sign. Other than that, the code looks the same as you would expect if you wrote it in Xcode!

Try printing out some of these variables to ensure you created them correctly:

```
(lldb) po $class
NSObject
(lldb) po $oldImp
(libobjc.A.dylib`-[NSObject init])
```

Now return to the multi-line feature of LLDB by typing po.

Create a new IMP using the imp_implementationWithBlock function:

```
id (^$block)(id) = ^id(id object) {
  if ((BOOL)[object isKindOfClass:[NSView class]]) {
    fprintf(stderr, "%s\n", (char *)[[[object class]
description] UTF8String]);
  }
  return object;
};
IMP $newImp = (IMP)imp_implementationWithBlock($block);
method_setImplementation($method, $newImp);
```

Once again, enter a blank line at the end to tell LLDB to process the expressions.

The aim of this code is to swizzle the –[NSObject init] method you just found. By default, –[NSObject init] doesn't do anything except return itself. The block checks to see if the object in question is of type NSView. If so, the object's class is printed out.

Here's how it works:

1. You create a block that takes an object reference.

2. The block checks if the object passed in is of type NSView.

3. If so, it prints a description of the view to stderr, which will appear on your **Xcode stderr** Terminal tab.

4. It then returns `object`, to perform the equivalent implementation of `-[NSObject init]` that it's swizzling. Ideally, swizzling these implementations would have been cleaner, and you could simply execute `$oldImp` with the right parameters. However, there is a bug in LLDB that will crash when executing IMPs inside of a block.

5. Finally, a new `IMP` is created from the block, and the method implementation is set to this new `IMP`. This has therefore swizzled `-[NSObject init]` with your new implementation.

Next, resume debugging by typing `continue`.

Observe the console output in the **Xcode stderr** Terminal tab. Check out all the classes created as you navigate around Xcode by clicking on different items.

You can do this to any program you attach LLDB to. If a particular Apple or third party application piques your interest, you can explore their class naming convention using the same trick. The only difference is that you must change the launch path to the appropriate executable.

Where to go from here?

This was a breadth-first, whirlwind introduction to using LLDB and attaching to a process where you don't have any source code to aid you. This chapter glossed over a lot of detail, but the goal was to get you right into the debugging process. There are lots of chapters remaining to get you into the details!

Keep reading to learn the essentials in the remainder of Section 1. Happy debugging!

Chapter 2: Help & Apropos

Just like any respectable developer tool, LLDB ships with a healthy amount of documentation. Knowing how to navigate through this documentation — including some of the more obscure command flags — is essential to mastering LLDB.

The "help" command

Open a Terminal window and type lldb. The LLDB prompt will appear. From there, simply type the help command:

```
(lldb) help
```

This will dump out all available commands, including the custom commands loaded from your ~/.lldbinit — but more on that later.

There are quite a few commands one can use with LLDB.

However, many commands have numerous subcommands, which in turn can have subcommands, which also have their own associated documentation. I told you it was a healthy amount of documentation!

Take the `breakpoint` command for instance. Run the documentation for `breakpoint` by typing the following:

```
(lldb) help breakpoint
```

You'll see the following output:

```
    Commands for operating on breakpoints (see 'help b' for
shorthand.)

Syntax: breakpoint <subcommand> [<command-options>]

The following subcommands are supported:

    clear   -- Delete or disable breakpoints matching the
specified source file and line.
    command -- Commands for adding, removing and listing LLDB
commands executed when a breakpoint is hit.
    delete  -- Delete the specified breakpoint(s).  If no
breakpoints are specified, delete them all.
    disable -- Disable the specified breakpoint(s) without
deleting them.  If none are specified, disable all breakpoints.
    enable  -- Enable the specified disabled breakpoint(s). If
no breakpoints are specified, enable all of them.
    list    -- List some or all breakpoints at configurable
levels of detail.
    modify  -- Modify the options on a breakpoint or set of
breakpoints in the executable.  If no breakpoint is specified,
            acts on the last created breakpoint.  With the
exception of -e, -d and -i, passing an empty argument clears
            the modification.
    name    -- Commands to manage name tags for breakpoints
    set     -- Sets a breakpoint or set of breakpoints in the
executable.

For more help on any particular subcommand, type 'help <command>
<subcommand>'.
```

From there, you can see several supported subcommands. Look up the documentation for `breakpoint name` by typing the following:

```
(lldb) help breakpoint name
```

You'll see the following output:

```
The following subcommands are supported:

      add    -- Add a name to the breakpoints provided.
      delete -- Delete a name from the breakpoints provided.
      list   -- List either the names for a breakpoint or the
breakpoints for a given name.

For more help on any particular subcommand, type 'help <command>
<subcommand>'.
```

If you can't quite understand `breakpoint name` at the moment, don't worry — you'll become intimately familiar with breakpoints and all of the subsequent commands soon. For now, the `help` command is the most important command you can remember.

The "apropos" command

Sometimes you don't know the name of the command you're searching for, but you know a certain word or phrase that might point you in the right direction. The `apropos` command can do this for you; it's a bit like using a search engine to find something on the web.

`apropos` will do a case-insensitive search for any word or string against the LLDB documentation and return any matching results. For example, try searching for anything pertaining to Swift:

```
(lldb) apropos swift
```

You'll see the following output:

```
The following built-in commands may relate to 'swift':
   breakpoint set            -- Sets a breakpoint or set of
breakpoints in the executable.
   expression                -- Evaluate an expression (ObjC++ or
Swift) in the current program context, using user defined
variables and variables
                              currently in scope.
   language swift            -- A set of commands for operating on
the Swift Language Runtime.
   language swift demangle -- Demangle a Swift mangled name
   language swift refcount -- Inspect the reference count data
for a Swift object

The following settings variables may relate to 'swift':
```

```
   target.swift-framework-search-paths -- List of directories to
be searched when locating frameworks for Swift.
   target.swift-module-search-paths -- List of directories to be
searched when locating modules for Swift.
   target.use-all-compiler-flags -- Try to use compiler flags for
all modules when setting up the Swift expression parser, not
just the main executable.
```

This dumped everything that might pertain to the word Swift: first the commands, and then the LLDB settings which can be used to control how LLDB operates.

You can also use `apropos` to search for a particular sentence. For example, if you were searching for something that can help with reference counting, you might try the following:

```
(lldb) apropos "reference count"
The following built-in commands may relate to 'reference count':
   language swift refcount -- Inspect the reference count data
for a Swift object
   target modules list    -- List current executable and
dependent shared library images.
```

Notice the quotes surrounding the words `"reference count"`. `apropos` will only accept one argument to search for, so the quotes are necessary to treat the input as a single argument.

Isn't that neat? `apropos` is a handy tool for querying. It's not quite as sophisticated as modern internet search engines, however with some playing around you can usually find what you're looking for.

Where to go from here?

It's easy to forget the onslaught of LLDB commands that will soon come, but try to commit these two commands, `help` and `apropos`, to heart. They're the foundation for querying information on commands and you'll be using them all the time as you master debugging.

Chapter 3: Attaching with LLDB

Now that you've learned about the two most essential commands, `help` and `apropos`, it's time to investigate how LLDB attaches itself to processes. You'll learn all the different ways you can attach LLDB to processes using various options, as well as what happens behind the scenes when attaching to processes.

The phrase of LLDB "attaching" is actually a bit misleading. A program named `debugserver` (found in `Xcode.app/Contents/SharedFrameworks/LLDB.framework/Resources/`) is responsible for attaching to a target process.

If it's a remote process, such as an iOS, watchOS or tvOS application running on a remote device, a remote `debugserver` gets launched on that remote device. It's LLDB's job to launch, connect, and coordinate with the `debugserver` to handle all the interactions in debugging an application.

Attaching to an existing process

As you've already seen in Chapter 1, you can attach to a process like so:

```
lldb -n Xcode
```

However, there are other ways to do the same thing. You can attach to Xcode by providing the process identifier, or **PID**, of a running program.

Open Xcode, then open a new `Terminal` session, and finally run the following:

```
pgrep -x Xcode
```

This will output the PID of the Xcode process.

Next, run the following, replacing `89944` with the number output from the command above:

```
lldb -p 89944
```

This tells LLDB to attach to the process with the given PID. In this case, this is your running Xcode process.

Attaching to a future process

The previous command only addresses a running process. If Xcode isn't running, or is already attached to a debugger, the previous commands will fail. How can you catch a process that is about to be launched, if you don't know the PID yet?

You can do that with the -w argument, which causes LLDB to wait until a process launches with a PID or executable name matching the criteria supplied to the -w argument.

For example, kill your existing LLDB session by pressing **Ctrl + D** in your Terminal window and type the following:

```
lldb -n Finder -w
```

This will tell LLDB to attach to the process named Finder whenever it next launches. Next, open a new Terminal tab, and enter the following:

```
pkill Finder
```

This will kill the Finder process and force it to restart. macOS will automatically relaunch Finder when it's killed. Switch back to your first Terminal tab and you'll notice LLDB has now attached itself to the newly created Finder process.

Another way to attach to a process is to specify the path to the executable and manually launch the process at your convenience:

```
lldb —f /System/Library/CoreServices/Finder.app/Contents/MacOS/
Finder
```

This will set Finder as the executable to launch. Once you're ready to begin the debug session, simply type the following into the LLDB session:

```
(lldb) process launch
```

> **Note:** An interesting side effect is that stderr output (i.e. NSLog & company) are automatically sent to the Terminal window when manually launching a process. Other LLDB attaching configurations don't do this automatically.

Options while launching

The process launch command comes with a suite of options worth further exploration. If you're curious and want to see the full list of all options available for process launch, simply type help process launch.

Close previous LLDB sessions, open a new Terminal window and type the following:

```
lldb —f /bin/ls
```

This tells LLDB to use /bin/ls (the file listing command) as the target executable. You'll see the following output:

```
(lldb) target create "/bin/ls"
Current executable set to '/bin/ls' (x86_64).
```

Since ls is a quick program (it launches, does its job, then exits) you'll run this program multiple times with different arguments to explore what each does.

Try launching ls from LLDB with no arguments at first. Enter the following:

```
(lldb) process launch
```

You'll see the following output:

```
Process 7681 launched: '/bin/ls' (x86_64)
... # Omitted directory listing output
Process 7681 exited with status = 0 (0x00000000)
```

An ls process will launch in the directory you started in. You can change the current working directory by telling LLDB where to launch with the –w option. Try the following:

```
(lldb) process launch -w /Applications
```

This will launch ls from within the /Applications directory. This is equivalent to the following:

```
$ cd /Applications
$ ls
```

There's yet *another* way to do this. Instead of telling LLDB to change to a directory then run the program, you can pass arguments to the program directly.

Try the following:

```
(lldb) process launch -- /Applications
```

This has the same effect as the previous command, but this time it's doing the following:

```
$ ls /Applications
```

Again, this spits out all your macOS programs, but you specified an argument instead of changing the starting directory. What about specifying your desktop directory as a launch argument? Try running this:

```
(lldb) process launch -- ~/Desktop
```

You'll see the following:

```
Process 8103 launched: '/bin/ls' (x86_64)
ls: ~/Desktop: No such file or directory
Process 8103 exited with status = 1 (0x00000001)
```

Uh-oh, that didn't work. You need the shell to expand the *tilde* in the argument. Try this instead:

```
(lldb) process launch -X true -- ~/Desktop
```

The –X argument expands any shell arguments you provide, such as the tilde. There's a shortcut in LLDB for this: simply type run. To learn more about creating your own command shortcuts, check out Chapter 8, "Persisting and Customizing Commands".

Type the following to see the documentation for run:

```
(lldb) help run
```

You'll see the following:

```
...
Command Options Usage:
  run [<run-args>]


'run' is an abbreviation for 'process launch -X true --'
```

See? It's an abbreviation of the command you just ran! Give the command a go by typing the following:

```
(lldb) run ~/Desktop
```

What about changing output to a different location? You've already tried changing stderr to a different Terminal tab in Chapter 1 using the –e flag, but how about stdout?

Type the following:

```
(lldb) process launch -o /tmp/ls_output.txt -- /Applications
```

The –o option tells LLDB to pipe stdout to the given file.

You'll see the following output:

```
Process 15194 launched: '/bin/ls' (x86_64)
Process 15194 exited with status = 0 (0x00000000)
```

Notice there's no output directly from ls.

Open another Terminal tab and run the following:

```
cat /tmp/ls_output.txt
```

It's your applications directory output again, as expected!

There is also an option –i for stdin as well. First, type the following:

```
(lldb) target delete
```

This removes ls as the target. Next, type this:

```
(lldb) target create /usr/bin/wc
```

This sets /usr/bin/wc as the new target. wc can be used to count characters, words or lines in the input given to stdin.

You've swapped target executables for your LLDB session from ls to wc. Now you need some data to provide to wc. Open a new Terminal tab and enter the following:

```
echo "hello world" > /tmp/wc_input.txt
```

You'll use this file to give wc some input.

Switch back to the LLDB session and enter the following:

```
(lldb) process launch —i /tmp/wc_input.txt
```

You'll see the following output:

```
Process 24511 launched: '/usr/bin/wc' (x86_64)
       1       2      12
Process 24511 exited with status = 0 (0x00000000)
```

This would be functionally equivalent to the following:

```
$ wc < /tmp/wc_input.txt
```

Sometimes you don't want a stdin (standard input). This is useful for GUI programs such as Xcode, but doesn't really help for Terminal commands such as ls and wc.

To illustrate, run the wc target with no arguments, like so:

```
(lldb) run
```

The program will just sit there and hang because it's expecting to read something from stdin.

Give it some input by typing in hello world, press Return, then press **Control + D**, which is the end of transmission character. wc will parse the input and exit. You'll see the same output as you did earlier when using the file as the input.

Now, launch the process like this:

```
(lldb) process launch —n
```

You'll see that wc exits immediately with the following output:

```
Process 28849 launched: '/usr/bin/wc' (x86_64)
Process 28849 exited with status = 0 (0x00000000)
```

The -n option tells LLDB not to create a stdin; therefore wc has no data to work with and exists immediately.

Where to go from here?

There are a few more interesting options to play with, and you'll explore them later in the book. In later chapters, you'll explore how LLDB attaches itself to a remote debugsever on iOS.

For now, try attaching to GUI and non-GUI programs alike. Try running Terminal commands that expect stdin or arguments and see what you find!

Chapter 4: Stopping in Code

Whether you're using Swift, Objective-C, C++, C, or an entirely different language in your technology stack, you'll need to learn how to create breakpoints. It's easy to click on the side panel in Xcode to create a breakpoint using the GUI, but the LLDB console can give you much more control over breakpoints.

In this chapter, you're going to learn all about breakpoints and how to create them using LLDB.

Signals

For this chapter, you'll be looking at a project I've supplied; it's called **Signals** and you'll find it in the resources bundle for this chapter.

Open up the **Signals** project using Xcode. **Signals** is a basic master-detail project themed as an American football app that displays some rather nerdily-named offensive play calls.

Internally, this project montors several Unix signals and displays them when the **Signals** program receives them.

Unix signals are a basic form of interprocess communication. For example, one of the signals, `SIGSTOP`, can be used to save the state and pause execution of a process, while its counterpart, `SIGCONT`, is sent to a program to resume execution. Both of these signals can be used by a debugger to pause and continue a program's execution.

This is an interesting application on several fronts, because it not only explores Unix signal handling, but also highlights what happens when a controlling process (LLDB) handles the passing of Unix signals to the controlled process. By default, LLDB has custom actions for handling different signals. Some signals are not passed onto the controlled process while LLDB is attached.

In order to display a signal, you can either `raise` a Signal from within the application, or send a signal externally from a different application, like Terminal.

In addition, there's a `UISwitch` that toggles the signal handling blocking, which calls the C function `sigprocmask` to disable or enable the signal handlers.

Finally, the Signal application has a **Timeout** bar button which raises the `SIGSTOP` signal from within the application, essentially "freezing" the program. However, if LLDB is attached to the Signals program (and by default it will be, when you build and run through Xcode), calling `SIGSTOP` will allow you to inspect the execution state with LLDB while in Xcode.

Make sure the **iPhone 7 Simulator** is selected as the target. Build and run the app. Once the project is running, navigate to the Xcode console and pause the debugger.

Resume Xcode and keep an eye on the Simulator. A new row will be added to the UITableView whenever the debugger stops then resumes execution. This is achieved by Signals monitoring the `SIGSTOP` Unix signal event and adding a row to the data model whenever it occurs. When a process is stopped, any new signals will not be immediately processed because the program is sort of, well, stopped.

Xcode breakpoints

Before you go off learning the cool, shiny breakpoints through the LLDB console, it's worth covering what you can achieve through Xcode alone.

Symbolic breakpoints are a great debugging feature of Xcode. They let you set a breakpoint on a certain **symbol** within your application. An example of a symbol is -[NSObject init], which refers to the init method of NSObject instances.

The neat thing about symbolic breakpoints in Xcode is that once you enter a symbolic breakpoint, you don't have to type it in again the next time the program launches.

You're now going to try using a symbolic breakpoint to show all the instances of NSObject being created.

Kill the app if it's currently running. Next, switch to the **Breakpoint Navigator**. In the bottom left, click the plus button to select the **Symbolic Breakpoint...** option.

A popup will appear. In the **Symbol** part of the popup type: -[NSObject init]. Under **Action**, select **Add Action** and then select **Debugger Command** from the dropdown. Next, enter po [$arg1 class] in the box below.

Finally, select **Automatically continue after evaluating actions**. Your popup should look similar to below:

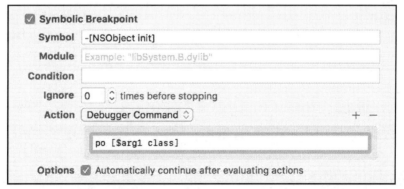

Build and run the app. Xcode will dump all the names of the classes it initializes while running the **Signals** program through the console... which, upon viewing, is quite a lot.

What you've done here is set a breakpoint that fires each time -[NSObject init] is called. When the breakpoint fires, a command runs in LLDB, and execution of the program continues automatically.

> **Note:** You'll learn how to properly use and manipulate registers in Chapter 10, "Assembly, Registers and Calling Convention", but for now, simply know **$arg1** is synonymous to the **$rdi** register and can be loosely thought of as holding the instance of a class when init is called.

Once you've finished inspecting all the class names dumped out, delete the symbolic breakpoint by right-clicking the breakpoint in the breakpoint navigator and selecting **Delete Breakpoint**.

In addition to symbolic breakpoints, Xcode also supports several types of error breakpoints. One of these is the **Exception Breakpoint**. Sometimes something goes wrong in your program and it just simply crashes. Your first reaction to this should be to enable an exception breakpoint, which will fire every time an exception is thrown. Xcode will show you the offending line, which greatly aids in hunting down the culprit responsible for the crash.

Finally, there is the **Swift Error Breakpoint**, which stops any time Swift throws an error by essentially creating a breakpoint on the swift_willThrow method. This is a great option to use if you're working with any APIs that can be error-prone, as it lets you diagnose the situation quickly without making false assumptions about the correctness of your code.

LLDB breakpoint syntax

Now that you've had a crash course in using the IDE debugging features of Xcode, it's time to learn how to create breakpoints through the LLDB console. In order to create useful breakpoints, you need to learn how to query what you're looking for.

The image command is an excellent tool to help introspect details that will be vital for setting breakpoints.

There are two configurations you'll use in this book for code hunting. The first is the following:

```
(lldb) image lookup -n "-[UIViewController viewDidLoad]"
```

This command dumps the load address of the function for –[UIViewController viewDidLoad]. The –n argument tells LLDB to look up either a symbol or function name. The output will be similar to below:

```
1 match found in /Applications/Xcode.app/Contents/Developer/
Platforms/iPhoneSimulator.platform/Developer/SDKs/
iPhoneSimulator.sdk//System/Library/Frameworks/UIKit.framework/
UIKit:
        Address: UIKit[0x00000000001c67c8] (UIKit.__TEXT.__text
+ 1854120)
        Summary: UIKit`-[UIViewController viewDidLoad]
```

Another useful, similar command is this:

```
(lldb) image lookup -rn test
```

This does a case-sensitive regex lookup for the word "test". If the lowercase word "test" is found anywhere, in any function, in any of the modules (i.e. UIKit, Foundation, Core Data, etc) loaded in the current executable (that are not stripped out of a release builds... more on that later), this command will spit out the results.

> **Note:** Use the –n argument when you want exact matches (with quotes around your query if it contains spaces) and use the –rn arguments to do a regex search. The –n only command helps figure out the exact parameters to match a breakpoint, especially when dealing with Swift, while the –rn argument option will be heavily favored in this book since a smart regex can eliminate quite a bit of typing — as you'll soon find out.

Objective-C properties

Learning how to query loaded code is essential for learning how to create breakpoints on that code. Both Objective-C and Swift have specific property signatures when they're created by the compiler, which results in different breakpoint strategies.

For example, the following Objective-C class is declared in the Signals project:

```
@interface TestClass : NSObject
@property (nonatomic, strong) NSString *name;
@end
```

The compiler will generate code for both the setter and getter of the property name. The getter will look like the following:

```
-[TestClass name]
```

...while the setter would look like below:

```
-[TestClass setName:]
```

Build and run the app, then pause the debugger. Next, verify these methods do exist by typing the following into LLDB:

```
(lldb) image lookup -n "-[TestClass name]"
```

In the console output, you'll get something similar to below:

```
1 match found in /Users/derekselander/Library/Developer/Xcode/
DerivedData/Signals-bqrjxlceauwfuihjesxmgfodimef/Build/Products/
Debug-iphonesimulator/Signals.app/Signals:
        Address: Signals[0x0000000100001470]
(Signals.__TEXT.__text + 0)
        Summary: Signals`-[TestClass name] at TestClass.h:28
```

LLDB will dump information about the function included in the executable. The output may look scary, but there are some good tidbits here.

The console output tells you LLDB was able to find out this function was implemented in the Signals executable, at an offset of `0x0000000100001470` in the __TEXT section to be exact. LLDB was also able to tell that this method was declared on line 28 in `TestClass.h`.

You can check for the setter as well, like so:

```
(lldb) image lookup -n "-[TestClass setName:]"
```

You'll get output similar to the previous command, this time showing the implementation address and of the setter's declaration for `name`.

Swift properties

The syntax for a property is much different in Swift. Take a look at the code in **SwiftTestClass.swift** which contains the following:

```
class SwiftTestClass: NSObject {
    var name: String!
}
```

Make sure the **Signals** project is running and paused in LLDB. Feel free to clear the LLDB console by typing **Command + K** in the debug window to start fresh.

In the LLDB console, type the following:

```
(lldb) image lookup -rn Signals.SwiftTestClass.name.setter
```

You'll get output similar to below:

```
2 matches found in /Users/derekselander/Library/Developer/Xcode/
DerivedData/Signals-bqrjxlceauwfuihjesxmgfodimef/Build/Products/
Debug-iphonesimulator/Signals.app/Signals:
        Address: Signals[0x000000010000aba0]
(Signals.__TEXT.__text + 38704)
        Summary: Signals`@objc
Signals.SwiftTestClass.name.setter :
Swift.ImplicitlyUnwrappedOptional<Swift.String> at
SwiftTestClass.swift         Address: Signals[0x000000010000ac60]
(Signals.__TEXT.__text + 38896)
        Summary: Signals`Signals.SwiftTestClass.name.setter :
Swift.ImplicitlyUnwrappedOptional<Swift.String> at
SwiftTestClass.swift
```

Hunt for the information after the word **Summary** in the output. There are a couple of interesting things to note here.

First, two symbols were found. The first has the same name as the second; however, the first is prefaced with `@objc`. This is a special function added by the compiler and known as a bridging function. This helps Objective-C and Swift play nicely together.

Second, did you see how long the function name is!? This whole thing needs to be typed out for *one* valid Swift breakpoint! If you wanted to set a breakpoint on this setter, you'd have to write something similar to below:

```
(lldb) b Signals.SwiftTestClass.name.setter :
Swift.ImplicitlyUnwrappedOptional<Swift.String>
```

Using regular expressions is an attractive alternative to typing out this monstrosity.

Apart from the length of the Swift function name you produced, note how the Swift property is formed. The function signature containing the property `name` has the word `setter` immediately following the property. Perhaps the same convention works for the getter method as well?

Try hunting for the `SwiftTestClass` setter and getter for the `name` property, at the same time, using the following regular expression query:

```
(lldb) image lookup -rn Signals.SwiftTestClass.name
```

This uses a regex query to dump everything that contains the phrase `Signals.SwiftTestClass.name`.

Since this is a regular expression, the periods (.) are evaluated as wildcards, which in turn matches periods in the actual function signatures.

You'll get a fair bit of output, but hone in every time you see the word **Summary** in the console ouput. You'll find the output matches the getter, (`Signals.SwiftTestClass.name.getter`) the setter, (`Signals.SwiftTestClass.name.setter`), the `@objc` bridging equivalents, as well as a method containing `materializeForSet`, which you'll learn about later.

There's a pattern for the function names for Swift properties:

```
ModuleName.Classname.PropertyName.(getter|setter)
```

The ability to dump methods, find a pattern, and narrow your search scope is a great way to uncover the Swift/Objective-C language internals as you work to create smart breakpoints in your code.

Finally... creating breakpoints

Now you know how to query the existence of functions and methods in your code, it's time to start creating breakpoints on them.

If you already have the Signals app running, stop and restart the application, then press the pause button to stop the application and bring up the LLDB console.

There are several different ways to create breakpoints. The most basic way is to simply type the letter **b** followed by the name of your breakpoint. This is fairly easy in Objective-C and C, since the names are short and easy to type (e.g. `-[NSObject init]`). They're quite tricky to type in C++ and Swift, since the compiler turns your methods into symbols with rather long names.

Since UIKit is primarily Objective-C (at the time of this writing at least!), try creating a breakpoint using the b argument, like so:

```
(lldb) b -[UIViewController viewDidLoad]
```

You'll see the following output:

```
Breakpoint 1: where = UIKit`-[UIViewController viewDidLoad],
address = 0x0000000102bbd788
```

When you create a valid breakpoint, the console will spit out some information about that breakpoint. In this particular case, the breakpoint was created as **Breakpoint 1** since this was the first breakpoint in this particular debugging session. As you create more breakpoints, this breakpoint ID will increment.

Resume the debugger. Once you've resumed execution, a new SIGSTOP signal will be displayed. Tap on the cell to bring up the detail UIViewController. The program should pause when viewDidLoad of the detail view controller is called.

> **Note:** Like a lot of shorthand commands, b is an abbreviation for another, longer LLDB command. Try running help with the b command to figure out the actual command yourself and learn all the cool tricks b can do under the hood.

In addition to the b command, there's another longer breakpoint set command, which has a slew of options available. You'll explore these options over the next couple of sections. Many of the commands will stem from various options of the breakpoint set command.

Regex breakpoints and scope

Another extremely powerful command is the regular expression breakpoint, rbreak, which is an abbreviation for breakpoint set -r %1. You can quickly create many breakpoints using smart regular expressions to stop wherever you want.

Going back to the previous example with the egregiously long Swift property function names, instead of typing:

```
(lldb) b Breakpoints.SwiftTestClass.name.setter :
Swift.ImplicitlyUnwrappedOptional<Swift.String>
```

You can simply type:

```
(lldb) rb SwiftTestClass.name.setter
```

Although this is much shorter, there is one annoyance with this breakpoint. This breakpoint will capture both the name setter as well as the Objective-C bridging method, forcing you to stop twice when this method gets called.

You can augment the breakpoint by adding ^(@).* to the breakpoint, essentially saying "don't let the function start with the @ character." In a future chapter, you'll build a command that performs a regex search to automatically filter out these bridging functions.

For now you'll just have to deal with two breakpoints. To be even more brief, you could simply use the following:

```
(lldb) rb name\.setter
```

This will produce a breakpoint on anything that contains the phrase `name.setter`. This will work if you know you don't have any other Swift properties called `name` within your project; otherwise you'll create multiple breakpoints for each of them.

Now try breaking on every Objective-C instance method of UIViewController. Type the following into your LLDB session:

```
(lldb) rb '\-\[UIViewController\ '
```

The ugly back slashes are escape characters to indicate you want the literal character to be in the regular expression search. As a result, this query breaks on every method containing the string `-[UIViewController` followed by a space.

But wait... what about Objective-C categories? They take on the form of `(-|+)` `[ClassName(categoryName) method]`. You'll have to rewrite the regular expression to include categories as well.

Type the following into your LLDB session and when prompted type y to confirm:

```
(lldb) breakpoint delete
```

This command deletes all the breakpoints you have set.

Next, type the following:

```
(lldb) rb '\-\[UIViewController(\(\w+\))?\ '
```

This provides an optional parenthesis with one or more alphanumeric characters followed by a space, after `UIViewController` in the breakpoint.

Regex breakpoints let you capture a wide variety of breakpoints with a single expression.

You can limit the scope of your breakpoints to a certain file, using the `-f` option. For example, you could type the following:

```
(lldb) rb . -f DetailViewController.swift
```

This would be useful if you were debugging **DetailViewController.swift**. It would set a breakpoint on all the property getters/setters, blocks/closures, extensions/categories, and functions/methods in this file. `-f` is known as a **scope limitation**.

If you were completely crazy and a fan of pain, you could omit the scope limitation and simply do this:

```
(lldb) rb .
```

This will create a breakpoint on everything... Yes, everything! This will create breakpoints on all the code in the **Signals** project, all the code in UIKit as well as Foundation, all the event run loop code that gets fired at (hopefully) 60 hertz — everything. As a result, expect to type `continue` in the debugger a fair bit if you execute this.

There are other ways to limit the scope of your searches. You can limit to a single library using the −s option:

```
(lldb) rb . -s Commons
```

This would set a breakpoint on everything within the `Commons` library, which is a dynamic library contained within the **Signals** project.

This is not limited to your code; you can use the same tactic to create a breakpoint on every function in UIKit, like so:

```
(lldb) rb . -s UIKit
```

Even *that* is still a little crazy. There are a lot of methods — around 66,189 UIKit methods in iOS 10.0. How about only stopping on the first method in UIKit you hit, and simply continue? The −o option offers a solution for this. It creates what is known as a "one-shot" breakpoint. When these breakpoints hit, the breakpoint is deleted. So it'll only ever hit once.

To see this in action, type the following in your LLDB session:

```
(lldb) breakpoint delete
(lldb) rb . -s UIKit -o
```

> **Note:** Be patient while your computer executes this command, as LLDB has to create a lot of breakpoints. Also make sure you are using the Simulator, or else you'll wait for a very long time! :]

Next, continue the debugger, and click on a cell in the table view. The debugger stops on the first UIKit method this action calls. Finally, continue the debugger, and the breakpoint will no longer fire.

Modifying and removing breakpoints

Now that you've a basic understanding of how to create these breakpoints, you might be wondering how you can alter them. What if you found the object you were interested in and wanted to delete the breakpoint, or temporarily disable it? What if you need to modify the breakpoint to perform a specific action next time it triggers?

First, you'll need to discover how to uniquely identify a breakpoint or a group of breakpoints. You can also name breakpoints when you create then using the –N option... if working with numbers is not really your thing. :]

Build and run the app to get a clean LLDB session. Next, pause the debugger and type the following into the LLDB session:

```
(lldb) b main
```

The output will look something like this:

```
Breakpoint 1: 20 locations.
```

This creates a breakpoint with 20 locations, matching the function "main" in various modules.

In this case, the breakpoint ID is 1, because it's the first breakpoint you created in this session. To see details about this breakpoint you can use the breakpoint list subcommand. Type the following:

```
(lldb) breakpoint list 1
```

The output will look similar to below:

```
1: name = 'main', locations = 20, resolved = 20, hit count = 0
  1.1: where = Breakpoints`main + 22 at AppDelegate.swift:12,
address = 0x00000001057676e6, resolved, hit count = 0
  1.2: where = Foundation`-[NSThread main], address =
0x000000010584d182, resolved, hit count = 0
  1.3: where = Foundation`-[NSBlockOperation main], address =
0x000000010585df4a, resolved, hit count = 0
  1.4: where = Foundation`-[NSFilesystemItemRemoveOperation
main], address = 0x00000001058990ff, resolved, hit count = 0
  1.5: where = Foundation`-[NSFilesystemItemMoveOperation main],
address = 0x0000000105899c23, resolved, hit count = 0
  1.6: where = Foundation`-[NSInvocationOperation main], address
= 0x00000001058c4fb9, resolved, hit count = 0
  1.7: where = Foundation`-[NSDirectoryTraversalOperation main],
address = 0x000000010590a87f, resolved, hit count = 0
  1.8: where = Foundation`-[NSOperation main], address =
0x000000010595209c, resolved, hit count = 0
  1.9: where = UIKit`-[UIStatusBarServerThread main], address =
0x00000001068b84f0, resolved, hit count = 0
  1.10: where = UIKit`-[_UIDocumentActivityItemProvider main],
address = 0x000000010691898c, resolved, hit count = 0
  1.11: where = UIKit`-[_UIDocumentActivityDownloadOperation
main], address = 0x0000000106975d51, resolved, hit count = 0
  1.12: where = UIKit`-[_UIGetAssetThread main], address =
0x000000010698ef4d, resolved, hit count = 0
```

```
   1.13: where = UIKit`-[UIWebPDFSearchOperation main], address =
0x0000000106ae7c99, resolved, hit count = 0
   1.14: where = UIKit`-[UIActivityItemProvider main], address =
0x0000000106c4e525, resolved, hit count = 0
   1.15: where = MobileCoreServices`-[LSOpenOperation main],
address = 0x000000010879703c, resolved, hit count = 0
   1.16: where = ImageIO`main, address = 0x000000010c87535d,
resolved, hit count = 0
   1.17: where = AppSupport`-[_CPPowerAssertionThread main],
address = 0x000000010ed95f03, resolved, hit count = 0
   1.18: where = AppSupport`-
[CPDistributedMessagingAsyncOperation main], address =
0x000000010ed9ba53, resolved, hit count = 0
   1.19: where = JavaScriptCore`WTF::RunLoop::main(), address =
0x0000000111c68af0, resolved, hit count = 0
   1.20: where = ConstantClasses`main, address =
0x0000000114329cd2, resolved, hit count = 0
```

This shows the details of that breakpoint, including all locations that include the word
"main".

A cleaner way to view this is to type the following:

```
(lldb) breakpoint list 1 -b
```

This will give you output that is a little easier on the visual senses. If you have a
breakpoint ID that encapsulates a lot of breakpoints, this brief flag is a good solution.

If you want to query all the breakpoints in your LLDB session, simply omit the ID like
so:

```
(lldb) breakpoint list
```

You can also specify multiple breakpoint IDs and ranges:

```
(lldb) breakpoint list 1 3
(lldb) breakpoint list 1-3
```

Using breakpoint delete to delete all breakpoints is a bit heavy-handed. You can
simply use the same ID pattern used in the breakpoint list command to delete a set.

You can delete a single breakpoint by specifying the ID like so:

```
(lldb) breakpoint delete 1
```

However, your breakpoint for "main" had 20 locations. You can also delete a single location, like so:

```
(lldb) breakpoint delete 1.1
```

This would delete the first sub-breakpoint of breakpoint 1.

Where to go from here?

You've covered a lot in this chapter. Breakpoints are a big topic and mastering the art of quickly finding an item of interest is essential to becoming a debugging expert. You've also started exploring function searching using regular expressions. Now would be a great time to brush up on regular expression syntax, as you'll be using lots of regular expressions in the rest of this book.

Check out https://docs.python.org/2/library/re.html to learn (or relearn) regular expressions. Try figuring out how to make a case-insensitive breakpoint query.

You've only begun to discover how the compiler generates functions in Objective-C and Swift. Try to figure out the syntax for stopping on Objective-C blocks or Swift closures. Once you've done that, try to design a breakpoint that only stops on Objective-C blocks within the Commons framework of the **Signals** project. These are regex skills you'll need in the future to construct ever more complicated breakpoints.

Chapter 5: Expression

Now that you've learned how to set breakpoints so the debugger will stop in your code, it's time to get useful information out of whatever software you're debugging.

You'll often want to inspect instance variables of objects. But, did you know you can even execute arbitrary code through LLDB? What's more, by using the Objective-C runtime you can declare, initialize, and inject code all on the fly to help aid in your understanding of the program.

In this chapter you'll learn about the **expression** command. This allows you to execute arbitrary code in the debugger.

Formatting p & po

You might be familiar with the go-to debugging command, **po**. po is often used in Swift & Objective-C code to print out an item of interest. This could be an instance variable in an object, a local reference to an object, or a register, as you've seen earlier in this book. It could even be an arbitrary memory reference — so long as there's an object at that address!

If you do a quick `help po` in the LLDB console, you'll find po is actually a shorthand expression for `expression -O --`. The –O arugment is used to print the object's description.

po's often overlooked sibling, **p**, is another abbreviation with the –O option omitted, resulting in `expression --`. The format of what p will print out is more dependent on the **LLDB type system**. LLDB's type formatting of values helps determine its output and is fully customizable (as you'll see in a second).

It's time to learn how the p & po commands get their content. You'll continue using the Signals project for this chapter.

Start by opening the Signals project in Xcode. Next, open **MasterViewController.swift** and add the following code at the top of the class:

```
override var description: String {
  return "Yay! debugging " + super.description
}
```

In `viewDidLoad`, add the following line of code below `super.viewDidLoad()`:

```
print("\(self)")
```

Now, put a breakpoint just after the print method you created in the `viewDidLoad()` of **MasterViewController.swift**. Do this using the Xcode GUI breakpoint side panel.

Build and run the application.

Once the Signals project stops at `viewDidLoad()`, type the following into the LLDB console:

```
(lldb) po self
```

You'll get output similar to the following:

```
Yay! debugging <Signals.MasterViewController: 0x7f8a0ac06b70>
```

Take note of the output of the `print` statement and how it matches the `po self` you just executed in the debugger.

You can also take it a step further. `NSObject` has an additional method description used for debugging called **debugDescription**. Try implementing that now. Add the following below your `description` variable definition:

```
override var debugDescription: String {
  return "debugDescription: " + super.debugDescription
}
```

Build and run the application. When the debugger stops at the breakpoint, print `self` again:

```
(lldb) po self
```

The output from the LLDB console will look similar to the following:

```
debugDescription: Yay! debugging <Signals.MasterViewController:
0x7fb71fd04080>
```

Notice how the `po self` and the output of `self` from the `print` command now differ, since you implemented `debugDescription`. When you print an object from LLDB, it's `debugDescription` gets called, rather than `description`. Neat!

As you can see, having a `description` or `debugDescription` when working with an `NSObject` class or subclass will influence the output of `po`.

So which objects override these description methods? You can easily hunt down which objects override these methods using the `image lookup` command with a smart regex query. Your learnings from previous chapters are already coming in handy!

For example, if you wanted to know all the Objective-C classes that override `debugDescription`, you can simply query all the methods by typing:

```
(lldb) image lookup -rn '\ debugDescription\]'
```

Based upon the output, the authors of the Foundation framework have added the debugDescription to a lot of foundation types (i.e. NSArray), to make our debugging lives easier. In addition, they're also private classes that have overridden debugDescription methods as well.

You may notice one of them in the listing is CALayer. Let's take a look at the difference between description and debugDescription in CALayer.

In your LLDB console, type the following:

```
(lldb) po self.view!.layer.description
```

You'll see something similar to the following:

```
"<CALayer: 0x61000022e980>"
```

That's a little boring. Now type the following:

```
(lldb) po self.view!.layer
```

You'll see something similar to the following:

```
<CALayer:0x61000022e980; position = CGPoint (187.5 333.5);
bounds = CGRect (0 0; 375 667); delegate = <UITableView:
0x7fdd04857c00; frame = (0 0; 375 667); clipsToBounds = YES;
autoresize = W+H; gestureRecognizers = <NSArray:
0x610000048220>; layer = <CALayer: 0x61000022e980>;
contentOffset: {0, 0}; contentSize: {375, 0}>; sublayers =
(<CALayer: 0x61000022d480>, <CALayer: 0x61000022da60>, <CALayer:
0x61000022d8c0>); masksToBounds = YES; allowsGroupOpacity = YES;
backgroundColor = <CGColor 0x6100000a64e0> [<CGColorSpace
0x61800002c580> (kCGColorSpaceICCBased; kCGColorSpaceModelRGB;
sRGB IEC61966-2.1; extended range)] ( 1 1 1 1 )>
```

That's much more interesting — and much more useful! Obviously the developers of Core Animation decided the plain description should be just the object reference, but if you're in the debugger, you'll want to see more information. It's unclear exactly why they made this difference. It might be some of the information in the debug description is expensive to calculate, so they only want to do it when absolutely necessary.

Next, while you're still stopped in the debugger (and if not, get back to the viewDidLoad() breakpoint), try executing the p command on self, like so:

```
(lldb) p self
```

You'll get something similar to the following:

```
(Signals.MasterViewController) $R2 = 0x00007fb71fd04080 {
  UIKit.UITableViewController = {
    baseUIViewController@0 = <extracting data from value failed>

    _tableViewStyle = 0
    _keyboardSupport = nil
    _staticDataSource = nil
    _filteredDataSource = 0x000061800024bd90
    _filteredDataType = 0
  }
  detailViewController = nil
}
```

This might look scary, but let's break it down.

First, LLDB spits out the class name of `self`. In this case, `Signals.MasterViewController`.

Next follows a reference you can use to refer to this object from now on within your LLDB session. In the example above, it's $R2. Yours will vary as this is a number LLDB increments as you use LLDB.

This reference is useful if you ever want to get back to this object later in the session, perhaps when you're in a different scope and `self` is no longer the same object. In that case, you can refer back to this object as $R2. To see how, type the following:

```
(lldb) p $R2
```

You'll see the same information printed out again. You'll learn more about these LLDB variables later in this chapter.

After the LLDB variable name is the address to this object, followed by some output specific to this type of class. In this case, it shows the details relevant to UITableViewController, which is the superclass of MasterViewController, followed by the `detailViewController` instance variable.

As you can see, the meat of the output of the p command is different to the po command. The output of p is dependent upon **type formatting**, internal data structures the LLDB authors have added to every (noteworthy) data structure in Objective-C, Swift, and other languages. It's important to note the formatting for Swift is under active development with every Xcode release, so the output of p for `MasterViewController` might be different for you.

Since these type formatters are held by LLDB, you have the power to change them if you so desire. In your LLDB session, type the following:

```
(lldb) type summary add Signals.MasterViewController --summary-
string "Wahoo!"
```

You've now told LLDB you just want to return the static string, **"Wahoo!"**, whenever you print out an instance of the MasterViewController class. The `Signals` prefix is essential for Swift classes since Swift includes the module in the classname to prevent namespace collisions. Try printing out `self` now, like so:

```
(lldb) p self
```

The output should look similar to the following:

```
(lldb) (Signals.MasterViewController) $R3 = 0x00007fb71fd04080
Wahoo!
```

This formatting will be remembered by LLDB across app launches, so be sure to remove it when you're done playing with the **p** command. Remove yours from your LLDB session like so:

```
(lldb) type summary clear
```

Typing **p** `self` will now go back to the default implementation created by the LLDB formatting authors. Type formatting is a detailed topic, which is worth further exploration in a future chapter since it can greatly help debug applications you don't have source code for.

Swift vs Objective-C debugging contexts

It's important to note there are two debugging contexts when debugging your program: a non-Swift debugging context and a Swift context. By default, when you stop in Objective-C code, LLDB will use the non-Swift (Objective-C) debugging context, while if you're stopped in Swift code, LLDB will use the Swift context. Sounds logical, right?

If you stop the debugger out of the blue, LLDB will choose the Objective-C context by default.

Make sure the GUI breakpoint you've created in the previous section is still enabled and build and run the app. When the breakpoint hits, type the following into your LLDB session:

```
(lldb) po [UIApplication sharedApplication]
```

LLDB will throw a cranky error at you:

```
error: <EXPR>:3:16: error: expected ',' separator
[UIApplication sharedApplication]
               ^
               ,
```

You've stopped in Swift code, so you're in the Swift context. But you're trying to execute Objective-C code. That won't work. Similarly, in the Objective-C context, doing a po on a Swift object will not work.

You can force the expression to be used in the Objective-C context with the −l flag to select the language. However, since the po expression is mapped to expression −O −−, you'll be unable to use the po command since the arguments you provide come *after* the −−, which means you'll have to type out the expression. In LLDB, type the following:

```
(lldb) expression -l objc -O -- [UIApplication
sharedApplication]
```

Here you've told LLDB to use the objc language for Objective-C. You can also use objc++ for Objective-C++ if necessary.

LLDB will spit out the reference to the shared application. Try the same thing in Swift. Since you're already stopped in the Swift context, try to print the UIApplication reference using Swift syntax, like so:

```
(lldb) po UIApplication.shared
```

You'll get the same output as you did printing with the Objective-C context. Resume the program, by typing continue, then pause the Signals application out of the blue. From there press, the up arrow to bring up the same Swift command you just executed and see what happens:

```
(lldb) po UIApplication.shared
```

Again, LLDB will be cranky:

```
error: property 'shared' not found on object of type
'UIApplication'
```

Remember, stopping out of the blue will put LLDB in the Objective-C context. That's why you're getting this error when trying to execute Swift code.

You should always be aware of the language in which you are currently paused in the debugger.

User defined variables

As you saw earlier, LLDB will automatically create local variables on your behalf when printing out objects. You can create your own variables as well.

Remove all the breakpoints from the program and build and run the app. Stop the debugger out of the blue so it defaults to the Objective-C context. From there type:

```
(lldb) po id test = [NSObject new]
```

LLDB will execute this code, which creates a new NSObject and stores it to the `test` variable. Now try to print it like so:

```
(lldb) po test
```

You'll get an error like the following:

```
error: use of undeclared identifier 'test'
```

This is because you need to prepend variables you want LLDB to remember with the **$** character.

Try declaring `test` again with the $ in front:

```
(lldb) po id $test = [NSObject new]
(lldb) po $test
<NSObject: 0x60000001d190>
```

This variable was created in the Objective-C object. But what happens if you try to access this from the Swift context? Try it, by typing the following:

```
(lldb) expression -l swift -O -- $test
```

So far so good. Now try executing a Swift-styled method on this Objective-C class.

```
(lldb) exppression -l swift -O -- $test.description
```

You'll get an error like this:

```
error: <EXPR>:3:1: error: use of unresolved identifier '$test'
$test.description
^~~~~
```

If you create an LLDB variable in the Objective-C context, then move to the Swift context, don't expect everything to "just work." This is an area under active development and the bridging between Objective-C and Swift through LLDB will likely see improvements over time.

So how could creating references in LLDB actually be used in a real life situation? You can grab the reference to an object and execute (as well as debug!) arbitrary methods of your choosing. To see this in action, create a symbolic breakpoint on MasterViewController's parent view controller, **MasterContainerViewController** using an Xcode symbolic breakpoint for MasterContainerViewController's `viewDidLoad`.

In the Symbol section type the following:

```
Signals.MasterContainerViewController.viewDidLoad () -> ()
```

Be aware of the spaces for the parameters and parameter return type, otherwise the breakpoint will not work.

Your breakpoint should look like the following:

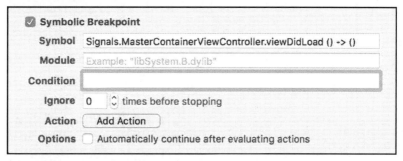

Build and run the app. Xcode will now break on `MasterContainerViewController.viewDidLoad()`. From there, type the following:

```
(lldb) p self
```

Since this is the first argument you executed in the Swift debugging context, LLDB will create the variable, **$R0**. Resume execution of the program by typing `continue` in LLDB.

Now you don't have a reference to the instance of `MasterContainerViewController` through the use of `self` since the execution has left `viewDidLoad()` and moved on to bigger and better run loop events. :]

Oh wait you still have that `$R0` variable! You can now reference `MasterContainerViewController` and even execute arbitrary methods to help debug your code.

Pause the app in the debugger manually, then type the following:

```
(lldb) po $R0.title
```

Unfortunately, you get:

```
error: use of undeclared identifier '$R0'
```

You stopped the debugger out of the blue! Remember, LLDB will default to Objective-C; you'll need to use the `−l` option to stay in the Swift context:

```
(lldb) expression −l swift −− $R0.title
```

This will output the following:

```
(String?) $R1 = "Quarterback"
```

Of course, this is the title of the view controller, shown in the navigation bar.

Now, type the following:

```
(lldb) expression −l swift −− $R0.title = "💩💩💩💩💩"
```

Resume the app by typing `continue` or pressing the play button in Xcode.

> **Note**: To quickly access a poop emoji on your macOS machine, hold down ⌘ + ^ + space. From there, you can easily hunt down the correct emoji by searching for the phrase "poop".

It's the small things in life you cherish!

As you can see, you can easily manipulate variables to your will.

In addition, you can also create a breakpoint on code, execute the code, and cause the breakpoint to be hit. This can be useful if you're in the middle of debugging something and want to step through a function with certain inputs to see how it operates.

For example, you still have the symbolic breakpoint in `viewDidLoad()`, so try executing that method to inspect the code. Pause execution of the program, then type:

```
(lldb) expression -l swift -O -- $R0.viewDidLoad()
```

Nothing happened. The breakpoint didn't hit. What gives? In fact, `MasterContainerViewController` *did* execute the method, but by default, LLDB will ignore any breakpoints when executing commands. You can disable this option with the `-i` option.

Type the following into your LLDB session:

```
(lldb) expression -l swift -O -i 0 -- $R0.viewDidLoad()
```

LLDB will now break on the `viewDidLoad()` symbolic breakpoint you created earlier. This tactic is a great way to test the logic of methods. For example, you can implement test-driven debugging, by giving a function different parameters to see how it handles different input.

Type formatting

One of the nice options LLDB has is the ability to format the output of basic data types. This makes LLDB a great tool to learn how the compiler formats basic C types. This is a must to know when you're exploring the assembly section, which you'll do later in this book.

Build and run the app, then pause the debugger out of the blue to make sure you're in the Objective-C context.

Type the following into your LLDB session:

```
(lldb) expression -G x -- 10
```

This -G option tells LLDB what format you want the output in. The G stands for **GDB format**. If you're not aware, GDB is the debugger that preceded LLDB. This therefore is saying whatever you specify is a GDB format specifier. In this case, x is used which indicates hexadecimal.

You'll see the following output:

```
(int) $0 = 0x0000000a
```

This is decimal 10 printed as hexadecimal. Wow!

But wait! There's more! LLDB lets you format types using a neat shorthand syntax. Type the following:

```
(lldb) p/x 10
```

You'll see the same output as before. But that's a lot less typing!

This is great for learning the representations behind C datatypes. For example, what's the binary representation of the integer 10?

```
(lldb) p/t 10
```

The /t specifies binary format. You'll see what decimal 10 looks like in binary. This can be particularly useful when you're dealing with a bit field for example, to double check what fields will be set for a given number.

What about negative 10?

```
(lldb) p/t -10
```

Decimal 10 in two's complement. Neat!

What about the floating point binary representation of 10.0?

```
(lldb) p/t 10.0
```

That could come in handy!

How about the ASCII value of the character 'D'?

```
(lldb) p/d 'D'
```

Ah so 'D' is 68! The /d specifies decimal format.

Finally, what is the acronym hidden behind this integer?

```
(lldb) p/c 1430672467
```

The /c specifies char format. It takes the number in binary, splits into 8 bit (1 byte) chunks, and converts each chunk into an ASCII character. In this case, it's a 4 character code (FourCC), saying STFU. Hey! Be nice now!

The full list of output formats is as follows (taken from https://sourceware.org/gdb/onlinedocs/gdb/Output-Formats.html):

- x: hexadecimal
- d: decimal
- u: unsigned decimal
- o: octal
- t: binary
- a: address
- c: character constant
- f: float
- s: string

If these formats aren't enough for you, you can use LLDB's extra formatters, although you'll be unable to use the GDB formatting syntax.

LLDB's formatters can be used like this:

```
(lldb) expression -f Y -- 1430672467
```

This gives you the following output:

```
(int) $0 = 53 54 46 55          STFU
```

This explains the FourCC code from earlier!

LLDB has the following formatters (taken from http://lldb.llvm.org/varformats.html):

- B: boolean
- b: binary
- y: bytes
- Y: bytes with ASCII
- c: character
- C: printable character
- F: complex float
- s: c-string
- i: decimal
- E: enumeration
- x: hex
- f: float
- o: octal
- O: OSType
- U: unicode16
- u: unsigned decimal
- p: pointer

Where to go from here?

Pat yourself on the back — this was another jam-packed round of what you can do with the expression command. Try exploring some of the other expression options yourself by executing help expression and see if you can figure out what they do.

Chapter 6: Thread, Frame & Stepping Around

You've learned how to create breakpoints, how to print and modify values, as well as how to execute code while paused in the debugger. But so far you've been left high and dry on how to move around in the debugger and inspect data beyond the immediate. It's time to fix that!

In this chapter, you'll learn how to move the debugger in and out of functions while LLDB is currently paused.

This is a critical skill to have since you often want to inspect values as they change over time when entering or exiting snippets of code.

Stack 101

When a computer program executes, it stores values in the **stack** and the **heap**. Both have their merits. As an advanced debugger, you'll need to have a good understand of how these work. Right now, let's take a brief look at the stack.

You may already know the whole spiel about what a stack is in computer science terms. In any case, it's worth having a basic understanding (or refresher) of how a process keeps track of code and variables when executing. This knowledge will come in handy as you're using LLDB to navigate around code.

The stack is a LIFO (Last-In-First-Out) queue that stores references to your currently executing code. This LIFO ordering means that whatever is added most recently, is removed first. Think of a stack of plates. Add a plate to the top, and it will be the one you take off first.

The **stack pointer** points to the current top of the stack. In the plate analogy, the stack pointer points to that top plate, telling you where to take the next plate from, or where to put the next plate on.

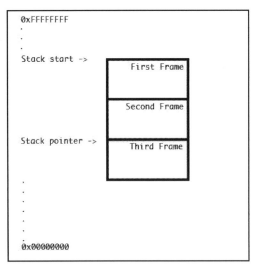

In this diagram, the high address is shown at the top (0xFFFFFFFF) and the low address is shown at the bottom (0x00000000) showcasing the stack would grow downwards.

Some illustrations like to have the high address at the bottom to match with the plate analogy as the stack would be shown growing upwards. However, I believe any diagrams showcasing the stack should be shown growing downwards from a high address because this will cause less headaches later on when talking about offsets from the stack pointer.

You'll take an in depth look at the stack pointer and other registers in Chapter 12, "Assembly and the Stack", but in this chapter you'll explore various ways to step through code that is on the stack.

Examining the stack's frames

You'll continue to use the **Signals** project for this chapter.

You'll glimpse some assembly in this chapter. Don't get scared! It's not that bad. However, be sure to use the iPhone 7 Simulator for this chapter since the assembly will be different if you were to generate the code on say, an actual iOS device. This is because a device uses the ARM architecture, whereas the simulator uses your Mac's native instruction set, x86_64 (or i386 if you are compiling on something lower than the iPhone 5s Simulator).

Open the Signals project in Xcode. Next, add a symbolic breakpoint with the following function name. Be sure to honor the spaces in the function signature or else the breakpoint will not be recognized.

```
Signals.MasterViewController.viewWillAppear (Swift.Bool) -> ()
```

This creates a symbolic breakpoint on `MasterViewController`'s `viewWillAppear(_:)` method.

Build and run the program. As expected, the debugger will pause the program on the `viewWillAppear(_:)` method of `MasterViewController`. Next, take a look at the stack trace in the left panel of Xcode. If you don't see it already, click on the **Debug Navigator** in the left panel (alternatively, press **Command + 6**, if you have the default Xcode keymap).

Make sure the three buttons in the bottom right corner are all disabled. These help filter stack functions to only functions you have source code for. Since you're learning about public as well as private code, you should always have these buttons disabled so you can see the full stack trace.

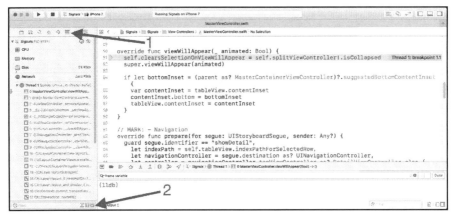

Within the Debug Navigator panel, the **stack trace** will appear, showing the list of **stack frames**, the first one being viewWillAppear(_:). Following that is the Swift/Objective-C bridging method, @objc MasterViewController.viewWillAppear(Bool) -> ():. This method is automatically generated so Objective-C can reach into Swift code.

After that, there's a few stack frames of Objective-C code coming from UIKit. Dig a little deeper, and you'll see some C++ code belonging to CoreAnimation. Even deeper, you'll see a couple of methods all containing the name CFRunLoop that belong to CoreFoundation. Finally, to cap it all off, is the **main** function (yes, Swift programs still have a main function, it's just hidden from you).

The stack trace you see in Xcode is simply a pretty printed version of what LLDB can tell you. Let's see that now.

In the LLDB console, type the following:

```
(lldb) thread backtrace
```

You could also simply type bt if you wished, which does the same. It's actually a different command and you can see the difference if you pull out your trusty friend, help.

After the command above, you'll see a stack trace much like you see in Xcode's Debug Navigator.

Type the following into LLDB:

```
(lldb) frame info
```

You'll get a bit of output similar to the following:

```
frame #0: 0x00000001075d0ae0
Signals`MasterViewController.viewWillAppear(animated=<invalid>
(0xd1), self=0x00007fff5862dac0) -> () at
```

```
MasterViewController.swift:47
```

As you can see, this output matches the content found in the Debug Navigator. So why is this even important if you can just see everything from the Debug Navigator? Well, using the LLDB console gives you finer-grained control of what information you want to see. In addition, you'll be making custom LLDB scripts in which these commands will become very useful. It's also nice to know where Xcode gets its information from, right?

Taking a look back at the Debug Navigator, you'll see some numbers starting from 0 and incrementing as you go down the **call stack**. This numbering helps you associate which **stack frame** you're looking at. Select a different stack by typing the following:

```
(lldb) frame select 1
```

Xcode will jump to the @objc bridging method, the method located at index 1 in the stack.

Provided you're using the Simulator and not an actual device, you'll get some assembly looking similar to the following.

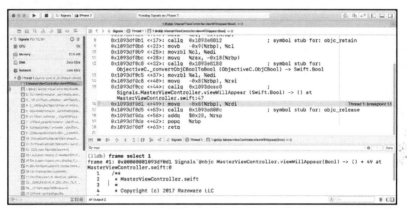

Take note of the green line in the assembly. Right before that line is the **callq** instruction that is responsible for executing viewWillAppear(_:) you set a breakpoint on earlier.

Don't let the assembly blur your eyes too much. You're not out of the assembly woods just yet...

Stepping

When mastering LLDB, the three most important navigation actions you can do while the program is paused revolve around **stepping** through a program. Through LLDB, you can **step over**, **step in**, or **step out** of code. Each of these allow you to continue executing your program's code, but in small chunks to allow you to examine how the program is executing.

Stepping over

Stepping over allows you to step to the next code statement (usually, the next line) in the context where the debugger is currently paused. This means if the current statement is calling another function, LLDB will run until this function has completed and returned.

Let's see this in action.

Type the following in the LLDB console:

```
(lldb) run
```

This will relaunch the Signals program without Xcode having to recompile. Neat! Xcode will stop on your symbolic breakpoint as before.

Next, type the following:

```
(lldb) next
```

The debugger will move one line forward. This is how you step over. Simple, but useful!

Stepping in

Stepping in means if the next statement is a function call, the debugger will move into the start of that function and then pause again.

Let's see this in action.

Relaunch the Breakpoints program from LLDB:

```
(lldb) run
```

Next, type the following:

```
(lldb) step
```

No luck. The program should've stepped in, because the line it's on contains a function call (well, actually it contains a few!).

In this case, LLDB acted more like a "step over" instead of a "step into". This is because LLDB will, by default, ignore stepping into a function if there are no debug symbols for that function. In this case, the function calls are all going into UIKit, for which you don't have debug symbols.

There is, however, a setting that specifies how LLDB should behave when stepping into a function for which no debug symbols exist. Execute the following command in LLDB to see where this setting is held:

```
(lldb) settings show target.process.thread.step-in-avoid-nodebug
```

If true, then stepping in will act as a step over in these instances. You can either change this setting (which you'll do in the future), or tell the debugger to ignore the setting, which you'll do now.

Type the following into LLDB:

```
(lldb) step -a0
```

This tells LLDB to step in regardless of whether you have the required debug symbols or not.

Stepping out

Stepping out means a function will continue for its duration then stop when it has returned. From a stack viewpoint, execution continues until the stack frame is popped off.

Run the Signals project again, and this time when the debugger pauses, take a quick look at the stack trace. Next, type the following into LLDB:

```
(lldb) finish
```

You'll notice that the debugger is now paused one function up in the stack trace. Try executing this command a few more times. Remember, by simply pressing **Enter**, LLDB will execute the last command you typed. The finish command will instruct LLDB to step out of the current function. Pay attention to the stack frames in the left panel as they disappear one by one.

Stepping in the Xcode GUI

Although you get much more finer-grained control using the console, Xcode already provides these options for you as buttons just above the LLDB console. These buttons appear when an application is running.

They appear, in order, as **step over**, **step in**, and **step out**.

Finally, the step over and step in buttons have one more cool trick. You can manually control the execution of different threads, by holding down **Control** and **Shift** while clicking on these buttons.

This will result in stepping through the thread on which the debugger is paused, while the rest of the threads remain paused. This is a great trick to have in the back of your toolbox if you are working with some hard-to-debug concurrency code like networking or something with Grand Central Dispatch.

Of course LLDB has the command line equivalent to do the same from the console by using the --run-mode option, or more simply -m followed by the appropriate option.

Examining data in the stack

A very interesting option of the frame command is the **frame variable** subcommand. This command will take the debug symbol information found in the headers of your executable (or a dYSM if your app is stripped... more on that later) and dump information out for that particular stack frame. Thanks to the debug information, the frame variable command can easily tell you the scope of all the variables in your function as well as any global variables within your program using the appropriate options.

Run the Signals project again and make sure you hit the viewWillAppear(_:) breakpoint. Next, navigate to the top of the stack by either clicking on the top stack frame in Xcode's Debug Navigator or by entering **frame select 0** in the console.

Next, type the following:

```
(lldb) frame variable
```

You'll get output similar to the following:

```
(Bool) animated = false
(Signals.MasterViewController) self = 0x00007fb3d160aad0 {
```

```
UIKit.UITableViewController = {
  baseUIViewController@0 = <extracting data from value failed>

  _tableViewStyle = 0
  _keyboardSupport = nil
  _staticDataSource = nil
  _filteredDataSource = 0x000061800005f0b0
  _filteredDataType = 0
}
detailViewController = nil
}
```

This dumps the variables available to the current stack frame and line of code. If possible, it'll also dump all the instance variables, both public and private, from the current available variables.

You, being the observant reader you are, might notice the output of `frame variable` also matches the content found in the **Variables View**, the panel to the left of the console window.

If it's not already, expand the Variables View by clicking on the left icon in the lower right corner of Xcode. You can compare the output of `frame variable` to the Variables View. You might notice `frame variable` will actually give you more information about the ivars of Apple's private API than the Variables View will.

Next, type the following:

```
(lldb) frame variable -F self
```

This is an easier way to look at all the private variables available to MasterViewController. It uses the -F option, which stands for "flat".

This will keep the indentation to 0 and only print out information about `self`, in **MasterViewController.swift**.

You'll get output similar to the truncated output below:

```
self = 0x00007fff5540eb40
self =
self =
self =
self = {}
self.detailViewController = 0x00007fc728816e00
self.detailViewController.some =
self.detailViewController.some =
self.detailViewController.some = {}
self.detailViewController.some.signal = 0x00007fc728509de0
```

As you can see, this is an attractive way to explore public variables when working with Apple's frameworks.

Where to go from here?

In this tutorial you've explored stack frames and the content in them. You've also learned how to navigate the stack by stepping in, out, and over code.

There are a lot of options in the `thread` command you didn't cover. Try exploring some of them with the `help thread` command, and seeing if you can learn some cool options.

Take a look at the `thread until`, `thread jump`, and `thread return` subcommands. You'll use them later, but they are fun commands so give them a shot now to see what they do!

Chapter 7: Image

By now, you have a solid foundation in debugging. You can find and attach to processes of interest, efficiently create regular expression breakpoints to cover a wide range of culprits, navigate the stack frame and tweak variables using the expression command.

However, it's time to explore one of the best tools for finding code of interest through the powers of LLDB. In this chapter, you'll take a deep dive into the **image** command.

The image command is an alias for the **target modules** subcommand. The image command specializes in querying information about **modules**; that is, the code loaded and executed in a process. Modules can comprise many things, including the main executable, frameworks, or plugins. However, the majority of these modules typically come in the form of **dynamic libraries**. Examples of dynamic libraries include UIKit for iOS or AppKit for macOS.

The image command is great for querying information about any private frameworks and its classes or methods not publicly disclosed in these header files.

Wait... modules?

You'll continue using the `Signals` project. Fire up the project, build on the iPhone 7 Simulator and run.

Pause the debugger and type the following into the LLDB console:

```
(lldb) image list
```

This command will list all the modules currently loaded. You'll see a lot! The start of the list should look something like the following:

```
[  0] 13A9466A-2576-3ABB-AD9D-D6BC16439B8F 0x00000001013aa000 /
usr/lib/dyld
[  1] 493D07DF-3F9F-30E0-96EF-4A398E59EC4A 0x000000010118e000 /
Applications/Xcode.app/Contents/Developer/Platforms/
iPhoneSimulator.platform/Developer/SDKs/iPhoneSimulator.sdk/usr/
lib/dyld_sim
[  2] 4969A6DB-CE85-3051-9FB2-7D7B2424F235 0x000000010115c000 /
Users/derekselander/Library/Developer/Xcode/DerivedData/Signals-
bqrjxlceauwfuihjesxmgfodimef/Build/Products/Debug-
iphonesimulator/Signals.app/Signals
```

The first two are the dynamic loaders: the base system one and then special additions for the iOS simulator. This is required code that allows your program to load dynamic libraries into memory for the program to operate. The third in this list is the app's main binary, `Signals`.

But there's a lot more in this list! You can filter out just those of interest to you. Type the following into LLDB:

```
(lldb) image list Foundation
```

The output will look similar to the following:

```
[  0] 4212F72C-2A19-323A-84A3-91FEABA7F900 0x0000000101435000 /
Applications/Xcode.app/Contents/Developer/Platforms/
iPhoneSimulator.platform/Developer/SDKs/iPhoneSimulator.sdk//
System/Library/Frameworks/Foundation.framework/Foundation
```

This is a useful way to find out information about just the module or modules you want.

Let's explore this output. There's a few interesting bits in there:

1. The module's UUID is printed out first (4212F72C-2A19-323A-84A3-91FEABA7F900). The UUID is important for hunting down symbolic information and uniquely identifies the Foundation module.

2. Following the UUID is the load address (0x0000000101435000). This identifies where the Foundation module is loaded into the Signals executable's process space.

3. Finally, you have the full path to the location of the binary for the module.

Let's take a deeper dive into another common module, UIKit. Type the following into LLDB:

```
(lldb) image dump symtab UIKit -s address
```

This will dump all the symbol table information available for UIKit. It's more output than you can shake a stick at! This command sorts the output by the address in which the functions are implemented in the UIKit module thanks to the -s address argument.

There's a lot of useful information in there, but you can't go reading all that, now can you? You need a way to effectively query the UIKit module with a flexible way to search for code of interest.

The **image lookup** command is perfect for filtering out all the data. Type the following into LLDB:

```
(lldb) image lookup -n "-[UIViewController viewDidLoad]"
```

This will dump out information relating just to UIViewController's viewDidLoad instance method. You'll see the name of the symbol relating to this method, and also where the code for that method is implemented inside the UIKit framework. This is good and all, but typing this is a little tedious and this can only dump out very specific instances.

This is where regular expressions come into play. The -r option will let you do a regular expression query. Type the following into LLDB:

```
(lldb) image lookup -rn UIViewController
```

Not only will this dump out all UIViewController methods, it'll also spit out results like UIViewControllerBuiltinTransitionViewAnimator since it contains the name UIViewController. You can be smart with the regular expression query to only spit out UIViewController methods. Type the following into LLDB:

```
(lldb) image lookup -rn '\[UIViewController\ '
```

This is good, but what about categories? They come in the form of UIViewController(CategoryName). Try searching for all UIViewController categories.

```
(lldb) image lookup -rn '\[UIViewController\(\w+\)\ '
```

This is starting to get complicated. The backslash at the beginning says you want the literal character for "[", then UIViewController. Finally the literal character of "(" then one or more alphanumeric or underscore characters (denoted by \w+), then ")", followed by a space.

Working knowledge of regular expressions will help you to creatively query any public or private code in any of the modules loaded into your binary.

Not only does this print out both public and private code, this will also give you hints to the methods the UIViewController class overrides from its parent classes.

Hunting for code

Regardless whether you're hunting for public or private code, sometimes it's just interesting trying to figure out how the compiler created the function name for a particular method. You briefly used the `image lookup` command above to find UIViewController methods. You also used it to hunt for how Swift property setters and getters are named in Chapter 4, "Stopping in Code".

However, there are many more cases where knowing how code is generated will give you a better understanding of where and how to create breakpoints for code you're interested in. One particularly interesting example to explore is the method signature for Objective-C's blocks.

So what is the best way to go about searching for a method signature for an Objective-C block? Since you don't have any clue on where to start searching for how blocks are named, a good way to start is by putting a breakpoint inside a block and then inspecting from there.

Open **UnixSignalHandler.m**, then find the singleton method **sharedHandler**. Within the function, look for the following code:

```
dispatch_once(&onceToken, ^{
  sharedSignalHandler = [[UnixSignalHandler alloc] initPrivate];
});
```

Put a breakpoint using the Xcode GUI in the line beginning with **sharedSignalHandler**. Then build and run. Xcode will now pause on the line of code you just set a breakpoint on. Check out the top stack frame in the debugging window.

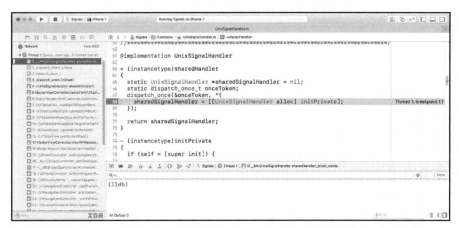

You can find the name of the function you're in using Xcode's GUI. In the Debug Navigator you'll see your stack trace and you can look at frame 0. That's a little hard to copy and paste (well, impossible, actually). Instead, type the following into LLDB:

```
(lldb) frame info
```

You'll get output similar to the following:

```
frame #0: 0x0000000100cb20a0 Commons`__34+[UnixSignalHandler
sharedHandler]_block_invoke((null)=0x0000000100cb7210) + 16 at
UnixSignalHandler.m:68
```

As you can see, the full function name is **__34+[UnixSignalHandler sharedHandler]_block_invoke**.

There's an interesting portion to the function name, **_block_invoke**. This might be the pattern you need to help uniquely identify blocks in Objective-C. Type the following into LLDB:

```
(lldb) image lookup -rn _block_invoke
```

This will do a regular expression search for the word **_block_invoke**. It will treat everything before and after the phrase as a wildcard.

But wait! You accidentally printed out *all* the Objective-C blocks loaded into the program. This search included anything from UIKit, Foundation, iPhoneSimulator SDK, etc. You should limit your search to only search for the Signals module. Type the following into LLDB:

```
(lldb) image lookup -rn _block_invoke Signals
```

Nothing is printed out. What gives? Open the right Xcode panel and click on the **File Inspector**. Alternatively, press ⌘ + **Option** + **1** if you have the default Xcode keymap.

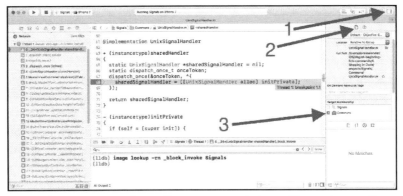

If you look to where **UnixSignalHandler.m** is compiled, you'll see it's actually compiled into the **Commons** framework. So, redo that search and look for Objective-C blocks in the Commons module. Type the following into LLDB:

```
(lldb) image lookup -rn _block_invoke Commons
```

Finally, you'll get some output!

You'll now see all the Objective-C blocks that you've searched for in the Commons framework.

Now, let's create a breakpoint to stop on a subset of these blocks you've found. Type the following into LLDB:

```
(lldb) rb appendSignal.*_block_invoke -s Commons
```

> **Note:** There is a subtle difference between searching for code in a module versus breaking in code for a module. Take the above commands as an example. When you wanted to search for all blocks in the Commons framework, you used `image lookup -rn _block_invoke Commons`. When you wanted to make breakpoints for blocks in the Commons framework, you used `rb appendSignal.*block_invoke -s Commons`. Take note of the `-s` argument vs the space.

The idea is this breakpoint will hit on any block within the `appendSignal` method.

Resume the program by clicking the play button or typing `continue` into LLDB. Jump over to Terminal and type the following:

```
pkill -SIGIO Signals
```

The signal you sent the program will be processed. However, before the signal gets visually updated to the tableview, your regex breakpoint will get hit.

The first breakpoint you will hit will be in:

```
___38-[UnixSignalHandler appendSignal:sig:]_block_invoke
```

Go past this by continuing the debugger.

Next you'll hit a breakpoint in:

```
___38-[UnixSignalHandler appendSignal:sig:]_block_invoke_2
```

There's an interesting item to note about this function name compared to the first; notice the number 2 in the method name. The compiler uses a base of `<FUNCTION_NAME>_block_invoke` for blocks defined within the function called `<FUNCTION_NAME>`. However, when there's more than one block in the function, a number is appended to the end to denote this.

As you learned in the previous chapter, the `frame variable` command will print all known local variable instances to a particular function. Try executing that command now to see the reference found in this particular block. Type the following into LLDB:

```
(lldb) frame variable
```

The output will look similar to the following:

```
(__block_literal_5 *) = 0x0000608000275e80
(int) sig = <read memory from 0x41 failed (0 of 4 bytes read)>

(siginfo_t *) siginfo = <read memory from 0x39 failed (0 of 8
bytes read)>

(UnixSignalHandler *const) self = <read memory from 0x31 failed
(0 of 8 bytes read)>
```

Those read memory failures don't look good! Step over once, either using the Xcode GUI or by typing `next` in LLDB. Next, execute `frame variable` again in LLDB. This time you'll see something similar to the following:

```
(__block_literal_5 *) = 0x0000608000275e80
(int) sig = 23
```

```
(siginfo_t *) siginfo = 0x00007fff587525e8
(UnixSignalHandler *) self = 0x000061800007d440
(UnixSignal *) unixSignal = 0x000000010bd9eebe
```

You needed to step over one statement, so the block executed some initial logic to setup the function, also known as the function prologue. The function prologue is a topic related to assembly, which you'll learn about in Section II.

This is actually quite interesting. First you see an object which references the block that's being invoked. In this case it's the type __block_literal_5. Then there are the sig and siginfo parameters that were passed into the Objective-C method where this block is invoked from. How did these get passed into the block?

Well, when a block is created, the compiler is smart enough to figure out what parameters are being used by it. It then creates a function that takes these as parameters. When the block is invoked, it's this function that is called, with the relevant parameters passed in.

Type the following into LLDB:

```
(lldb) image dump symfile Commons
```

You'll get a *lot* of output. Use ⌘ + F to search for the block type declared by the compiler: **__block_literal_5**. It's important to note your type could potentially differ when there are updates to LLVM, so make sure you have the correct type from the output of the frame variable command.

When searching for the declaration of the block type, there will be several different hits. Search for the declaration of the struct that matches the line number of the block. For example, the breakpoint you created initially stopped on line 123, so search for that in the declaration as well. You'll eventually find output that looks like the following:

```
0x7fefe24bcf90:    Type{0x100000e06} , name =
"__block_literal_5", size = 52, decl = UnixSignalHandler.m:123,
compiler_type = 0x00007fefd86d0410 struct __block_literal_5 {
        void *__isa;
        int __flags;
        int __reserved;
        void (*__FuncPtr)();
        __block_descriptor_withcopydispose *__descriptor;
        UnixSignalHandler *const self;
        siginfo_t *siginfo;
        int sig;
    }
```

This is the object that defines the block! Neat!

As you can see, this is almost as good as a header file for telling you how to navigate the memory in the block. Provided you cast the reference in memory to the type __block_literal_5, you can easily print out all the variables referenced by the block.

Start by getting the stack frame's variable information again by typing the following:

```
(lldb) frame variable
```

Next, find the address of the __block_literal_5 object and print it out like so:

```
(lldb) po ((__block_literal_5 *)0x0000618000070200)
```

You should see something similar to the following:

```
<__NSMallocBlock__: 0x0000618000070200>
```

If you don't, make sure the address you're casting to a __block_literal_5 is the address of your block as it will differ each time the project is run.

Now you can query the members of the __block_literal_5 struct. Type the following into LLDB:

```
(lldb) p/x ((__block_literal_5 *)0x0000618000070200)->__FuncPtr
```

This will dump the location of the function pointer for the block. The output will look like the following:

```
(void (*)()) $1 = 0x000000010756d8a0 (Commons`__38-
[UnixSignalHandler appendSignal:sig:]_block_invoke_2 at
UnixSignalHandler.m:123)
```

The function pointer for the block points to the function which is run when the block is invoked. It's the same address that is being executed right now! You can confirm this by typing the following, replacing the address with the address of your function pointer printed in the command you last executed:

```
(lldb) image lookup -a 0x000000010756d8a0
```

This uses the -a (address) option of image lookup to find out which symbol a given address relates to.

Jumping back to the block struct's members, you can also print out all the parameters passed to the block as well. Type the following, again replacing the address with the address of your block:

```
(lldb) po ((__block_literal_5 *)0x0000618000070200)->sig
```

This will output the signal number that was sent in as a parameter to the block's parent function.

There is also a reference to the `UnixSignalHandler` in a member of the struct called `self`. Why is that? Take a look at the block and hunt for this line of code:

```
[(NSMutableArray *)self.signals addObject:unixSignal];
```

It's the reference to `self` the block captured, and uses to find the offset of where the `signals` array is. So the block needs to know what `self` is. Pretty cool, eh?

Using the `image dump symfile` command in combination with the module is a great way to learn how a certain unknown data type works. It's also a great tool to understand how the compiler generates code for your sources.

Additionally, you can inspect how blocks hold references to pointers outside the block — a very useful tool when debugging memory retain cycle problems.

Snooping around

OK, you've discovered how to inspect a private class's instance variables in a static manner, but that block memory address is too tantalizing to be left alone. Try printing it out and exploring it using dynamic analysis. Type the following, replacing the address with the address of your block:

```
po 0x0000618000070200
```

LLDB will dump out a class indicating it's an Objective-C class.

```
<__NSMallocBlock__: 0x618000070200>
```

This is interesting. The class is `__NSMallocBlock__`. Now that you've learned how to dump methods for both private and public classes, it's time to explore what methods `__NSMallocBlock__` implements. In LLDB, type:

```
(lldb) image lookup -rn __NSMallocBlock__
```

Nothing. Hmm. This means `__NSMallocBlock__` doesn't override any methods implemented by its super class. Type the following in LLDB to figure out the parent class of `__NSMallocBlock__`.

```
(lldb) po [__NSMallocBlock__ superclass]
```

This will produce a similarly named class named **__NSMallocBlock** — notice the lack of trailing underscores. What can you find out about this class? Does this class implement or override any methods? Type the following into LLDB:

```
(lldb) image lookup -rn __NSMallocBlock
```

The methods dumped by this command seems to indicate that __NSMallocBlock is responsible for memory management, since it implements methods like retain and release. What is the parent class of __NSMallocBlock? Type the following into LLDB:

```
(lldb) po [__NSMallocBlock superclass]
```

You'll get another class named NSBlock. What about this class? Does it implement any methods? Type the following into LLDB:

```
(lldb) image lookup -rn 'NSBlock\ '
```

Notice the backslash and space at the end. This ensures there are no other classes that will match this query — remember, without it, a different class could be returned that *contains* the name NSBlock. A few more methods will be spat out. One of them, **invoke**, looks incredibly interesting:

```
Address: CoreFoundation[0x000000000018fd80]
(CoreFoundation.__TEXT.__text + 1629760)
        Summary: CoreFoundation`-[NSBlock invoke]
```

You're now going to try to invoke this method on the block. However, you don't want the block to disappear when the references that are retaining this block release their control, thus lowering the retainCount, and potentially deallocating the block.

There's a simple way to hold onto this block — just **retain** it! Type the following into LLDB, replacing the address with the address of your block:

```
(lldb) po id $block = (id)0x0000618000070200
(lldb) po [$block retain]
(lldb) po [$block invoke]
```

For the final line, you'll see the following output:

```
Appending new signal: SIGIO
  nil
```

This shows you the block has been invoked again! Pretty neat!

It only worked because everything was already set up in the right way for the block to be invoked, since you're currently paused right at the start of the block.

This type of methodology for exploring both public and private classes, and then exploring what methods they implement, is a great way to learn what goes on underneath the covers of a program. You'll later use the same process of discovery for methods and then analyze the assembly these methods execute, giving you a very close approximation of the source code of the original method.

Private debugging methods

The `image lookup` command does a beautiful job of searching for private methods as well the public methods you've seen throughout your Apple development career. However, there are some hidden methods which are quite useful when debugging your own code.

For example, a method beginning with _ usually denotes itself as being a private (and potentially important!) method.

Let's try to search for any Objective-C methods in all of the modules that begin with the underscore character and contain the word "description" in it.

Build and run the project again. When your breakpoint in `sharedHandler` is hit, type the following into LLDB:

```
(lldb) image lookup -rn (?i)\ _\w+description\]
```

This regular expression is a bit complex so let's break it down.

The expression searches for a space (\) followed by an underscore (_). Next, the expression searches for one or more alphanumeric or underscore characters (\w+) followed by the word `description`, followed by the] character.

The beginning of the regular expression has an interesting set of characters, (?i). This states you want this to be a case insensitive search.

This regular expression has backslashes prepending characters. This means you want the literal character, instead of its regular expression meaning. It's called "escaping". For example, in a regular expression, the] character has meaning, so to match the literal "]" character, you need to use \].

The exception to this in the regular expression above is the \w character. This is a special search item returning an alphanumeric character or an underscore (i.e. _, a-z, A-Z, 0-9).

If you had the deer in the headlights expression when reading this line of code, it's strongly recommended to carefully scan https://docs.python.org/2/library/re.html to brush up on your regular expression queries; it's only going to get more complicated from here on out.

Carefully scan through the output of image lookup. It's often this tedious scanning that gives you the best answers, so please make sure you go through all the output.

You'll notice a slew of interesting methods belonging to an **NSObject** category named **IvarDescription** belonging in UIKit.

Try redoing the search so only contents in this category get printed out. Type the following into LLDB:

```
(lldb) image lookup -rn NSObject\(IvarDescription\)
```

The console will dump out all the methods this category implements. Of the group of methods, there are a couple very interesting methods that stand out:

```
_ivarDescription
_propertyDescription
_methodDescription
```

Since this category is on **NSObject**, any subclass of **NSObject** can use these methods. This is pretty much everything, of course!

Try executing these methods on **UIApplication**. Type the following into LLDB:

```
(lldb) po [[UIApplication sharedApplication] _ivarDescription]
```

You'll get a slew of output since **UIApplication** holds many instance variables behind the scenes. Scan carefully and find something that interests you. Don't come back to reading until you find something of interest. This is important. :]

After carefully scanning the output, you can see a reference to the private class **UIStatusBar**. Which Objective-C setter methods does **UIStatusBar** have, I hear you ask? Let's find out! Type the following into LLDB:

```
(lldb) image lookup -rn '\[UIStatusBar\ set'
```

This dumps all the setter methods available to **UIStatusBar**. In addition to the declared and overriden methods available in UIStatusBar, you have access to all the methods available to its parent class. Check to see if the UIStatusBar is a subclass of the UIView class

```
(lldb) po (BOOL)[[UIStatusBar class] isSubclassOfClass:[UIView class]]
```

Alternatively, you can repeatedly use the **superclass** method to jump up the class hierarchy. As you can see, it looks like this class is a subclass of UIView, so the **backgroundColor** property is available to you in this class. Let's play with it.

First, type the following into LLDB:

```
(lldb) po [[UIApplication sharedApplication] statusBar]
```

You'll see something similar to the following:

```
<UIStatusBar: 0x7fb8d400d200; frame = (0 0; 375 20); opaque =
NO; autoresize = W+BM; layer = <CALayer: 0x61800003aec0>>
```

This prints out the UIStatusBar instance for your app. Next, using the address of the status bar, type the following into LLDB:

```
(lldb) po [0x7fb8d400d200 setBackgroundColor:[UIColor
purpleColor]]
```

In LLDB, remove any of the previous breakpoints you created.

```
(lldb) breakpoint delete
```

Continue the app and see the beauty you've unleashed upon the world through your fingertips!

Not the prettiest of apps now, but at least you've managed to inspect a private method and used it to do something fun!

Where to go from here?

As a challenge, try figuring out a pattern using `image lookup` to find all Swift closures within the Signals module. Once you do that, create a breakpoint on every Swift closure within the Signals module. If that's too easy, try looking at code that can stop on **didSet/ willSet** property helpers, or do/try/catch blocks.

Also, try looking for more private methods hidden away in Foundation and UIKit. Have fun!

Chapter 8: Persisting & Customizing Commands

As you might have noticed in your development career, typing the same thing over and over really sucks. If you use a particular command that is difficult to type, there's no reason you should have to type the whole thing out. Just as you've learned when creating breakpoints using regular expressions, you'd go crazy typing out the full names of some of those Swift functions.

The same idea can be applied to any commands, settings, or code executed in LLDB. However, there are two problems that haven't been addressed until now: persisting your commands and creating shortcuts for them! Every time you run a new LLDB session, all your previous commands you've executed will vanish!

In this chapter, you'll learn how to persist these choices through the `.lldbinit` file. By persisting your choices and making convenience commands for yourself, your debugging sessions will run much more smoothly and efficiently. This is also an important concept because from here on out, you'll use the `.lldbinit` file on a regular basis.

Persisting... how?

Whenever LLDB is invoked, it'll search several directories for special initialization files. If found, these files will be loaded into LLDB as soon as LLDB starts up but before LLDB has attached to the process (important to know if you're trying to execute arbitrary code in the init file). You can use these files to specify settings or create custom commands to do your debugging bidding.

LLDB searches for an initialization file in the following places:

1. **~/.lldbinit**-[**context**] where [context] is **Xcode**, if you are debugging with Xcode, or **lldb** if you are using the command line incarnation of LLDB. For example, if you wanted commands that were only available in LLDB while debugging in the Terminal, you'd add content to `~/.lldbinit-lldb`, while if you wanted to have commands only available to Xcode you'd use `~/.lldbinit-Xcode`.

2. Next, LLDB searches for content found in **~/.lldbinit**. This is the ideal file for most of your logic, since you want to use commands in both Xcode and terminal sessions of LLDB.

3. Finally, LLDB will search the directory where it was invoked. Unfortunately, when Xcode launches LLDB, it'll launch LLDB at / directory. This isn't an ideal place to stick an `.lldbinit` file, so this particular implementation will be ignored throughout the book.

Creating the .lldbinit file

In this section you're going to create your first `.lldbinit` file.

First, open a Terminal window and type the following:

```
nano ~/.lldbinit
```

This uses the `nano` text editor to open up your `.lldbinit` file. If you already have an existing file in the location, `nano` will open up the file instead of creating a new one.

> **Note:** You really should be using some form of **vi** or **emacs** for editing .lldbinit, and then angrily blog about how unconventional the other editor is. :] I'm suggesting `nano` to stay out of the great debate.

Once open in the nano editor, add the following line of code to the end of
your .lldbinit file:

```
command alias -- Yay_Autolayout expression -l objc -O --
[[[[UIApplication sharedApplication] keyWindow]
rootViewController] view] recursiveDescription]
```

You've just created an **alias** — a shortcut command for a longer expression. The alias's
name is called Yay_Autolayout and it'll execute an expression command to get the root
UIView (iOS only) and dump the position and layout of the root view and all of it's
subviews.

Save your work by pressing **Ctrl + O**, but don't exit nano just yet.

Open the Signals Xcode project — you know, the one you've been playing with
throughout this section. Build and run the Signals application. Once running, pause
execution and type the alias in the debugger:

```
(lldb) Yay_Autolayout
```

This will dump out all the views in the applications! Neat!

> **Note:** The cool thing about this command is it'll work equally well for apps you
> do — and don't — have source code for. You could, hypothetically, attach LLDB
> to the Simulator's SpringBoard and dump all the views using the exact same
> method.

Now, try getting the help for this new command:

```
(lldb) help Yay_Autolayout
```

The output will look kinda meh. You can do better. Go back to the nano Terminal
window and rewrite the command alias to include some helpful information, like so:

```
command alias -H "Yay_Autolayout will get the root view and
recursively dump all the subviews and their frames" -h
"Recursively dump views" -- Yay_Autolayout expression -l objc -O
-- [[[[UIApplication sharedApplication] keyWindow]
rootViewController] view] recursiveDescription]
```

Make sure nano saves the file by pressing **Ctrl + O**. Next, build and run the Signals
project.

Now when you stop the debugger and type help Yay_Autolayout, you'll get help text
at the bottom of the output. This is done with the -H command. You can also get a brief

summary by just typing `help`, which gives the `-h` description along with the rest of the commands.

This may seem a bit pointless now, but when you have many, many custom commands in your `.lldbinit` file, you'll be thankful you provided documentation for yourself.

Command aliases with arguments

You've just created a standalone command alias that doesn't require any arguments. However, you'll often want to create aliases to which you can supply input.

Go back to the `nano` window in Terminal. Add the following at the bottom of the file:

```
command alias cpo expression -l objc -O --
```

You've just created a new command called **cpo**. The `cpo` command will do a normal `po` (print object), but it'll use the Objective-C context instead. This is an ideal command to use when you're in a Swift context, but want to use Objective-C to print out an address or register of something you know is a valid Objective-C object.

Save your work in nano, and jump over to the Signals project. Navigate to **MasterViewController**'s `viewDidLoad` and set a breakpoint at the top of the function. Build and run the application.

To best understand the importance of the `cpo` command, first get the reference to the MasterViewController.

```
(lldb) po self
```

You'll get output similar to the following:

```
<Signals.MasterViewController: 0x7fc8295071a0>
```

Take the memory address you get at the end of the output (as usual, yours will likely be different), and try printing that in the debugger.

```
(lldb) po 0x7fc8295071a0
```

This will not produce any meaningful output, since you've stopped in a Swift file, and Swift is a type-safe language. Simply printing an address in Swift will not do anything. This is why the Objective-C context is so useful when debugging, especially when dealing with assembly where there only references to memory addresses.

Now, try using the new command you've just created on the address:

```
(lldb) cpo 0x7fc8295071a0
```

You'll see the same output as you did with `po self`:

```
<Signals.MasterViewController: 0x7fc8295071a0>
```

This is a helpful command to get the object's description, whether it's created with Objective-C or Swift.

This is a rather contrived example, because you could just use `po self` as you've seen. However if you just have a memory address, then you can't use `po`, as you've also seen. Therefore `cpo` is useful in these cases.

Where to go from here?

You've learned how to create aliases for simple commands as well as persist them in the `.lldbinit` file. This will work across both Xcode and Terminal invocations of LLDB.

As an exercise, add help messages to your newly created `cpo` command in the `~/.lldbinit` file so you'll be able to remember how to use it when you have an onslaught of custom commands. Remember the –h option is the short help message, while the –H option is the longer help command. Remember to use the –– to separate your help input arguments to the rest of your command.

In addition, write a command alias for something you often use. Put this alias in your `~/.lldbinit` file and try it out!

Chapter 9: Regex Commands

In the previous chapter, you learned about the `command alias` command as well as how to persist commands through the `lldbinit` file. Unfortunately, `command alias` has some limitations.

An alias created this way will work great if you're trying to execute a static command, but usually you'd want to feed input into a command in order to get some useful output.

Where `command alias` falls short is it essentially *replaces* the alias with the actual command. What if you wanted to have input supplied into the middle of a command, such as a command to get the class of a given object instance, providing the object as an input?

One horribly ugly solution would be using a `command alias` to do the following (please don't *ever* do this):

```
(lldb) po id $INPUT = @"input test";
(lldb) command alias getcls po -l objc -O -- [$INPUT class]
```

This creates a temporary variable in LLDB called `$INPUT` then uses $INPUT to get the class. But this is awful, not to mention ugly. You'd have to redeclare $INPUT every time, which completely negates the point of using a shorthand convenience command in the first place!

However, don't despair — there *is* an elegant solution to supplying input.

command regex

The LLDB command **command regex** acts much like command alias, except you can provide a regular expression for input which will be parsed and applied to the action part of the command.

command regex takes an input syntax that looks similar to the following:

```
s/<regex>/<subst>/
```

This is a normal regular expression. It starts with 's/', which specifies a stream editor input to use the **substitute command**. The <regex> part is the bit that specifies what should be replaced. The <subst> part says what to replace it with.

> **Note:** This syntax is derived from the **sed** Terminal command. This is important to know, because if you're experimenting using advanced patterns, you can check the **man** pages of sed to see what is possible within the substitute formatting syntax.

Time to look at a concrete example. Open up the **Signals** Xcode project. Build and run, then pause the application in the debugger. Once the LLDB console is up and ready to receive input, enter the following command in LLDB:

```
(lldb) command regex rlook 's/(.+)/image lookup -rn %1/'
```

This command you've entered will make your image regex searches much easier. You've created a new command called rlook. This new command takes everything after the rlook and prefixes it with image lookup -rn. It does this through a regex with a single matcher (the parentheses) which matches on one or more characters, and replaces the whole thing with image lookup -rn %1. The %1 specifies the contents of the matcher.

So, for example, if you enter this:

```
rlook FOO
```

LLDB will actually execute the following:

```
image lookup -rn FOO
```

Now instead of having to type the soul-crushingly long image lookup -rn, you can just type rlook!

But wait, it gets better. Provided there are no conflicts with the characters rl, you can simply use that instead. You can specify any command, be it built-in or your own, by using any prefix which is not shared with another command.

This means that you can easily search for methods like viewDidLoad using a much more convenient amount of typing. Try it out now:

```
(lldb) rl viewDidLoad
```

This will produce all the viewDidLoad implementations across all modules in the current executable. Try limiting it to only code in the Signals app:

```
(lldb) rl viewDidLoad Signals
```

Now you're satisfied with the command, add the following line of code to your ~/.lldbinit file:

```
command regex rlook 's/(.+)/image lookup -rn %1/'
```

> **Note:** The best way to implement a regex command is to use LLDB while a program is running. This lets you iterate on the command regex (by redeclaring it if you're not happy with it) and test it out without having to relaunch LLDB. Once you're happy with the command, add it to your ~/.lldbinit file so it will be available every time LLDB starts up.

Now the rlook command will be available to you from here on out, resulting in no more painful typing of the full image lookup -rn command. Yay!

Executing complex logic

Time to take the command regex up a level. You can actually use this command to execute multiple commands for a single alias. While LLDB is still paused, implement this new command:

```
(lldb) command regex -- tv 's/(.+)/expression -l objc -O --
@import QuartzCore; [%1 setHidden:!(BOOL)[%1 isHidden]]; (void)
[CATransaction flush];/'
```

This complicated, yet useful command, will create a command named **tv** (toggle view), which toggles a UIView (or NSView) on or off while the debugger is paused.

Packed into this command are three separate lines of code:

1. `@import QuartzCore` imports the QuartzCore framework into the debugger's address space. This is required because the debugger won't understand what code you're executing until it's declared. You're about to execute code from the QuartzCore framework, so just in case it hasn't been imported yet, you're doing it now.

2. `[%1 setHidden:!(BOOL)[%1 isHidden]];` toggles the view to either hidden or visible, depending what the previous state was. Note that `isHidden` doesn't know the return type, so you need to cast it to an Objective-C `BOOL`

3. The final command, `[CATransaction flush]`, will flush the CATransaction queue. Manipulating the UI in the debugger will normally mean the screen will not reflect any updates until the debugger resumes execution. However, this method will update the screen resulting in LLDB not needing to `continue` in order to show visual changes.

> **Note**: Due to the limitations of the input params, specifying multiline input is not allowed so you have to join all the commands onto one line. This is ugly but necessary when crafting these regex commands. However, if you ever do this in actual Objective-C/Swift source code, may the Apple Gods punish you with extra-long app review times! :]

Provided LLDB is still paused, execute this newly created `tv` command:

```
(lldb) tv [[[UIApp keyWindow] rootViewController] view]
```

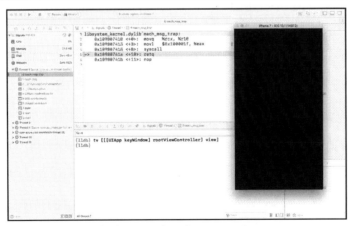

Bring up the Simulator to verify the view has disappeared.

Now simply press **Enter** in the LLDB console, as LLDB will repeat the last command you've entered. The view will flash back to normal.

Now you're done implementing the tv command, add it to your ~/.lldbinit file:

```
command regex -- tv 's/(.+)/expression -l objc -O -- @import
QuartzCore; [%1 setHidden:!(BOOL)[%1 isHidden]]; (void)
[CATransaction flush];/'
```

Chaining regex inputs

There's a reason why that weird stream editor input was chosen for using this command: this format lets you easily specify multiple actions for the same command. When given multiple commands, the regex will try to match each input. If the input matches, that particular <subst> is applied to the command. If the input doesn't match for a particular stream, it'll go to the next command and see if the regex can match that input.

It's generally necessary to use the Objective-C context when working with objects in memory and registers. Also, anything that begins with the square open bracket or the '@' character is Objective-C. This is because Swift makes it difficult to work with memory, and it won't let you access registers, nor do Swift expressions usually ever begin with an open bracket or '@' character.

You can use this information to automatically detect which context you need to use for a given input.

Let's see how you'd you go about building a command which gets the class information out of an object, which honors the above requirements.

- In Objective-C, you'd use **[objcObject class]**

- In Swift, you'd use **type(of: swiftObject)**.

In Xcode, create a Symbolic breakpoint on MasterViewController.viewDidLoad () -> () (make sure to keep the spacing).

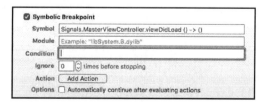

Build and run, then wait for the breakpoint to be triggered. As usual, head on over to the debugger.

First, build out the Objective-C implementation of this new command, **getcls**.

```
(lldb) command regex getcls 's/(([0-9]|\$|\@|\[).*)/cpo [%1
class]/'
```

Wow, that regex makes the eyes blur. Time to break it down:

At first, there's an inner grouping saying the following characters can be used to match the start:

- [0-9] means the numbers from 0-9 can be used.

- \$ means the literal character '$' will be matched

- \@ means the literal character '@' will be matched

- \[means the literal character '[' will be matched

Any characters that start with the above will generate a match. Following that is .* which means zero or more characters will produce a match.

Overall, this means that a number, $, @, or [, followed by any characters will result in the command matching and running cpo [%1 class]. Once again, %1 is replaced with the first matcher from the regex. In this case, it's the entire command. The inner matcher (matching a number, $, or so on) would be %2.

Try throwing a couple of commands at the getcls command to see how it works:

```
(lldb) getcls @"hello world"
__NSCFString

(lldb) getcls @[@"hello world"]
__NSSingleObjectArrayI

(lldb) getcls [UIDevice currentDevice]
UIDevice

(lldb) cpo [UIDevice currentDevice]
<UIDevice: 0x60800002b520>

(lldb) getcls 0x60800002b520
UIDevice
```

Awesome!

However, this only handles references that make sense in the Objective-C context and that match your command. For example, try the following:

```
(lldb) getcls self
```

You'll get an error:

```
error: getcls
```

This is because there was no matching regex for the input you provided. Let's add one which catches other forms of input to `getcls`. Type the following into LLDB now:

```
(lldb) command regex getcls 's/(([0-9]|\$|\@|\[).*)/cpo [%1
class]/' 's/(.+)/expression -l swift -O -- type(of: %1)/'
```

This looks a bit more complex, but it's not too bad. The first part of the command is the same as you added before. But now you've added another regex to the end. This one is a catch-all, just like the `rlook` command you added. This catch-all simply calls `type(of:)` with the input as the parameter.

Try executing the command again for `self`:

```
(lldb) getcls self
```

You'll now get the expected `Signals.MasterViewController` output. Since you made using the Swift context as a catch-all, you can use this command in interesting ways.

```
(lldb) getcls self .title
```

Notice the space in there, and it still works. This is because you told the Swift context to quite literally take anything except newlines. :]

Once, you're done playing with this new and improved `getcls` command, be sure to add it to your `~/.lldbinit` file.

Limitations of command regex

There are a few limits to the number of creative applications of the `command regex` LLDB command. The `command regex` LLDB command has a limit of only one parameter you can supply to the `<subst>` command. This means advanced commands where you supply multiple parameters are out of the question.

Fortunately, LLDB has the **script bridging** interface — a fully featured Python implementation for creating advanced LLDB commands to do your debugging bidding. You'll take an in depth look at script bridging in a later section.

For now, simply use either `command alias` or `command regex` to suit your debugging needs.

Where to go from here?

Go back to the regex commands you've created in this chapter and add **syntax** and **help** help documentation.

As mentioned previously, you'll thank yourself you've provided this documentation to remind you of your command's functionality when it's 11 PM on a Friday night and you just want to figure out this gosh darn bug.

Section II: Understanding Assembly

Knowing what the computer is doing with all those 1s and 0s underneath your code is an excellent skill to have when digging for useful information about a program. This section will set you up with the theory you'll need for the remainder of this book in order to create complex debugging scripts — and introduce you to the basic theory behind reverse-engineering code.

Chapter 10: Assembly Register Calling Convention

Chapter 11: Assembly & Memory

Chapter 12: Assembly and the Stack

Chapter 10: Assembly Register Calling Convention

Now you've gained a basic understanding of how to maneuver around the debugger, it's time to take a step down the executable Jenga tower and explore the 1s and 0s that make up your source code. This section will focus on the low-level aspects of debugging.

In this chapter, you'll look at registers the CPU uses and explore and modify parameters passed into function calls. You'll also learn about common Apple computer architectures and how their registers are used within a function. This is known as an architecture's **calling convention**.

Knowing how assembly works and how a specific architecture's calling convention works is an extremely important skill to have. It lets you observe function parameters you don't have the source code for and lets you modify the parameters passed into a function. In addition, it's sometimes even better to go to the assembly level because your source code could have different or unknown names for variables you're not aware of.

For example, let's say you always wanted to know the second parameter of a function call, regardless of what the parameter's name is. Knowledge of assembly gives you a great base layer to manipulate and observe parameters in functions.

Assembly 101

Wait, so what's assembly again?

Have you ever stopped in a function you didn't have source code for, and saw an onslaught of memory addresses followed by scary, short commands? Did you huddle in a ball and quietly whisper to yourself you'll never look at this dense stuff again? Well... that stuff is known as assembly!

Here's a picture of a backtrace in Xcode, which showcases the assembly of a function within the Simulator.

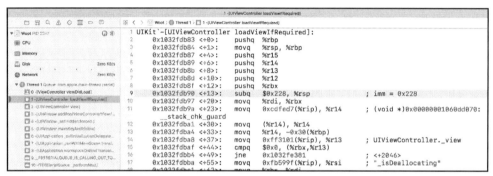

Looking at the image above, the assembly can be broken into several parts. Each line in a assembly instruction contains an **opcode**, which can be thought of as an extremely simple instruction for the computer.

So what does an opcode look like? An opcode is an instruction that performs a simple task on the computer. For example, consider the following snippet of assembly:

```
pushq   %rbx
subq    $0x228, %rsp
movq    %rdi, %rbx
```

In this block of assembly, you see three opcodes, **pushq**, **subq**, and **movq**. Think of the opcode items as the action to perform. The things following the opcode are the source and destination labels. That is, these are the items the opcode acts upon.

In the above example, there are several **registers**, shown as **rbx**, **rsp**, **rdi**, and **rbp**. The **%** before each tells you this is a register.

In addition, you can also find a numeric constant in hexadecimal shown as **0x228**. The **$** before this constant tells you it's an absolute number.

There's no need to know what this code is doing at the moment, since you'll first need to learn about the registers and calling convention of functions. Then you'll learn more about the opcodes and write your own assembly in a future chapter.

> **Note:** In the above example, take note there are a bunch of %'s and $'s that precede the registers and constants. This is how the disassembler formats the assembly. However, there are two main ways that assembly can be showcased. The first is **Intel** assembly, and the second is **AT&T** assembly.
>
> By default, Apple's disassembler tools ship with assembly displayed in the AT&T format, as it is in the example above. Although this is a good format to work with, it can be a little hard on the eyes. In the next chapter, you'll change the assembly format to Intel, and will work exclusively with Intel assembly syntax from there on out.

x86_64 vs ARM64

As a developer for Apple platforms, there are two primary architectures you'll deal with when learning assembly: **x86_64** architecture and **ARM64** architecture. x86_64 is the architecture most likely used on your macOS computer, unless you are running an "ancient" Macintosh.

x86_64 is a **64-bit** architecture, which means every address can hold up to 64 1s or 0s. Alternatively, older Macs use a **32-bit** architecture, but Apple stopped making 32-bit Macs at the end of the 2010's. Programs running under macOS are likely to be 64-bit compatible, including programs on the Simulator. That being said, even if your macOS is x86_64, it can still run 32-bit programs.

If you have any doubt of what hardware architecture you're working with, you can get your computer's hardware architecture by running the following command in Terminal:

```
uname -m
```

ARM64 architecture is used on mobile devices such as your iPhone where limiting energy consumption is critical.

ARM emphasizes power conservation, so it has a reduced set of opcodes that help facilitate energy consumption over complex assembly instructions. This is good news for you, because there are fewer instructions for you to learn on the ARM architecture.

Here's a screenshot of the same method shown earlier, except this time in ARM64 assembly on an iPhone 7:

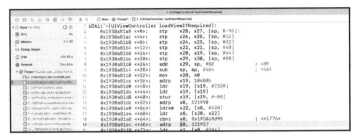

You might not be able to differentiate between the two architectures now, but you'll soon know them like the back of your hand.

Apple originally shipped 32-bit ARM processors in many of their devices, but have since moved to 64-bit ARM processors. 32-bit devices are almost obsolete as Apple has phased them out through various iOS versions. For example, the iPhone 4s is a 32-bit device which is not supported in iOS 10. All that remains in the 32-bit iPhone lineup is the iPhone 5, which iOS 10 does support.

Interestingly, all Apple Watch devices are currently 32-bit. This is likely because 32-bit ARM CPUs typically draw less power than their 64-bit cousins. This is really important for the watch as the battery is tiny.

Since it's best to focus on what you'll need for the future, this book will focus primarily on 64-bit assembly for both architectures. In addition, you'll start learning x86_64 assembly first and then transition to learning ARM64 assembly so you don't get confused. Well, not *too* confused.

x86_64 register calling convention

Your CPU uses a set of registers in order to manipulate data in your running program. These are storage holders, just like the RAM in your computer. However they're located on the CPU itself very close to the parts of the CPU that need them. So these parts of the CPU can access these registers incredibly quickly.

Most instructions involve one or more registers and perform operations such as writing the contents of a register to memory, reading the contents of memory to a register or performing arithmetic operations (add, subtract, etc.) on two registers.

In **x64** (from here on out, x64 is an abbreviation for x86_64), there are **16 general purpose registers** used by the machine to manipulate data.

These registers are **RAX, RBX, RCX, RDX, RDI, RSI, RSP, RBP** and **R8** through **R15**.

These names will not mean much to you now, but you'll explore the importance of each register soon.

When you call a function in x64, the manner and use of the registers follows a very specific convention. This dictates where the parameters to the function should go and where the return value from the function will be when the function finishes. This is important so code compiled with one compiler can be used with code compiled with another compiler.

For example, take a look at this simple Objective-C code:

```
NSString *name = @"Zoltan";
NSLog(@"Hello world, I am %@. I'm %d, and I live in %@.", name,
30, @"my father's basement");
```

There are four parameters passed into the NSLog function call. Some of these values are passed as-is, while one parameter is stored in a local variable, then referenced as a parameter in the function. However, when viewing code through assembly, the computer doesn't care about names for variables; it only cares about locations in memory.

The following registers are used as parameters when a function is called in x64 assembly. Try and commit these to memory, as you'll use these frequently in the future:

- First Argument: RDI

- Second Argument: RSI

- Third Argument: RDX

- Fourth Argument: RCX

- Fifth Argument: R8

- Sixth Argument: R9

If there are more than six parameters, then the program's stack is used to pass in additional parameters to the function.

Going back to that simple Objective-C code, you can re-imagine the registers being passed like the following pseudo-code:

```
RDI = @"Hello world, I am %@. I'm %d, and I live in %@.";
RSI = @"Zoltan";
RDX = 30;
RCX = @"my father's basement";
NSLog(RDI, RSI, RDX, RCX);
```

As soon as the NSLog function starts, the given registers will contain the appropriate values as shown above.

However, as soon as the **function prologue** (the beginning section of a function that prepares the stack and registers) finishes executing, the values in these registers will likely change. The generated assembly will likely overwrite the values stored in these registers, or just simply discard these references when the code has no more need of them.

This means as soon as you leave the start of a function (through stepping over, stepping in, or stepping out), you can no longer assume these registers will hold the expected values you want to observe, unless you actually look at the assembly code to see what it's doing.

This calling convention heavily influences your debugging (and breakpoint) strategy. If you were to automate any type of breaking and exploring, you would have to stop at the start of a function call in order to inspect or modify the parameters without having to actually dive into the assembly.

Objective-C and registers

As you learned in the previous section, registers use a specific calling convention. You can take that same knowledge and apply it to other languages as well.

When Objective-C executes a method, a special C function is executed named **objc_msgSend**. There's actually several different types of these functions, but more on that later. This is the heart of message dispatch. As the first parameter, objc_msgSend takes the reference of the object upon which the message is being sent. This is followed by a **selector**, which is simply just a char * specifying the name of the method being called on the object. Finally, objc_msgSend takes a variable amount of arguments within the function if the selector specifies there should be parameters.

Let's look at a concrete example of this in an iOS context:

```
[UIApplication sharedApplication];
```

The compiler will take this code and create the following pseudocode:

```
id UIApplicationClass = [UIApplication class];
objc_msgSend(UIApplicationClass, "sharedApplication");
```

The first parameter is a reference to the UIApplication class, followed by the sharedApplication selector. An easy way to tell if there are any parameters is to simply check for colons in the Objective-C selector. Each colon will represent a parameter in a Selector.

Here's another Objective-C example:

```
NSString *helloWorldString = [@"Can't Sleep; "
stringByAppendingString:@"Clowns will eat me"];
```

The compiler will create the following (shown below in pseudocode):

```
NSString *helloWorldString;
helloWorldString = objc_msgSend(@"Can't Sleep; ",
"stringByAppendingString:", @"Clowns will eat me");
```

The first argument is an instance of an NSString (@"Can't Sleep; "), followed by the selector, followed by a parameter which is also an NSString instance.

Using this knowledge of objc_msgSend, you can use the registers in x64 to help explore content, which you'll do very shortly.

Putting theory to practice

For this section, you'll be using a project supplied in this chapter's resource bundle called **Registers**.

Open this project up through Xcode and give it a run.

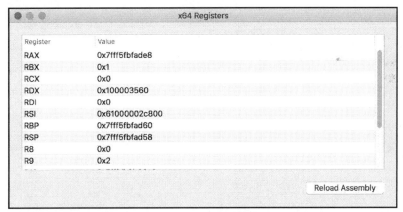

This is a rather simple application which merely displays the contents of some x64 registers. It's important to note that this application can't display the values of registers at any given moment, it can only display the values of registers during a specific function call. This means that you won't see too many changes to the values of these registers since they'll likely have the same (or similar) value when the function to grab the register values is called.

Now that you've got an understanding of the functionality behind the Registers macOS application, create a symbolic breakpoint for NSViewController's viewDidLoad method. Remember to use "NS" instead of "UI", since you're working on a Cocoa application.

Build and rerun the application. Once the debugger has stopped, type the following into the LLDB console:

```
(lldb) register read
```

This will list all of the main registers at the paused state of execution. However, this is too much information. You should selectively print out registers and treat them as Objective-C objects instead.

If you recall, −[NSViewController viewDidLoad] will be translated into the following assembly pseudocode:

```
RDI = UIViewControllerInstance
RSI = "viewDidLoad"
objc_msgSend(RDI, RSI)
```

With the x64 calling convention in mind, and knowing how objc_msgSend works, you can find the specific NSViewController that is being loaded.

Type the following into the LLDB console:

```
(lldb) po $rdi
```

You'll get output similar to the following:

```
<Registers.ViewController: 0x6080000c13b0>
```

This will dump out the NSViewController reference held in the RDI register, which as you now know, is the location of the first argument to the method.

In LLDB, it's important to prefix registers with the $ character, so LLDB knows you want the value of a register and not a variable related to your scope in the source code. Yes, that's different than the assembly you see in the disassembly view! Annoying, eh?

> **Note:** The observant among you might notice whenever you stop on an
> Objective-C method, you'll never see the objc_msgSend in the LLDB backtrace.
> This is because the objc_msgSend family of functions perfoms a **jmp**, or jump
> opcode command in assembly. This means that objc_msgSend acts as a
> trampoline function, and once the Objective-C code starts executing, all stack
> trace history of objc_msgSend will be gone. This is an optimization known as
> **tail call optimization.**

Try printing out the RSI register, which will hopefully contain the selector that was
called. Type the following into the LLDB console:

```
(lldb) po $rsi
```

Unfortunately, you'll get garbage output that looks something like this:

```
140735181830794
```

Why is this?

An Objective-C selector is basically just a char *. This means, like all C types, LLDB
does not know how to format this data. As a result, you must explicitly cast this reference
to the data type you want.

Try casting it to the correct type:

```
(lldb) po (char *)$rsi
```

You'll now get the expected:

```
"viewDidLoad"
```

Of course, you can also cast it to the Selector type to produce the same result:

```
(lldb) po (SEL)$rsi
```

Now, it's time to explore an Objective-C method with arguments. Since you've stopped
on viewDidLoad, you can safely assume the NSView instance has loaded. A method of
interest is the **mouseUp:** selector implemented by NSView's parent class, NSResponder.

In LLDB, create a breakpoint on NSResponder's mouseUp: selector and resume
execution. If you can't remember how to do that, here are the commands you need:

```
(lldb) b -[NSResponder mouseUp:]
(lldb) continue
```

Now, click on the application's window. Make sure to click on the outside of the NSScrollView as it will gobble up your click and the –[NSResponder mouseUp:] breakpoint will not get hit.

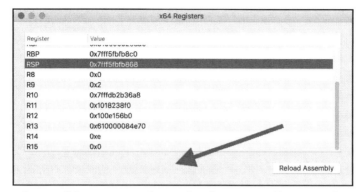

As soon as you let go of the mouse or the trackpad, LLDB will stop on the mouseUp: breakpoint. Print out the reference of the NSResponder by typing the following into the LLDB console:

```
(lldb) po $rdi
```

You'll get something similar to the following:

```
<NSView: 0x608000120140>
```

However, there's something interesting with the selector. There's a colon in it, meaning there's an argument to explore! Type the following into the LLDB console:

```
(lldb) po $rdx
```

You'll get the description of the NSEvent:

```
NSEvent: type=LMouseUp loc=(351.672,137.914) time=175929.4
flags=0 win=0x6100001e0400 winNum=8622 ctxt=0x0 evNum=10956
click=1 buttonNumber=0 pressure=0 deviceID:0x300000014400000
subtype=NSEventSubtypeTouch
```

How can you tell it's an NSEvent? Well, you can either look online for documentation on –[NSResponder mouseUp:] or, you can simply use Objective-C to get the type:

```
(lldb) po [$rdx class]
```

Pretty cool, eh?

Sometimes it's useful to use registers and breakpoints in order to get a reference to an object you know is alive in memory.

For example, what if you wanted to change the front NSWindow to red, but you had no reference to this view in your code, and you didn't want to recompile with any code changes? You can simply create a breakpoint you can easily trip, get the reference from the register and manipulate the instance of the object as you please. You'll try changing the main window to red now.

> **Note:** Even though `NSResponder` implements `mouseDown:`, `NSWindow` overrides this method since it's a subclass of `NSResponder`. You can dump all classes that implement `mouseDown:` and figure out which of those classes inherit from `NSResponder` to determine if the method is overridden without having access to the source code. An example of dumping all the Objective-C classes that implement `mouseDown:` is `image lookup -rn '\ mouseDown:'`

First remove any previous breakpoints using the LLDB console:

```
(lldb) breakpoint delete
About to delete all breakpoints, do you want to do that?: [Y/n]
```

Then type the following into the LLDB console:

```
(lldb) breakpoint set -o -S "-[NSWindow mouseDown:]"
(lldb) continue
```

This sets a breakpoint which will fire only once — a one-shot breakpoint.

Tap on the application. Immediately after tapping, the breakpoint should trip. Then type the following into the LLDB console:

```
(lldb) po [$rdi setBackgroundColor:[NSColor redColor]]
(lldb) continue
```

Upon resuming, the NSWindow will change to red!

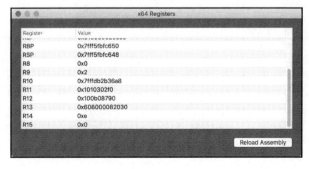

Swift and registers

When exploring registers in Swift you'll hit two hurdles that make assembly debugging harder than it is in Objective-C.

1. First, registers are **not** available in the Swift debugging context. This means you have to get whatever data you want and then use the Objective-C debugging context to print out the registers passed into the Swift function. Remember that you can use the `expression -l objc -O --` command, or alternatively use the `cpo` custom command you made in Chapter 8, "Persisting and Customizing Commands". Fortunately, the `register read` command is available in the Swift context.

2. Second, Swift is not as dynamic as Objective-C. In fact, it's sometimes best to assume that Swift is like C, except with a very, very cranky and bossy compiler. If you have a memory address, you need to explicitly cast it to the object you expect it to be; otherwise, the Swift debugging context has no clue how to interpret a memory address.

That being said, the same register calling convention is used in Swift. However, there's one *very* important difference. When Swift calls a function, it has no need to use `objc_msgSend`, unless of course you mark up a method to use **dynamic**. This means when Swift calls a function, the previously used RSI register assigned to the selector will actually contain the function's second parameter.

Enough theory — time to see this in action.

In the Registers project, navigate to **ViewController.swift** and add the following function to the class:

```
func executeLotsOfArguments(one: Int, two: Int, three: Int,
                            four: Int, five: Int, six: Int,
                            seven: Int, eight: Int, nine: Int,
                            ten: Int) {
    print("arguments are: \(one), \(two), \(three),
        \(four), \(five), \(six), \(seven),
        \(eight), \(nine), \(ten)")
}
```

Now, in `viewDidLoad`, call this function with the appropriate arguments:

```
override func viewDidLoad() {
  super.viewDidLoad()
  self.executeLotsOfArguments(one: 1, two: 2, three: 3, four: 4,
                              five: 5, six: 6, seven: 7,
                              eight: 8, nine: 9, ten: 10)
}
```

Put a breakpoint on the very same line as of the declaration of
executeLotsOfArguments so the debugger will stop at the very beginning of the
function. This is important, or else the registers might get clobbered if the function is
actually executing.

Then remove the symbolic breakpoint you set on -[NSViewController
viewDidLoad].

Build and run the app, then wait for the executeLotsOfArguments breakpoint to stop
execution.

Again, a good way to start investigating is to dump the list registers. In LLDB, type the
following:

```
(lldb) register read -f d
```

This will dump the registers and display the format in decimal by using the -f d option.
The output will look similar to this:

```
General Purpose Registers:
       rax = 7
       rbx = 9
       rcx = 4
       rdx = 3
       rdi = 1
       rsi = 2
       rbp = 140734799801424
       rsp = 140734799801264
        r8 = 5
        r9 = 6
       r10 = 10
       r11 = 8
       r12 = 107202385676032
       r13 = 106652628550688
       r14 = 10
       r15 = 4298620128   libswiftCore.dylib`swift_isaMask
       rip = 4294972615
Registers`Registers.ViewController.viewDidLoad () -> () + 167 at
ViewController.swift:16
     rflags = 518
         cs = 43
         fs = 0
         gs = 0
```

As you can see, the registers follow the x64 calling convention. RDI, RSI, RDX, RCX, R8
and R9 hold your first six parameters.

You may also notice other parameters are stored in some of the other registers. While this
is true, it's simply a leftover from the code that sets up the stack for the remaining
parameters. Remember, parameters after the sixth one go on the stack.

RAX, the return register

But wait — there's more! So far, you've learned how six registers are called in a function, but what about return values?

Fortunately, there is only one designated register for return values from functions: **RAX**. Go back to executeLotsOfArguments and modify the function to return a String, like so:

```
func executeLotsOfArguments(one: Int, two: Int, three: Int,
                    four: Int, five: Int, six: Int,
                    seven: Int, eight: Int, nine: Int,
                    ten: Int) -> String {
    print("arguments are: \(one), \(two), \(three), \(four),
        \(five), \(six), \(seven), \(eight), \(nine), \(ten)")
    return "Mom, what happened to the cat?"
}
```

In viewDidLoad, modify the function call to receive and ignore the String value.

```
override func viewDidLoad() {
    super.viewDidLoad()
    let _ = self.executeLotsOfArguments(one: 1, two: 2,
        three: 3, four: 4, five: 5, six: 6, seven: 7,
        eight: 8, nine: 9, ten: 10)
}
```

Create a breakpoint somewhere in executeLotsOfArguments. Build and run again, and wait for execution to stop in the function. Next, type the following into the LLDB console:

```
(lldb) finish
```

This will finish executing the current function and pause the debugger again. At this point, the return value from the function should be in RAX. Type the following into LLDB:

```
(lldb) register read rax
```

You'll get something similar to the following:

```
rax = 0x0000000100003760   "Mom, what happened to the cat?"
```

Boom! Your return value!

Knowledge of the return value in RAX is extremely important as it will form the foundation of debugging scripts you'll write in later sections.

Changing around values in registers

In order to solidify your understanding of registers, you'll modify registers in an already-compiled application.

Close Xcode and the Registers project. Open a Terminal window and launch the iPhone 7 Simulator. Do this by typing the following:

```
xcrun simctl list
```

You'll see a long list of devices. Search for the latest iOS version for which you have a simulator installed. Underneath that section, find the iPhone 7 device. It will look something like this:

```
iPhone 7 (269B10E1-15BE-40B4-AD24-B6EED125BC28) (Shutdown)
```

The UUID is what you're after. Use that to open the iOS Simulator by typing the following, replacing your UUID as appropriate:

```
open /Applications/Xcode.app/Contents/Developer/Applications/
Simulator.app --args -CurrentDeviceUDID 269B10E1-15BE-40B4-AD24-
B6EED125BC28
```

Make sure the simulator is launched and is sitting on the home screen. You can get to the home screen by pressing **Command + Shift + H**. Once your simulator is set up, head over to the Terminal window and attach LLDB to the SpringBoard application:

```
lldb -n SpringBoard
```

This attaches LLDB to the SpringBoard instance running on the iOS Simulator! SpringBoard is the program that controls the home screen on iOS.

Once attached, type the following into LLDB:

```
(lldb) p/x @"Yay! Debugging"
```

You should get some output similar to the following:

```
(__NSCFString *) $3 = 0x0000618000644080 @"Yay! Debugging!"
```

Take a note of the memory reference of this newly created NSString instance as you'll use it soon. Now, create a breakpoint on UILabel's setText: method in LLDB:

```
(lldb) b -[UILabel setText:]
```

Next, type the following in LLDB:

```
(lldb) breakpoint command add
```

LLDB will spew some output and go into multi-line edit mode. This command lets you add extra commands to execute when the breakpoint you just added is hit. Type the following, replacing the memory address with the address of your NSString from above:

```
> po $rdx = 0x0000618000644080
> continue
> DONE
```

Take a step back and review what you've just done. You've created a breakpoint on UILabel's setText: method. Whenever this method gets hit, you're replacing what's in RDX — the third parameter — with a different NSString instance that says **Yay! Debugging!**.

Resume the debugger by using the **continue** command:

```
(lldb) continue
```

Try exploring the SpringBoard Simulator app and see what content has changed. Swipe up from the bottom to bring up the Control Center, and observe the changes:

Try exploring other areas where modal presentations can occur, as this will likely result in a new UIViewController (and all of its subviews) being lazily loaded, causing the breakpoint action to be hit.

Although this might seem like a cool gimmicky programming trick, it provides an insightful look into how a limited knowledge of registers and assembly can produce big changes in applications you don't have the source for.

This is also useful from a debugging standpoint, as you can quickly visually verify where the -[UILabel setText:] is executed within the SpringBoard application and run breakpoint conditions to find the exact line of code that sets a particular UILabel's text.

To continue this thought, any UILabel instances whose text did not change also tells you something. For example, the UIButtons whose text didn't change to Yay! Debugging! speaks for itself. Perhaps the UILabel's setText: was called at an earlier time? Or maybe the developers of the SpringBoard application chose to use setAttributedText: instead? Or maybe they're using a private method that is not publicly available to third-party developers?

As you can see, using and manipulating registers can give you a lot of insight into how an application functions. :]

Where to go from here?

Whew! That was a long one, wasn't it? Sit back and take a break with your favorite form of liquid; you've earned it.

So what did you learn?

• Architectures define a calling convention which dictates where parameters to a function and its return value are stored.

> * In Objective-C, the `RDI` register is the reference of the calling `NSObject`, `RSI` is the Selector, `RDX` is the first parameter and so on.

- In Swift, RDI is the first argument, RSI is the second parameter, and so on provided that the Swift method isn't using dynamic dispatch.

- The RAX register is used for return values in functions regardless of whether you're working with Objective-C or Swift.

- Make sure you use the Objective-C context when printing registers with $.

There's a lot you can do with registers. Try exploring apps you don't have the source code for; it's a lot of fun and will build a good foundation for tackling tough debugging problems.

Try attaching to an application on the iOS Simulator and map out the UIViewControllers as they appear using assembly, a smart breakpoint, and a breakpoint command.

Chapter 11: Assembly & Memory

You've begun the journey and learned the dark arts of the x64 calling convention in the previous chapter. When a function is called, you now know how parameters are passed to functions, and how function return values come back. What you haven't learned yet is how code is executed when it's loaded into memory.

In this chapter, you'll explore how a program executes. You'll look at a special register used to tell the processor where it should read the next instruction from, as well as how different sizes and groupings of memory can produce *very* different results.

Setting up the Intel-Flavored Assembly Experience™

As mentioned in the previous chapter, there are two main ways to display assembly. One type, **AT&T** assembly, is the default assembly set for LLDB. This flavor has the following format:

```
opcode  source  destination
```

Take a look at a concrete example:

```
movq  $0x78, %rax
```

This will move the hexadecimal value 0x78 into the RAX register. Although this assembly flavor is nice for some, you'll use the **Intel** flavor instead from here on out.

> **Note:** The choice of assembly flavor is somewhat of a flame war — check out this discussion in StackOverflow: https://stackoverflow.com/questions/972602/att-vs-intel-syntax-and-limitations.
>
> The choice to use Intel was based on the admittedly loose consensus that Intel is better for reading, but at times, worse for writing. Since you're learning about debugging, the majority of time you'll be reading assembly as opposed to writing it.

Add the following lines to the bottom of your **~/.lldbinit** file:

```
settings set target.x86-disassembly-flavor intel
settings set target.skip-prologue false
```

The first line tells LLDB to display x86 assembly (both 32-bit and 64-bit) in the Intel flavor.

The second line tells LLDB to not skip the function prologue. You came across this earlier in this book, and from now on it's prudent to not skip the prologue since you'll be inspecting assembly right from the first instruction in a function.

> **Note:** When editing your **~/.lldbinit** file, make sure you don't use a program like TextEdit for this, as it will add unnecessary characters into the file that could

> result in LLDB not correctly parsing the file. An easy (although dangerous) way to add this is through a terminal command like so: `echo "settings set target.x86-disassembly-flavor intel" >> ~/.lldbinit`.
>
> Make sure you have two '>>' in there or else you'll overwrite all your previous content in your **~/.lldbinit** file. If you're not comfortable with the Terminal, editors like `nano` (which you've used earlier) are your best bet.

The Intel flavor will swap the source and destination values, remove the '%' and '$' characters as well as do many, many other changes. Since you'll not use the AT&T syntax, it's better to not explain the full differences between the two assembly flavors, and instead just learn the Intel format.

Take a look at the previous example, now shown in the Intel flavor and see how much cleaner it looks:

```
mov  rax, 0x78
```

Again, this will move the hexadecimal value `0x78` into the `RAX` register.

Compared to the AT&T flavor shown earlier, the Intel flavor swaps the source and destination operands. The destination operand now precedes the source operand. When working with assembly, it's important you always identify the correct flavor, since you could expect a different action to occur if you're not clear which flavor you're working with.

From here on out, the Intel flavor will be the path forward. If you ever see a numeric hexadecimal constant that begins with a $ character, or a register that begins with %, know that you're in the wrong assembly flavor and should change it using the process described above.

Creating the cpx command

First of all, you're going to create your own LLDB command to help later on.

Open `~/.lldbinit` again in your favorite text editor (vim, right?). Then add the following to the bottom of the file:

```
command alias -H "Print value in ObjC context in hexadecimal" -h
"Print in hex" -- cpx expression -f x -l objc --
```

This command, **cpx**, is a convenience command you can use to print out something in hexadecimal format, using the Objective-C context. This will be useful when printing out register contents.

Remember, registers aren't available in the Swift context, so you need to use the Objective-C context instead.

Now you have the tools needed to explore memory in this chapter through an assembly point of view!

Bits, bytes, and other terminology

Before you begin exploring memory, you need to be aware of some vocabulary about how memory is grouped.

A value that can contain either a 1 or a 0 is known as a **bit**. You can say there are 64 bits per address in a 64-bit architecture. Simple enough.

When there are 8 bits grouped together, they're known as a **byte**. How many unique values can a byte hold? You can determine that by calculating 2^8 which will be 256 values, starting from 0 and going to 255.

Lots of information is expressed in bytes. For example, the C `sizeof()` function returns the size of the object in bytes.

If you are familiar with ASCII character encoding, you'll recall all ASCII characters can be held in a single byte.

It's time to take a look at this terminology in action and learn some tricks along the way.

Open up the **Registers** macOS application which you'll find in the resources folder for this chapter. Next, build and run the app. Once it's running, pause the program and bring up the LLDB console. As mentioned previously, this will result in the non-Swift debugging context being used.

```
(lldb) p sizeof('A')
```

This will print out the number of bytes required to make up the 'A' character:

```
(unsigned long) $0 = 1
```

Next, type the following:

```
(lldb) p/t 'A'
```

You'll get the following output:

```
(char) $1 = 0b01000001
```

This is the binary representation for the character A in ASCII.

Another more common way to display a byte of information is using hexadecimal values. Two hexadecimal digits are required to represent a byte of information in hexadecimal.

Print out the hexadecimal representation of 'A':

```
(lldb) p/x 'A'
```

You'll get the following output:

```
(char) $2 = 0x41
```

Hexadecimal is great for viewing memory because a single hexadecimal digit represents exactly 4 bits. So if you have 2 hexadecimal digits, you have 1 byte. If you have 8 hexadecimal digits, you have 4 bytes. And so on.

Here's a few more terms for you that you'll find useful in the chapters to come:

- **Nybble**: 4 bits, a single value in hexadecimal

- **Half word**: 16 bits, or 2 bytes

- **Word**: 32 bits, or 4 bytes

- **Double word** or **Giant word**: 64 bits or 8 bytes.

With this terminology, you're all set to explore the different memory chunks.

The RIP register

Ah, the exact register to put on your gravestone.

When a program executes, code to be executed is loaded into memory. The location of which code to execute next in the program is determined by one magically important register: the **RIP** or **instruction pointer** register.

Let's take a look at that in action. Open the **Registers** application again and navigate to the **AppDelegate.swift** file. Modify the file so it contains the following code:

```
@NSApplicationMain
class AppDelegate: NSObject, NSApplicationDelegate {

  func applicationWillBecomeActive(
    _ notification: Notification) {
      print("\(#function)")
      self.aBadMethod()
  }

  func aBadMethod() {
```

```
    print("\(#function)")
  }

  func aGoodMethod() {
    print("\(#function)")
  }
}
```

Build and run the application. Unsuprisingly, the method name will get spat out in `applicationWillBecomeActive(_:)` to the debug console, followed by the `aBadMethod` output. There will be no execution of `aGoodMethod`.

Create a breakpoint at the very begining of the `aBadMethod` using the Xcode GUI:

```
 9  import Cocoa
10
11  @NSApplicationMain
12  class AppDelegate: NSObject, NSApplicationDelegate {
13
14    func applicationWillFinishLaunching(_ notification: Notification) {
15      print("\(#function)")
16      self.aBadMethod()
17    }
18
19    func aBadMethod() {
20      print("\(#function)")
21    }
22
23    func aGoodMethod() {
24      print("\(#function)")
25    }
26  }
27
28
```

Build and run again. Once the breakpoint is hit at the beginning of the `aBadMethod`, navigate to **Debug\Debug Workflow\Always Show Disassembly** in Xcode. You'll now see the actual assembly of the program!

Next, type the following into the LLDB console:

```
(lldb) cpx $rip
```

This prints out the instruction pointer register using the `cpx` command you created earlier.

You'll notice the output LLDB spits out will match the address highlighted by the green line in Xcode:

```
(unsigned long) $1 = 0x0000000100006b70
```

It's worth noting your address could be different than the above output, but the address of the green line and the RIP console output will match. Now, enter the following command in LLDB:

```
(lldb) image lookup -vrn ^Registers.*aGoodMethod
```

This is the tried-and-true `image lookup` command with the typical regular expression arguments plus an added argument, `-v`, which dumps the verbose output.

You'll get a fair bit of content. Search for the content immediately following `range = [`; **Command + F** will prove useful here. It's the first value in the range brackets that you're looking for.

This address is known as the **load address**. This is the actual physical address of this function in memory.

This differs from the usual output you've seen in the `image lookup` command, in it only displays the offset of the function relative to the executable, also known as the **implementation offset**. When hunting for a function's address, it's important to differentiate the load address from the implementation offset in an executable, as it will differ.

Copy this new address at the beginning of the range brackets. For this particular example, the load address of `aGoodMethod` is located at `0x0000000100003a10`. Now, write this address which points the beginning of the `aGoodMethod` method to the RIP register.

```
(lldb) register write rip 0x0000000100003a10
```

Click **continue** using the Xcode debug button. It's important you do this instead of typing `continue` in LLDB, as there is a bug that will trip you up when modifying the RIP register and continuing in the console.

After pressing the Xcode continue button, you'll see that aBadMethod() is not executed and aGoodMethod() is executed instead. Verify this by viewing the output in the console log.

> **Note:** Modifying the RIP register is actually a bit dangerous. You need to make sure the registers holding data for a previous value in the RIP register do not get applied to a new function which makes an incorrect assumption with the registers. Since aGoodMethod and aBadMethod are very similar in functionality, you've stopped at the beginning, and as no optimizations were applied to the Registers application, this is not a worry.

Registers and breaking up the bits

As mentioned in the previous chapter, x64 has 16 general purpose registers: RDI, RSI, RAX, RDX, RBP, RSP, RCX, RDX, R8, R9, R10, R11, R12, R13, R14 and R15.

In order to maintain compatibility with previous architectures, such as i386's 32-bit architecture, registers can be broken up into their 32, 16, or 8-bit values.

For registers that have had a history across different architectures, the frontmost character in the name given to the register determines the size of the register. For example, the RIP register starts with R, which signifies 64 bits. If you wanted the 32 bit equivalent of the RIP register, you'd swap out the R character with an E, to get the EIP register.

64-bit Register	32-bit Register	16-bit Register	8-bit Register
rax	eax	ax	al
rbx	ebx	bx	bl
rcx	ecx	cx	cl
rdx	edx	dx	dl
rsi	esi	si	sil
rdi	edi	di	dil
rbp	ebp	bp	bpl
rsp	esp	sp	spl
r8	r8d	r8w	r8l
r9	r9d	r9w	r9l
r10	r10d	r10w	r10l
r11	r11d	r11w	r11l
r12	r12d	r12w	r12l
r13	r13d	r13w	r13l
r14	r14d	r14w	r14l
r15	r15d	r15w	r15l

Why is this useful? When working with registers, sometimes the value passed into a register does not need to use all 64 bits. For example, consider the Boolean data type. All you really need is a 1 or a 0 to indicate true or false, right? Based upon the languages features and constraints, the compiler knows this and will sometimes only write information to certain parts of a register.

Let's see this in action.

Remove all breakpoints in the Registers project. Build and run the project. Now, pause the program out of the blue.

Once stopped, type the following:

```
(lldb) register write rdx 0x0123456789ABCDEF
```

This writes a value to the RDX register.

Let's halt for a minute. A word of warning: You should be aware that writing to registers could cause your program to tank, especially if the register you write to is expected to have a certain type of data. But you're doing this in the name of science, so don't worry if your program does crash!

Confirm that this value has been successfully written to the RDX register:

```
(lldb) p/x $rdx
```

Since this is a 64-bit program, you'll get a double word, i.e. 64 bits, or 8 bytes, or 16 hexadecimal digits.

Now, try printing out the EDX register:

```
(lldb) p/x $edx
```

The EDX register is the least-significant half of the RDX register. So you'll only see the least-significant half of the double word, i.e., a word. You should see the following:

```
0x89abcdef
```

Next, type the following:

```
(lldb) p/x $dx
```

This will print out the DX register, which is the least-significant half of the EDX register. It is therefore a half word. You should see the following:

```
0xcdef
```

Next, type the following:

```
(lldb) p/x $dl
```

This prints out the DL register, which is the least-significant half of the DX register — a byte this time. You should see the following:

```
0xef
```

Finally, type the following:

```
(lldb) p/x $dh
```

This gives you the most significant half of the DX register, i.e. the other half to that given by DL. It should come as no surprise that the L in DL stands for "low" and the H in DH stands for "high".

Keep an eye out for registers with different sizes when exploring assembly. The size of the registers can give clues about the values contained within. For example, you can easily hunt down functions that return Booleans by looking for registers having the L suffix, since a Boolean needs only a single bit to be used.

Registers R8 to R15

Since the R8 to R15 family of registers were created only for 64-bit architectures, they use a completely different format for signifying their smaller counterparts.

Now you'll explore R9's different sizing options. Build and run the Registers application, and pause the debugger. Like before, write the same hex value to the R9 register:

```
(lldb) register write $r9 0x0123456789abcdef
```

Confirm that you've set the R9 register by typing the following:

```
(lldb) p/x $r9
```

Next type the following:

```
(lldb) p/x $r9d
```

This will print the lower 32 bits of the R9 register. Note how it's different than how you specified the lower 32 bits for RDX (that is, EDX, if you've forgotten already).

Next, type the following:

```
(lldb) p/x $r9w
```

This time you get the lower 16 bits of R9. Again, this is different than how you did this for RDX.

Finally, type the following:

```
(lldb) p/x $r9l
```

This prints out the lower 8 bits of R9.

Although this seems a bit tedious, you're building up the skills to read an onslaught of assembly.

Breaking down the memory

Now that you've taken a look at the instruction pointer, it's time to further explore the memory behind it. As its name suggests, the instruction pointer is actually a **pointer**. It's not executing the instructions stored in the RIP register — it's executing the instructions pointed to in the RIP register.

Seeing this in LLDB will perhaps describe it better. Back in the Registers application, open **AppDelegate.swift** and once again set a breakpoint on aBadMethod. Build and run the app.

Once the breakpoint is hit and the program is stopped, navigate back to the assembly view. If you forgot, and haven't created a keyboard shortcut for it, it's found under Debug\Debug Workflow\Always Show Disassembly.

You'll be greeted by the onslaught of opcodes and registers. Take a look at the location of the RIP register which should be pointing to the very beginning of the function.

For this particular build, the beginning address of aBadMethod begins as **0x1000017c0**. As usual, your address will likely be different.

In the LLDB console, type the following:

```
(lldb) cpx $rip
```

As you know by now, this prints out the contents of the instruction pointer register.

As expected, you'll get the address of the start of aBadMethod. But again, the RIP register points to a value in memory. What is it pointing to? Well... you could dust off your mad C coding skillz (you remember those, right?) and dereference the pointer, but there's a much more elegant way to go about it using LLDB.

Type the following, replacing the address with the address of your aBadMethod function:

```
(lldb) memory read -fi -c1 0x1000017c0
```

Wow, what the heck does that command do?!

memory read takes a value and reads the contents pointed at by the memory address you supply. The -f command is a formatting argument; in this case, it's the assembly **instruction** format. Finally you're saying you only want one assembly instruction to be printed out with the **count**, or -c argument.

You'll get output that looks similar to this:

```
-> 0x1000017c0: 55  pushq  %rbp
```

This here is some gooooooooood output. It's telling you the assembly instruction, as well as the opcode, provided in hexadecimal (**0x55**) that is responsible for the pushq %rbp operation.

> **Note:** Wait, did you see a '%' preceeding a register?! There's a bug in LLDB that doesn't honor your assembly flavor when printing code in the instruction format. Remember, if you see this kind of thing the source and destination operands are reversed!

Let's look at that "55" there in the output some more. This is an encoding of the entire instruction, i.e. the whole pushq %rbp. Don't believe me? You can verify it. Type the following into LLDB:

```
(lldb) expression -f i -l objc -- 0x55
```

This effectively asks LLDB to decode 0x55. You'll get the following output:

```
$1 = 55  pushq  %rbp
```

That command is a little long, but it's because you need the required switch to Objective-C context if you are in the Swift debugging context. However, if you move to the Objective-C debugging context, you can use a convenience expression that is a lot shorter.

Try clicking on a different frame in the left panel of Xcode to get into an Objective-C context which doesn't contain Swift or Objective-C/Swift bridging code. Click on any frame which is in an Objective-C function.

Next, type the following into the LLDB console:

```
(lldb) p/i 0x55
```

Much better, right?

Now, back to the application in hand. Type the following into LLDB, replacing the address once again with your aBadMethod function address:

```
(lldb) memory read –fi –c10 0x1000017c0
```

You'll get 10x the output! That's something worthy to put on that LinkedIn résumé...

```
->  0x100003840: 55                 pushq   %rbp
    0x100003841: 48 89 e5           movq    %rsp, %rbp
    0x100003844: 48 83 ec 60        subq    $0x60, %rsp
    0x100003848: b8 01 00 00 00     movl    $0x1, %eax
    0x10000384d: 89 c1              movl    %eax, %ecx
    0x10000384f: 48 89 7d f8        movq    %rdi, -0x8(%rbp)
    0x100003853: 48 89 cf           movq    %rcx, %rdi
    0x100003856: e8 75 05 00 00     callq   0x100003dd0
; symbol stub for: generic specialization <preserving fragile
attribute, Any> of Swift._allocateUninitializedArray <A>
(Builtin.Word) -> (Swift.Array<A>, Builtin.RawPointer)
    0x10000385b: be 03 00 00 00     movl    $0x3, %esi
    0x100003860: 89 f7              movl    %esi, %edi
```

There's something interesting to note here: assembly instructions can have variable lengths. Take a look at the first instruction, versus the rest of the instructions in the output. The first instruction is 1 byte long, represented by 0x55. The following instruction is 3 bytes long.

Make sure you are still in an Objective-C context, and try to print out the opcode responsible for this instruction. It's just 3 bytes, so all you have to do is join them together, right?

```
(lldb) p/i 0x4889e5
```

You'll get a different instruction completely unrelated to the mov %rsp, %rbp instruction! You'll see this:

```
e5 89  inl    $0x89, %eax
```

What gives? Perhaps now would be a good time to talk about **endianness**.

Endianness... this stuff is reversed?

The x64 as well as the ARM family architecture devices all use **little-endian**, which means that data is stored in memory with the least significant byte first. If you were to store the number 0xabcd in memory, the 0xcd byte would be stored first, followed by the 0xab byte.

Back to the instruction example, this means that the instruction 0x4889e5 will be stored in memory as 0xe5, followed by 0x89, followed by 0x48.

Jumping back to that mov instruction you encountered earlier, try reversing the bytes that used to make up the assembly instruction. Type the following into LLDB:

```
(lldb) p/i 0xe58948
```

You'll now get your expected assembly instruction:

```
$2 = 48 89 e5  movq   %rsp, %rbp
```

Let's see some more examples of little-endian in action. Type the following into LLDB:

```
(lldb) memory read -s1 -c20 -fx 0x100003840
```

This command reads the memory at address 0x100003840. It reads in size chunks of 1 byte thanks to the -s1 option, and a count of 20 thanks to the -c20 option. You'll see something like this:

```
0x100003840: 0x55 0x48 0x89 0xe5 0x48 0x83 0xec 0x60
0x100003848: 0xb8 0x01 0x00 0x00 0x00 0x89 0xc1 0x48
0x100003850: 0x89 0x7d 0xf8 0x48
```

Now, double the size and half the count like so:

```
(lldb) memory read -s2 -c10 -fx 0x100003840
```

You will see something like this:

```
0x100003840: 0x4855 0xe589 0x8348 0x60ec 0x01b8 0x0000 0x8900
0x48c1
0x100003850: 0x7d89 0x48f8
```

Notice how when the memory values are grouped together, they are reversed thanks to being in little-endian.

Now double the size and half the count again:

```
(lldb) memory read -s4 -c5 -fx 0x100003840
```

And now you'll get something like this:

```
0x100003840: 0xe5894855 0x60ec8348 0x000001b8 0x48c18900
0x100003850: 0x48f87d89
```

Once again the values are reversed compared to the previous output.

This is *very* important to remember and also a source of confusion when exploring memory. Not only will the size of memory give you a potentially incorrect answer, but also the order. Remember this when you start yelling at your computer when you're trying to figure out how something should work!

Where to go from here?

Good job getting through this one. Memory layout can be a confusing topic. Try exploring memory on other devices to make sure you have a solid understanding of the little-endian architecture and how assembly is grouped together.

In the next chapter, you'll explore the stack frame and how a function gets called.

Chapter 12: Assembly and the Stack

When there are more than six parameters passed into a function, the excess parameters are passed through the stack (there's situations when this is not true, but one thing at a time, young grasshopper). But what does *being passed on the stack* mean exactly? It's time to take a deeper dive into what happens when a function is called from an assembly standpoint by exploring some "stack related" registers as well as the contents in the stack.

Understanding how the stack works is useful when you're reverse engineering programs, since you can help deduce what parameters are being manipulated in a certain function when no debugging symbols are available. In a later section, you'll use the knowledge from this chapter to build a command in LLDB which scrapes through functions in memory to find potentially interesting classes to explore.

Let's begin.

The stack, revisited

As discussed previously in Chapter 6, "Thread, Frame & Stepping Around", when a program executes, the memory is laid out so the stack starts at a "high address" and grows downward, towards a lower address; that is, towards the heap.

> **Note**: In some architectures, the stack grows upwards. But for x64 and ARM for iOS devices, the two you care about, both grow the the stack downwards.

Confused? Here's an image to help clarify how the stack moves.

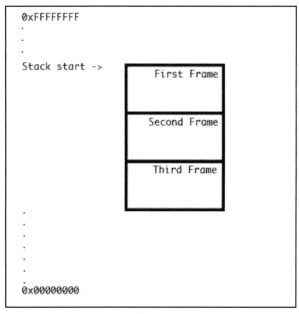

The stack starts at a high address. How high, exactly, is determined by the operating system's kernel. The kernel gives stack space to each running program (well, each thread).

The stack is finite in size and increases by growing downwards in memory address space. As space on the stack is used up, the pointer to the "top" of the stack moves down from the highest address to the lowest address.

Once the stack reaches the finite size given by the kernel, or if it crosses the bounds of the heap, the stack is said to *overflow*. This is a fatal error, often referred to as a *stack overflow*. Now you know where that website resource you often use gets its name from!

Stack pointer & base pointer registers

Two very important registers you've yet to learn about are the **RSP** and **RBP**. The stack pointer register, RSP, points to the head of the stack for a particular thread. The head of the stack will grow downwards, so the RSP will decrement when items are added to the stack. The RSP will *always* point to the head of the stack.

Here's a visual of the stack pointer changing when a function is called.

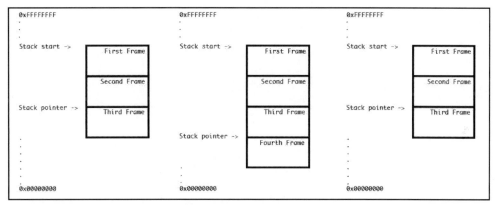

In the above image, the sequence of the stack pointer follows:

1. The stack pointer currently points to Frame 3

2. The code pointed to by the instruction pointer register calls a new function. The stack pointer gets updated to point to a new frame, Frame 4, which is potentially responsible for scratchspace and data inside this newly called function from the instruction pointer.

3. Execution is completed in Frame 4 and control resumes back in Frame 3. The stack pointer's previous reference to Frame 4 gets popped off and resumes pointing to Frame 3

The other important register, the base pointer register (RBP), has multiple uses during a function being executed. Programs use offsets from the RBP to access local variables or function parameters while execution is inside the method/function. This happens because the RBP is set to the value of the RSP register at the beginning of a function in the **function prologue**.

The interesting thing here is the previous contents of the base pointer is stored on the stack *before* it's set to the value of the RSP register. This is the first thing that happens in the function prologue. Since the base pointer is saved onto the stack and set to the current stack pointer, you can traverse the stack just by knowing the value in the base pointer register. A debugger does this when it shows you the stack trace.

> **Note:** Some systems don't use a base pointer, and it's possible to compile your application to omit using the base pointer. The logic is it might be beneficial to have an extra register to use. But this means you can't unwind the stack easily, which makes debugging much harder.

Yeah, an image is definitely needed to help explain :].

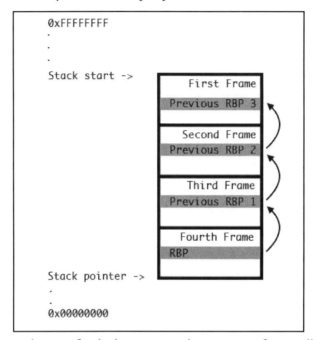

When a function prologue is finished setting up, the contents of RBP will point to the previous RBP a stack frame lower.

> **Note:** When you jump to a different stack frame by clicking on a frame in Xcode or using LLDB, both the RBP & RSP registers will change values to correspond to the new frame! This is expected because local variables for a function use offsets of RBP to get their values.
>
> If the RBP didn't change, you'd be unable to print local variables to that function, and the program might even crash. This might result in a source of confusion when exploring the RBP & RSP registers, so always keep this in mind. You can verify this in LLDB by selecting different frames and typing cpx $rbp or cpx $rsp in the LLDB console.

So why are these two registers important to learn about? When a program is compiled with debug information, the debug information references offsets from the base pointer register to get a variable. These offsets are given names, the same names you gave your variables in your source code.

When a program is compiled and optimized for release, the debug information that comes packaged into the binary is removed. Although the names to the references of these variables and parameters are removed, you can still use offsets of the stack pointer and base pointer to find the location of where these references are stored.

Stack related opcodes

So far, you've learned about the calling convention and how the memory is laid out, but haven't really explored what the many opcodes actually *do* in x64 assembly. It's time to focus on several stack related opcodes in more detail.

The 'push' opcode

When anything such as an `int`, Objective-C instance, Swift class or a reference needs to be saved onto the stack, the **push** opcode is used. `push` decrements the stack pointer (remember, the stack grows downward), then stores the value assigned to the memory address pointed at by the new RSP value.

After a `push` instruction, the most recently pushed value will be located at the address pointed to by RSP. The previous value would be at RSP plus the size of the most recently pushed value — usually 8 bytes for 64-bit architecture.

To see at a concrete example, consider the following opcode:

```
push 0x5
```

This would decrement the RSP, then store the value 5 in the memory address pointed to by RSP. So, in C pseudocode:

```
RSP = RSP - 0x8
*RSP = 0x5
```

The 'pop' opcode

The **pop** opcode is the exact opposite of the `push` opcode. `pop` takes the value from the RSP register and stores it to a destination. Next, the RSP is incremented by `0x8` because, again, as the stack gets smaller, it will grow to a higher address.

Below is an example of pop:

```
pop rdx
```

This stores the value of the RSP register into the RDX register, then increments the RSP register. Here's the pseudocode below:

```
RDX = *RSP
RSP = RSP + 0x8
```

The 'call' opcode

The **call** opcode is responsible for executing a function. call pushes the address of where to return to after the called function completes; then jumps to the function.

Imagine a function at 0x7fffb34df410 in memory like so:

```
0x7fffb34de913 <+227>: call    0x7fffb34df410
0x7fffb34de918 <+232>: mov     edx, eax
```

When an instruction is executed, first the RIP register is incremented, then the instruction is executed. So, when the call instruction is executed, the RIP register will increment to 0x7fffb34de918, then execute the instruction pointed to by 0x7fffb34de913. Since this is a call instruction, the RIP register is pushed onto the stack (just as if a push had been executed) then the RIP register is set to the value 0x7fffb34df410, the address of the function to be executed.

The pseudocode would look similar to the following:

```
RIP = 0x7fffb34de918
RSP = RSP - 0x8
*RSP = RIP
RIP = 0x7fffb34df410
```

From there, execution continues at the location 0x7fffb34df410.

Computers are pretty cool, aren't they?

The 'ret' opcode

The **ret** opcode is the opposite of the call opcode, in that it pops the top value off the stack (which will be the return address pushed on by the call opcode, provided the assembly's pushes and pops match) then sets the RIP register to this address. Thus execution goes back to where the function was called from.

Now that you have a basic understanding of these four important opcodes, it's time to see them in action.

It's *very* important to have all push opcodes match your pop opcodes, or else the stack will get out of sync. For example, if there was no corresponding pop for a push, when the ret happened at the end of the function, the wrong value would be popped off. Execution would return to some random place, potentially not even a valid place in the program. Fortunately, the compiler will take care of synchronizing your push and pop opcodes. You only need to worry about this when you're writing your own assembly... which you'll be doing in the next chapter. Muahaha!

Observing RBP & RSP in action

Now you've an understanding of the RBP and RSP registers, as well as the four opcodes that manipulate the stack, it's time to see it all in action.

In the Registers application lives a function named **StackWalkthrough(int)**. This C function takes one integer as a parameter and is written in assembly (AT&T assembly, remember to be able to spot the correct location for the source and destination operands) and is located in **StackWalkthrough.s**. Open this file and have a look around; there's no need to understand it all just now. You'll learn how it works in a minute.

This function is made available to Swift through a bridging header **Registers-Bridging-Header.h**, so you can call this method written in assembly from Swift.

Now to make use of this.

Open **ViewController.swift**, and add the following below viewDidLoad():

```
override func awakeFromNib() {
  super.awakeFromNib()
  StackWalkthrough(5)
}
```

This will call StackWalkThrough with a parameter of 5. The 5 is simply a value used to show how the stack works.

Before exploring RSP and RBP in depth, it's best to get a quick overview of what is happening in StackWalkthrough. Create a **symbolic breakpoint** on the StackWalkthrough function.

Once created, build and run.

Xcode will break on StackWalkthrough, which contains the following assembly:

```
push   %rbp         ; Push contents of RBP onto the stack (*RSP =
RBP, RSP decreases)
movq   %rsp, %rbp ; RBP = RSP
movq   $0x0, %rdx ; RDX = 0
movq   %rdi, %rdx ; RDX = RDI
push   %rdx         ; Push contents of RDX onto the stack (*RSP =
RDX, RSP decreases)
movq   $0x0, %rdx ; RDX = 0
pop    %rdx         ; Pop top of stack into RDX (RDX = *RSP, RSP
increases)
pop    %rbp         ; Pop top of stack into RBP (RBP = *RSP, RSP
increases)
ret                 ; Return from function (RIP = *RSP, RSP
increases)
```

Comments have been added to help understand what's happening. Read it through and try to understand it if you can. You're already familiar with the mov instruction, and the rest of the assembly consists of function related opcodes you've just learned about.

This function takes the integer parameter passed into it (as you'll recall, the first parameter is passed in RDI), stores it into the RDX register, and pushes this parameter onto the stack. RDX is then set to 0x0, then the value popped off the stack is stored back into the RDX register.

Make sure you have a good mental understanding of what is happening in this function, as you'll be exploring the registers in LLDB next.

Back in Xcode, create a breakpoint using Xcode's GUI on the StackWalkthrough(5) line in the awakeFromNib function of **ViewController.swift**. Leave the previous StackWalkthrough symbolic breakpoint alive, since you'll want to stop at the beginning of the StackWalkthrough function when exploring the registers.

Build and run and wait for the GUI breakpoint to trigger.

Now click **Debug\Debug Workflow\Always Show Disassembly**, to show the disassembly. You'll be greeted with scary looking stuff!

Wow! Look at that! You've landed right on a `call` opcode instruction. Do you wonder what function you're about to enter?

From here on out, you'll step through every assembly instruction while printing out four registers of interest: RBP, RSP, RDI and RDX. To help with this, type the following into LLDB:

```
(lldb) command alias dumpreg register read rsp rbp rdi rdx
```

This creates the command **dumpreg** that will dump the four registers of interest. Execute dumpreg now:

```
(lldb) dumpreg
```

You'll see something similar to the following:

```
rsp = 0x00007fff5fbfe820
rbp = 0x00007fff5fbfe850
rdi = 0x0000000000000005
rdx = 0x0040000000000000
```

For this section, the output of dumpreg will be overlaid on each assembly instruction to show exactly what is happening with each of the registers during each instruction. Again, even though the values are provided for you, it's very important you execute and understand these commands yourself.

Your screen will look similar to the following:

```
 6    0x10000240c <+12>: mov    qword ptr [rbp - 0x2    (lldb) .dumpreg               retain
 7    0x100002410 <+16>: call   0x100008b28                 rsp = 0x00007fff5bfe760
 8    0x100002415 <+21>: mov    rdi, qword ptr [rbp -       rbp = 0x00007fff5bfe790
 9    0x100002419 <+25>: mov    qword ptr [rbp - 0x2        rdi = 0x0000000000000005
10    0x10000241d <+29>: mov    qword ptr [rbp - 0x3        rdx = 0x0040000000000000
11    0x100002421 <+33>: call   0x100002380                 ; type metadata accessor for
      Registers.ViewController at ViewController.swift
12    0x100002426 <+38>: lea    rdi, [rbp - 0x18]
13    0x10000242a <+42>: mov    rcx, qword ptr [rbp - 0x30]
14    0x10000242e <+46>: mov    qword ptr [rbp - 0x18], rcx
15    0x100002432 <+50>: mov    qword ptr [rbp - 0x10], rax
16    0x100002436 <+54>: mov    rsi, qword ptr [rip + 0xaa4b] ; "awakeFromNib"
17    0x10000243d <+61>: call   0x100008b1c              ; symbol stub for: objc_msgSendSuper2
18    0x100002442 <+66>: mov    rdi, qword ptr [rbp - 0x20]
19    0x100002446 <+70>: call   0x100008b22              ; symbol stub for: objc_release
20    0x10000244b <+75>: mov    edi, 0x5
21 -> 0x100002450 <+80>: call   0x100002020             ; StackWalkthrough       Thread 1: breakpoint 2.1
22    0x100002455 <+85>: add    rsp, 0x30
23    0x100002459 <+89>: pop    rbp
24    0x10000245a <+90>: ret
25
```

Once you jump into the function call, keep a *very* close eye on the RSP register, as it's about to change once RIP jumps to the beginning of StackWalkthrough. As you've learned earlier, the RDI register will contain the value for the first parameter, which is 0x5 in this case.

In LLDB, type the following:

```
(lldb) si
```

This is an alias for thread step-inst, which tells LLDB to execute the next instruction and then pause the debugger.

You've now stepped into StackWalkthrough. Again for each step, dump out the registers using dumpreg.

```
 1    Registers`StackWalkthrough:
 2 -> 0x100002020 <+0>:  push   rbp          (lldb) dumpreg                          Thread 1: breakpoint 1.1
 3    0x100002021 <+1>:  mov    rbp, rsp          rsp = 0x00007fff5bfe758
 4    0x100002024 <+4>:  mov    rdx, 0x0          rbp = 0x00007fff5bfe790
 5    0x10000202b <+11>: mov    rdx, rdi          rdi = 0x0000000000000005
 6    0x10000202e <+14>: push   rdx               rdx = 0x0040000000000000
 7    0x10000202f <+15>: mov    rdx, 0x0
 8    0x100002036 <+22>: pop    rdx
 9    0x100002037 <+23>: pop    rbp
10    0x100002038 <+24>: ret
```

Take note of the difference in the RSP register. The value pointed at by RSP will now contain the return address to the previous function. For this particular example, RSP, which points to 0x7fff5bfe758, will contain the value 0x100002455 — the address immediately following the call in awakeFromNib.

Verify this now through LLDB:

```
(lldb) x/gx $rsp
```

The output will match the address immediately following the call opcode in awakeFromNib.

Next, perform an `si`, then `dumpreg` for the next instruction.

```
 1 Registers`StackWalkthrough:                     (lldb) dumpreg
 2    0x100002020 <+0>:   push   rbp                 rsp = 0x00007fff5fbfe750
 3 -> 0x100002021 <+1>:   mov    rbp, rsp            rbp = 0x00007fff5fbfe790   Thread 1: instruction step into
 4    0x100002024 <+4>:   mov    rdx, 0x0            rdi = 0x0000000000000005
 5    0x10000202b <+11>:  mov    rdx, rdi            rdx = 0x0040000000000000
 6    0x10000202e <+14>:  push   rdx
 7    0x10000202f <+15>:  mov    rdx, 0x0
 8    0x100002036 <+22>:  pop    rdx
 9    0x100002037 <+23>:  pop    rbp
10    0x100002038 <+24>:  ret
```

The value of RBP is pushed onto the stack. This means the following two commands will produce the same output. Execute both of them to verify.

```
(lldb) x/gx $rsp
```

This looks at the memory address pointed at by the stack pointer register.

> **Note:** Wait, I just threw a new command at you with no context. The x command is a shortcut for the `memory read` command. The `/gx` says to format the memory in a giant word (8 bytes, remember that terminology from Chapter 11, "Assembly & Memory"?) in hexadecimal format. The weird formatting is due to the popularity of this command in **gdb**, which saw this command syntax ported into **lldb** to make the transition from debuggers easier.

Now look at the value in the base pointer register.

```
(lldb) p/x $rbp
```

Next, step into the next instruction, using `si` again:

```
 1 Registers`StackWalkthrough:                     (lldb) dumpreg
 2    0x100002020 <+0>:   push   rbp                 rsp = 0x00007fff5fbfe750
 3    0x100002021 <+1>:   mov    rbp, rsp            rbp = 0x00007fff5fbfe750
 4 -> 0x100002024 <+4>:   mov    rdx, 0x0            rdi = 0x0000000000000005   Thread 1: instruction step into
 5    0x10000202b <+11>:  mov    rdx, rdi            rdx = 0x0040000000000000
 6    0x10000202e <+14>:  push   rdx
 7    0x10000202f <+15>:  mov    rdx, 0x0
 8    0x100002036 <+22>:  pop    rdx
 9    0x100002037 <+23>:  pop    rbp
10    0x100002038 <+24>:  ret
```

The base pointer is assigned to the value of the stack pointer. Verify both have the same value using `dumpreg` as well as the following LLDB command:

```
(lldb) p (BOOL)($rbp == $rsp)
```

It's important you put parentheses around the expression, else LLDB won't parse it correctly.

Execute `si` and `dumpreg` again. This time it looks like the following:

```
 1  Registers`StackWalkthrough:                          (lldb) dumpreg
 2      0x100002020 <+0>:   push   rbp                      rsp = 0x00007fff5fbfe750
 3      0x100002021 <+1>:   mov    rbp, rsp                 rbp = 0x00007fff5fbfe750
 4      0x100002024 <+4>:   mov    rdx, 0x0                 rdi = 0x0000000000000005
 5  ->  0x10000202b <+11>:  mov    rdx, rdi                 rdx = 0x0000000000000000    Thread 1: instruction step into
 6      0x10000202e <+14>:  push   rdx
 7      0x10000202f <+15>:  mov    rdx, 0x0
 8      0x100002036 <+22>:  pop    rdx
 9      0x100002037 <+23>:  pop    rbp
10      0x100002038 <+24>:  ret
```

RDX is cleared to 0.

Execute `si` and `dumpreg` again. This time the output looks the following:

```
 1  Registers`StackWalkthrough:                          (lldb) dumpreg
 2      0x100002020 <+0>:   push   rbp                      rsp = 0x00007fff5fbfe750
 3      0x100002021 <+1>:   mov    rbp, rsp                 rbp = 0x00007fff5fbfe750
 4      0x100002024 <+4>:   mov    rdx, 0x0                 rdi = 0x0000000000000005
 5      0x10000202b <+11>:  mov    rdx, rdi                 rdx = 0x0000000000000005
 6  ->  0x10000202e <+14>:  push   rdx                                                 Thread 1: instruction step into
 7      0x10000202f <+15>:  mov    rdx, 0x0
 8      0x100002036 <+22>:  pop    rdx
 9      0x100002037 <+23>:  pop    rbp
10      0x100002038 <+24>:  ret
```

RDX is set to RDI. You can verify both have the same value with `dumpreg` again.

Execute `si` and `dumpreg`. This time it looks the following:

```
 1  Registers`StackWalkthrough:                          (lldb) dumpreg
 2      0x100002020 <+0>:   push   rbp                      rsp = 0x00007fff5fbfe748
 3      0x100002021 <+1>:   mov    rbp, rsp                 rbp = 0x00007fff5fbfe750
 4      0x100002024 <+4>:   mov    rdx, 0x0                 rdi = 0x0000000000000005
 5      0x10000202b <+11>:  mov    rdx, rdi                 rdx = 0x0000000000000005
 6      0x10000202e <+14>:  push   rdx
 7  ->  0x10000202f <+15>:  mov    rdx, 0x0                                            Thread 1: instruction step into
 8      0x100002036 <+22>:  pop    rdx
 9      0x100002037 <+23>:  pop    rbp
10      0x100002038 <+24>:  ret
```

RDX is pushed onto the stack. This means the stack pointer was decremented, and RSP points to a value which will point to the value of `0x5`. Confirm that now:

```
(lldb) p/x $rsp
```

This gives the current value pointed at RSP. What does the value here point to?

```
(lldb) x/gx $rsp
```

You'll get the expected `0x5`. Type `si` again to execute the next instruction:

```
 1  Registers`StackWalkthrough:                          (lldb) dumpreg
 2      0x100002020 <+0>:   push   rbp                      rsp = 0x00007fff5fbfe748
 3      0x100002021 <+1>:   mov    rbp, rsp                 rbp = 0x00007fff5fbfe750
 4      0x100002024 <+4>:   mov    rdx, 0x0                 rdi = 0x0000000000000005
 5      0x10000202b <+11>:  mov    rdx, rdi                 rdx = 0x0000000000000000
 6      0x10000202e <+14>:  push   rdx
 7      0x10000202f <+15>:  mov    rdx, 0x0
 8  ->  0x100002036 <+22>:  pop    rdx                                                 Thread 1: instruction step into
 9      0x100002037 <+23>:  pop    rbp
10      0x100002038 <+24>:  ret
```

RDX is set to `0x0`. Nothing too exciting here, move along... move along. Type `si` and `dumpreg` again:

```
 1 Registers`StackWalkthrough:                       (lldb) dumpreg
 2    0x100002020 <+0>:   push   rbp                      rsp = 0x00007fff5fbfe750
 3    0x100002021 <+1>:   mov    rbp, rsp                 rbp = 0x00007fff5fbfe750
 4    0x100002024 <+4>:   mov    rdx, 0x0                 rdi = 0x0000000000000005
 5    0x10000202b <+11>:  mov    rdx, rdi                 rdx = 0x0000000000000005
 6    0x10000202e <+14>:  push   rdx
 7    0x10000202f <+15>:  mov    rdx, 0x0
 8    0x100002036 <+22>:  pop    rdx
 9 -> 0x100002037 <+23>:  pop    rbp                                Thread 1: instruction step into
10    0x100002038 <+24>:  ret
```

The top of the stack is popped into RDX, which you know was recently set to `0x5`. The RSP is incremented by `0x8`. Type `si` and `dumpreg` again:

```
 1 Registers`StackWalkthrough:                       (lldb) dumpreg
 2    0x100002020 <+0>:   push   rbp                      rsp = 0x00007fff5fbfe758
 3    0x100002021 <+1>:   mov    rbp, rsp                 rbp = 0x00007fff5fbfe790
 4    0x100002024 <+4>:   mov    rdx, 0x0                 rdi = 0x0000000000000005
 5    0x10000202b <+11>:  mov    rdx, rdi                 rdx = 0x0000000000000005
 6    0x10000202e <+14>:  push   rdx
 7    0x10000202f <+15>:  mov    rdx, 0x0
 8    0x100002036 <+22>:  pop    rdx
 9    0x100002037 <+23>:  pop    rbp
10 -> 0x100002038 <+24>:  ret                                       Thread 1: instruction step into
```

The base pointer is popped off of the stack and reassigned back to the value it originally had when entering this function. The calling convention specifies RBP should remain consistent across function calls. That is, the RBP can't change to a different value once it leaves a function, so we're being a good citizen and restoring its value.

Onto the `ret` opcode. Keep an eye out for the RSP value about to change. Type `si` and `dumpreg` again:

```
      0x10000240c <+12>:  mov    qword ptr [rbp - 0x(lldb) dumpreg
 6    0x100002410 <+16>:  call   0x100008b28              rsp = 0x00007fff5fbfe760  etain
 7    0x100002415 <+21>:  mov    rdi, qword ptr [rbp      rbp = 0x00007fff5fbfe790
 8    0x100002419 <+25>:  mov    qword ptr [rbp - 0x2     rdi = 0x0000000000000005
 9    0x10000241d <+29>:  mov    qword ptr [rbp - 0x3     rdx = 0x0000000000000005
10    0x100002421 <+33>:  call   0x100002380              ; type metadata accessor for
         Registers.ViewController at ViewController.swift
12    0x100002426 <+38>:  lea    rdi, [rbp - 0x18]
13    0x10000242a <+42>:  mov    rcx, qword ptr [rbp - 0x30]
14    0x10000242e <+46>:  mov    qword ptr [rbp - 0x18], rcx
15    0x100002432 <+50>:  mov    qword ptr [rbp - 0x10], rax
16    0x100002436 <+54>:  mov    rsi, qword ptr [rip + 0xaa4b] ; "awakeFromNib"
17    0x10000243d <+61>:  call   0x100008b1c              ; symbol stub for: objc_msgSendSuper2
18    0x100002442 <+66>:  mov    rdi, qword ptr [rbp - 0x20]
19    0x100002446 <+70>:  call   0x100008b22              ; symbol stub for: objc_release
20    0x10000244b <+75>:  mov    edi, 0x5
21    0x100002450 <+80>:  call   0x100002020              ; StackWalkthrough
22 -> 0x100002455 <+85>:  add    rsp, 0x30                          Thread 1: instruction step into
23    0x100002459 <+89>:  pop    rbp
24    0x10000245a <+90>:  ret
```

The return address was pushed off the stack and set to the RIP register; you know this because you've gone back to where the function was called. Control then resumes in `awakeFromNib`,

Wowza! That was fun! A simple function, but it illustrates how the stack works through `call`, `push`, `pop` and `ret` instructions.

The stack and 7+ parameters

As described in Chapter 10, the calling convention for x86_64 will use the following registers for function parameters in order: RDI, RSI, RDX, RCX, R8, R9. When a function requires more than six parameters, the stack needs to be used.

> **Note**: The stack may also need to be used when a large struct is passed to a function. Each parameter register can only hold 8 bytes (on 64-bit architecture), so if the struct needs more than 8 bytes, it will need to be passed on the stack as well. There are strict rules defining how this works in the calling convention, which all compilers must adhere to.

Open **ViewController.swift** and find the function named executeLotsOfArguments(one:two:three:four:five:six:seven:eight:nine:ten:). You used this function in Chapter 10 to explore the registers. You'll use it again now to see how parameters 7 and beyond get passed to the function.

Add the following code to the end of viewDidLoad:

```
_ = self.executeLotsOfArguments(one: 1, two: 2, three: 3, four:
4,
                              five: 5, six: 6, seven: 7, eight: 8,
                              nine: 9, ten: 10)
```

Next, using the Xcode GUI, create a breakpoint on the line you just added. Build and run the app, and wait for this breakpoint to hit. You should see the disassembly view again, but if you don't, use the **Always Show Disassembly** option.

As you've learned in the **Stack Related Opcodes** section, call is responsible for the execution of a function. Since there's only one call opcode between where RIP is right now and the end of viewDidLoad, this means this call must be the one responsible for calling executeLotsOfArguments(one:two:three:four:five:six:seven:eight:nine:ten:).

But what are all the rest of the instructions before `call`? Let's find out.

These instructions set up the stack as necessary to pass the additional parameters. You have your usual 6 parameters being put into the appropriate registers, as seen by the instructions before where RIP is now, from `mov edx, 0x1` onwards.

But parameters 7 and beyond need to be passed on the stack. This is done with the following instructions:

```
0x1000013e2 <+178>: mov    qword ptr [rsp], 0x7
0x1000013ea <+186>: mov    qword ptr [rsp + 0x8], 0x8
0x1000013f3 <+195>: mov    qword ptr [rsp + 0x10], 0x9
0x1000013fc <+204>: mov    qword ptr [rsp + 0x18], 0xa
```

Looks scary, doesn't it? I'll explain.

The brackets containing RSP and an optional value indicate a dereference, just like a * would in C programming. The first line above says "put 0x7 into the memory address pointed to by RSP." The second line says "put 0x8 into the memory address pointed to by RSP plus 0x8." And so on.

This is placing values onto the stack. But take note the values are not explicitly pushed using the push instruction, which would decrease the RSP register. Why is that?

Well, as you've learned, during a `call` instruction the return address is pushed onto the stack. Then, in the function prologue, the base pointer is pushed onto the stack, and then the base pointer gets set to the stack pointer.

What you haven't learned yet is the compiler will actually make room on the stack for "scratch space". That is, the compiler allocates space on the stack for local variables in a function as necessary.

You can easily determine if extra scratch space is allocated for a stack frame by looking for the `sub rsp, VALUE` instruction in the function prologue. For example, click on the `viewDidLoad` stack frame and scroll to the top. Observe how much scratch space has been created:

The compiler has been a little bit clever here; instead of doing lots of pushes, it knows it has allocated some space on the stack for itself, and fills in values before the function call passing these extra parameters. Individual push instructions would involve more writes to RSP, which would be less efficient.

Time to look at this scratch space in more depth.

The stack and debugging info

The stack is not only used when calling functions, but it's also used as a scratch space for a function's local variables. Speaking of which, how does the debugger know which addresses to reference when printing out the names of variables that belong to that function?

Let's find out!

Clear all the breakpoints you've set and create a new Symbolic breakpoint on executeLotsOfArguments.

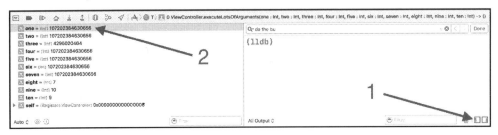

Build and run the app, then wait for the breakpoint to hit.

As expected, control should stop at the ever-so-short name of a function: executeLotsOfArguments(one:two:three:four:five:six:seven:eight:nine:t en:), from here on, now referred to as executeLotsOfArguments, because its full name is a bit of a mouthful!

In the lower right corner of Xcode, click on **Show the Variables View**:

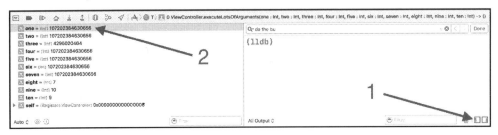

From there, look at the value pointed at by the one variable... it definitely ain't holding the value of 0x1 at the moment. This value seems to be gibberish!

Why is one referencing a seemingly random value?

The answer is stored by the **DWARF Debugging Information** embedded into the debug build of the Registers application. You can dump this information to help give you insight into what the one variable is referencing in memory.

In LLDB, type the following:

```
(lldb) image dump symfile Registers
```

You'll get a crazy amount of output. Search for (Cmd + F) the word **"one"**; include the quotes within your search.

Below is a truncated output that includes the relevant information:

```
0x7fc9e1730bf0:       Function{0x3000001e8}, mangled =
_TFC9Registers14ViewController22executeLotsOfArgumentsfT3oneSi3t
woSi5threeSi4fourSi4fiveSi3sixSi5sevenSi5eightSi4nineSi3tenSi_T_
, demangled = Registers.ViewController.executeLotsOfArguments
(one : Swift.Int, two : Swift.Int, three : Swift.Int, four :
Swift.Int, five : Swift.Int, six : Swift.Int, seven : Swift.Int,
eight : Swift.Int, nine : Swift.Int, ten : Swift.Int) -> (),
type_uid = 0x3000001e8
0x7fc9e1730c28:       Block{0x3000001e8}, ranges =
[0x1000024a0-0x100002a83)
0x7fc9d25492f0:        Variable{0x30000020a}, name = "one", type
= {3c0e000003000000} 0x00007fc9d25490f0 (Swift.Int), scope =
parameter, decl = ViewController.swift:30, location =
DW_OP_fbreg(-40)
```

Based upon the output, the variable named one is of type **Swift.Int**, found in executeLotsOfArguments, whose location can be found at **DW_OP_fbreg(-40)**. This rather obfuscated code actually means base pointer minus 40, i.e. RBP – 40. Or in hexadecimal, RBP – 0x28.

This is important information. It tells the debugger the variable called one can always be found in this memory address. Well, not always, but always when that variable is valid, i.e. it's in scope.

You may wonder why it can't just be RDI, since that's where the value is passed to the function, and it's also the first parameter. Well, RDI may need to be reused later on within the function, so using the stack is a safer bet for storage.

The debugger should still be stopped on executeLotsOfArguments. Make sure you're viewing the **Always Show Disassembly** output and hunt for the assembly. It should be line 16:

```
mov    qword ptr [rbp - 0x28], rdi
```

Once you've found it in the assembly output of executeLotsOfArguments, create a breakpoint on this line of assembly.

Continue execution so LLDB will stop on this line of assembly.

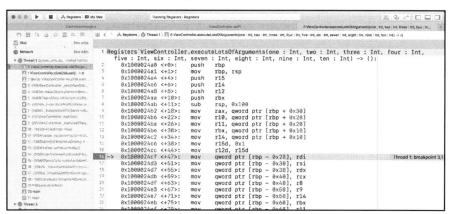

Try printing out the output of one in LLDB:

```
(lldb) po one
```

Gibberish, still. Hmph.

Remember, RDI will contain the first parameter passed into the function. So to make the debugger be able to see the value that one should be, RDI needs to be written to the address where one is stored. In this case, RBP - 0x28.

Now, perform an assembly instruction step in LLDB:

```
(lldb) si
```

Print the value of one again.

```
(lldb) po one
```

Awwww.... yeah! It's working! The value one is referencing is correctly holding the value 0x1.

You may be wondering what happens if one changes. Well, RBP − 0x28 needs to change in that case too. This would potentially be another instruction needed to write it there as well as wherever the value is used. This is why debug builds are so much slower than release builds.

Stack exploration takeaways

Don't worry. This chapter is almost done. But there are some very important takeaways that should be remembered from your stack explorations.

Provided you're in a function, and the function has finished executing the function prologue, the following items will hold true to x64 assembly:

- RBP will point to the start of the stack frame for this function.

- *RBP will contain the address of the start of the previous stack frame. (Use x/gx $rbp in LLDB to see it).

- *(RBP + 0x8) will point to the return address to the previous function in the stack trace (Use x/gx '$rbp + 0x8' in LLDB to see it).

- *(RBP + 0x10) will point to the 7th parameter (if there is one).

- *(RBP + 0x18) will point to the 8th parameter (if there is one).

- *(RBP + 0x20) will point to the 9th parameter (if there is one).

- *(RBP + 0x28) will point to the 10th parameter (if there is one).

- RBP − X where X is multiples of 0x8, will reference local variables to that function.

Where to go from here?

Now that you're familiar with the RBP and RSP registers, you've got a homework assignment!

Attach LLDB to a program (any program, source or no source) and traverse the stack frame using only the RBP register. Create a breakpoint on an easily triggerable method. One good example is -[NSView hitTest:], if you attach to a macOS application such as Xcode, and click on a view.

It's important to ensure the breakpoint you choose to add is *not* a Swift function. You're going to inspect registers, — and recall you can't (easily) do this in the Swift context.

Once the breakpoint has been triggered, make sure you're on frame 0 by typing the following into LLDB:

```
(lldb) f 0
```

The f command is an alias for `frame select`.

You should see the following two instructions at the top of this function:

```
push    rbp
mov     rbp, rsp
```

These instructions form the start of the function prologue and push RBP onto the stack and then set RBP to RSP.

Step over both of these instructions using `si`.

Now the base pointer is set up for this stack frame, you can traverse the stack frames yourself by inspecting the base pointer.

Execute the following in LLDB:

```
(lldb) p uintptr_t $Previous_RBP = *(uintptr_t *)$rsp
```

So now $Previous_RBP equals the old RBP, i.e. the start of the stack frame from the function that called this one.

Recall the first thing on the stack frame is the address to where the function should return. So you can find out where the *previous* function will return to. This will therefore be where the debugger is stopped in frame 2.

To find this out and check that you're right, execute the following in LLDB:

```
(lldb) x/gx '$Previous_RBP + 0x8'
```

This will print something like this:

```
0x7fff5fbfd718: 0x00007fffa83ed11b
```

Confirm this address equals the return address in frame 1 with LLDB:

```
(lldb) f 2
```

It will look something like this, depending on what you decided to set the initial breakpoint in:

```
frame #2: 0x00007fffa83ed11b AppKit`-[NSWindow
_setFrameCommon:display:stashSize:] + 3234
```

```
AppKit`-[NSWindow _setFrameCommon:display:stashSize:]:
    0x7fffa83ed11b <+3234>: xor     ebx, ebx
    0x7fffa83ed11d <+3236>: mov     rsi, qword ptr [rip +
0x1c5a9d8c] ; "_bindingAdaptor"
    0x7fffa83ed124 <+3243>: mov     rdi, r12
    0x7fffa83ed127 <+3246>: call    qword ptr [rip +
0x1c319f53] ; (void *)0x00007fffbee77b40: objc_msgSend
```

The first address that it spits out should match the output of your earlier x/gx command.

Good luck and may the assembly be with you!

Section III: Low Level

With a foundation of assembler theory solidly below you, it's time to explore other aspects of how programs work. This section is an eclectic grab-bag of weird and fun studies into reverse engineering, seldom-used APIs and debugging strategies.

Chapter 13: Hello, Ptrace

Chapter 14: Dynamic Frameworks

Chapter 15: Hooking & Executing Code with dlopen & dlsym

Chapter 16: Exploring and Method Swizzling Objective-C Frameworks

Chapter 13: Hello, Ptrace

As alluded to in the introduction to this book, debugging is not entirely about just fixing stuff. Debugging is the process of gaining a better understanding of what's happening behind the scenes. In this chapter, you'll explore the foundation of debugging, namely, a system call responsible for a process attaching itself to another process: **ptrace**.

In addition, you'll learn some common security tricks developers use with ptrace to prevent a process from attaching to their programs. You'll also learn some easy workarounds for these developer-imposed restrictions.

System calls

Wait wait wait... `ptrace` is a system call. What's a *system* call?

A **system call** is a powerful, lower-level service provided by the kernel. System calls are the foundations user-land frameworks, such as C's stdlib, Cocoa, UIKit, or even your own brilliant frameworks are built upon.

macOS Sierra has about 500 system calls. Open a Terminal window and run the following command to get a very close estimate of the number of systems calls available in your system:

```
sudo dtrace -ln 'syscall:::entry' | wc -l
```

This command uses an incredibly powerful tool named **DTrace** to inspect system calls present on your macOS machine.

> **Note**: You'll need `sudo` for the `DTrace` command as DTrace can monitor processes across multiple users, as well as perform some incredibly powerful actions. With great power comes great responsibility — that's why you need `sudo`.

You'll learn more about how to bend DTrace to your will in a later chapter. For now you'll use simple DTrace commands to get system call information out of `ptrace`.

The foundation of attachment, ptrace

You're now going to take a look at the `ptrace` system call in more depth. Open a Terminal console, or reuse an old one. Before you start, make sure to clear the Terminal console by pressing ⌘ + K. Next, execute the following DTrace inline script in Terminal to see how `ptrace` is called:

```
sudo dtrace -qn 'syscall::ptrace:entry { printf("%s(%d, %d, %d,
%d) from %s\n", probefunc, arg0, arg1, arg2, arg3, execname); }'
```

This creates a `DTrace` probe that will execute every time the `ptrace` function executes; it will spit out the arguments of the `ptrace` system call as well as the executable responsible for calling.

Don't worry about the semantics of this `DTrace` script; you'll become uncomfortably familiar with this tool in a later set of chapters. For now, just focus on what's returned from the Terminal.

Create a new tab in Terminal with the shortcut ⌘ + T.

> **Note:** If you haven't disabled Rootless yet, you'll need to check out Chapter 1 for more information on how to disable it, or else ptrace will fail when attaching to Xcode.

Once Rootless is disabled, type the following into the new Terminal tab:

```
lldb —n Finder
```

Once you've attached to the Finder application, the DTrace probe you set up on your first Terminal tab will spit out some information similar to the following:

```
ptrace(14, 459, 0, 0) from debugserver
```

It seems a process named **debugserver** is responsible for calling ptrace and attaching to the Finder process. But how was debugserver called? You attached to Finder using LLDB, not debugserver. And is this debugserver process even still alive?

Time to answer these questions. Create a new tab in Terminal (⌘ + T). Next, type the following into the Terminal window:

```
pgrep debugserver
```

Provided LLDB has attached successfully and is running, you'll receive an integer output representing debugserver's process ID, or **PID**, indicating debugserver is alive and well and running on your computer.

Since debugserver is currently running, you can find out how debugserver was started. Type the following:

```
ps —fp `pgrep —x debugserver`
```

Be sure to note that the above commands uses *backticks*, not single quotes, to make the command work.

This will give you the full path to the location of debugserver, along with all arguments used to launch this process.

You'll see something similar to the following:

```
/Applications/Xcode—beta.app/Contents/SharedFrameworks/
LLDB.framework/Resources/debugserver ——native—regs ——setsid ——
reverse—connect 127.0.0.1:59297
```

Cool! This probably makes you wonder how the functionality changes when you subtract or modify certain launch arguments. For instance, what would happen if you got rid of `--reverse-connect 127.0.0.1:59297`?

So which process launched `debugserver`? Type the following:

```
ps -o ppid= $(pgrep -x debugserver)
```

This will dump out the parent PID responsible for launching `debugserver`. You'll get an integer similar to the following:

```
82122
```

As always when working with PIDs, they will very likely be different on your computer (and from run to run) than what you see here.

All right, numbers are interesting, but you're dying to know the actual name associated with this PID. You can get this information by executing the following in Terminal, replacing the number with the PID you discovered in the previous step:

```
ps -a 82122
```

You'll get the name, fullpath, and launch arguments of the process responsible for launching `debugserver`:

```
PID   TT  STAT      TIME COMMAND
82122 s000 S+     0:05.35 /Applications/Xcode-beta.app/
Contents/Developer/usr/bin/lldb -n Finder
```

As you can see, LLDB was responsible for launching the debugserver process, which then attached itself to `Finder` using the `ptrace` system call. Now you know where this call is coming from, you can take a deeper dive into the function arguments passed into `ptrace`.

ptrace arguments

You're able to infer the process and arguments executed when `ptrace` was called. Unfortunately, they're just numbers, which are rather useless to you at the moment. It's time to make sense of these numbers using the **<sys/ptrace.h>** header file. To do this, you'll use a macOS application to guide your understanding.

Open up the **helloptrace** application, which you'll find in the resources folder for this chapter. This is a macOS Terminal command application and is as barebones as they come. All it does is launch then complete with no output to `stdout` at all.

The only thing of interest in this project is a bridging header used to import the `ptrace` system call API into Swift.

Open **main.swift** and add the following code to the end of the file:

```
while true {
    sleep(2)
    print("helloptrace")
}
```

Next, position Xcode and the DTrace Terminal window so they are both visible on the same screen.

Build and run the application. Once your app has launched and `debugserver` has attached, observe the output generated by the DTrace script.

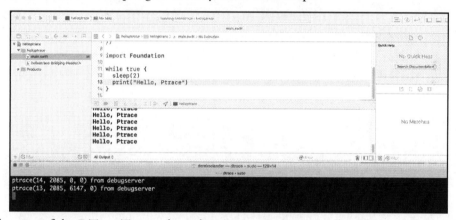

Take note of the DTrace Terminal window. Two new `ptrace` calls will happen when the `helloptrace` process starts running. The output of the DTrace script will look similar to this:

```
ptrace(14, 17768, 0, 0) from debugserver
ptrace(13, 17768, 6147, 0) from debugserver
```

Pause the application. At the time of writing, there's a bug in Xcode that won't retrieve the proper documentation for `ptrace`. To work around this, try to use the **Open Quickly** Xcode feature (⌘ + Shift + O) and type **sys/ptrace.h**.

If Xcode hangs on `Generating interface`, then you're not completely out of luck. In this case, navigate to **main.swift** and type the following on a line by itself:

```
PT_DENY_ATTACH
```

⌘ + click on the above word to go to the correct header file. "It just works", right? :]

Be sure to remove this line when you're done, as you don't need it quite yet.

One way or another, you'll be in the sys/ptrace.h header. Time to compare the ptrace function signature to the expected parameters.

A look in **ptrace.h** gives the following function prototype for ptrace:

```
int ptrace(int _request, pid_t _pid, caddr_t _addr, int _data);
```

The first parameter is what you want ptrace to do. The second parameter is the PID you want to act upon. The third and fourth parameters depend on the first parameter.

Take a look back at your earlier DTrace output. Your first line of output was something similar to the following:

```
ptrace(14, 17768, 0, 0) from debugserver
```

Compare the first parameter to **ptrace.h** header and you'll see the first parameter, 14, actually stands for **PT_ATTACHEXC**. What does this PT_ATTACHEXC mean? To get information about this parameter, open a Terminal window. Next, type **man ptrace** and search for PT_ATTACHEXC.

Note: You can perform case-sensitive searches on man pages by pressing /, followed by your search query. You can search downwards to the next hit by pressing **N** or upwards to the previous hit by pressing **Shift + N**.

You'll find some relevant info about PT_ATTACHEXC with the following output obtained from the ptrace man page:

```
This request allows a process to gain control of an otherwise
unrelated process and begin tracing it. It does not need any
cooperation from the to-be-traced process. In this case, pid
specifies the process ID of the to-be-traced process, and the
other two arguments are ignored.
```

With this information, the reason for the first call of ptrace should be clear. This call says "hey, attach to this process", and attaches to the process provided in the second parameter.

Onto the next ptrace call from your DTrace output:

```
ptrace(13, 459, 6147, 0) from debugserver
```

This one is a bit trickier to understand, since Apple decided to not give any man documentation about this one. Er, thanks, Apple. This call relates to the internals of a process attaching to another one.

If you look at the ptrace API header, 13 stands for **PT_THUPDATE** and relates to how the controlling process, in this case, debugserver, handles UNIX signals and Mach messages passed to the controlled process, in this case helloptrace.

The kernel needs to know how to handle signal passing from a process controlled by another process, as in the Signals project from Section 1. The controlling process could say it doesn't want to send any signals to the controlled process.

This specific ptrace action is an implementation detail of how the Mach kernel handles ptrace internally; there's no need to dwell on it.

Fortunately, there are other *documented* signals definitely worth exploring through man. One of them is the **PT_DENY_ATTACH** action, which you'll learn about now.

Creating attachment issues

A process can actually specify it doesn't want to be attached to by calling ptrace and supplying the PT_DENY_ATTACH argument. This is often used as a security implementation to prevent unwelcome reverse engineers from discovering a program's secrets.

You'll now experiment with this argument. Open **main.swift** and add the following line of code before the while loop:

```
ptrace(PT_DENY_ATTACH, 0, nil, 0)
```

Build and run, keep on eye on the debugger console and see what happens.

The program will exit and output the following to the debugger console:

```
Program ended with exit code: 45
```

> **Note:** You may need to open up the debug console by clicking **View\Debug Area\Activate Console** to see this.

This happened because Xcode launches the helloptrace program by default with LLDB automatically attached. If you execute the ptrace function with PT_DENY_ATTACH, LLDB will exit early and the program will stop executing.

If you were to try and execute the helloptrace program, and tried later to attach to it, LLDB will fail in attaching and the helloptrace program would happily continue execution, oblivious to debugserver's attachment issues.

There are numerous macOS (and iOS) programs that perform this very action in their production builds. However, it's rather trivial to circumvent this security precaution. Ninja debug mode activated!

Getting around PT_DENY_ATTACH

Once a process executes ptrace with the PT_DENY_ATTACH argument, making an attachment greatly escalates in complexity. However, there's a *much* easier way of getting around this problem.

Typically a developer will execute ptrace(PT_DENY_ATTACH, 0, 0, 0) somewhere in the main executable's code — oftentimes, right in the main function.

Since LLDB has the -w argument to wait for the launching of a process, you can use LLDB to "catch" the launch of a process and perform logic to augment or ignore the PT_DENY_ATTACH command before the process has a chance to execute ptrace!

Open a new Terminal window and type the following:

```
sudo lldb -n "helloptrace" -w
```

This starts an lldb session and attaches to the helloptrace program, but this time -w tells lldb to wait until a process of this program has started.

You need to use sudo due to an ongoing bug with LLDB and macOS security when you tell LLDB to wait for a Terminal program to launch.

In the Project Navigator, open the **Products** folder and right click on the **helloptrace** executable. Next, select **Show in Finder**.

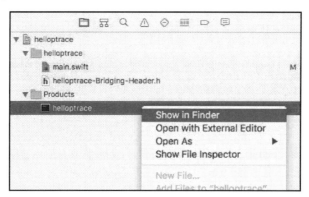

Next, drag the `helloptrace` executable into a new Terminal tab. Finally, press **Enter** to start the executable.

Now, open the previously created Terminal tab, where you had LLDB sit and wait for the `helloptrace` executable.

If everything went as expected, LLDB will see `helloptrace` has started and will launch itself, attaching to this newly created `helloptrace` process.

In LLDB, create the following regex breakpoint to stop on any type of function containing the word `ptrace`:

```
(lldb) rb ptrace -s libsystem_kernel.dylib
```

This will add a breakpoint on the kernel implementation of the `ptrace` function. Next, type `continue` into the Terminal window.

```
(lldb) continue
```

You'll break right before the `ptrace` function is about to be executed. However, you can simply use LLDB to return early and not execute that function. Do that now like so:

```
(lldb) thread return 0
```

Next, simply just continue:

```
(lldb) continue
```

Although the program entered the `ptrace` kernel function, you told LLDB to return early and not execute any logic within `ptrace`.

Navigate to the `helloptrace` output tab and verify it's outputting "helloptrace" over and over. If so, you've successfully bypassed `PT_DENY_ATTACH` and are running LLDB while still attached to the `helloptrace` command!

This is great if you already know what process you're interested in beforehand, but what about the occasions when you don't know *when* a process will execute the `ptrace` system call to lock you out of taking control?

In an upcoming chapter, you'll let DTrace monitor your macOS system and automatically augment this ptrace function if the developers were foolish enough to try using PT_DENY_ATTACH and automatically change the parameters around to do nothing. Until then, use the -w LLDB argument to catch a process and create breakpoints to catch and return early from this ptrace call.

Where to go from here?

With the DTrace dumping script you used in this chapter, explore parts of your system and see when ptrace is called.

If you're feeling cocky, read up on the ptrace man pages and see if you can create a program that will automatically attach itself to another program on your system.

Remember, having attachment issues is not always a bad thing! :]

Chapter 14: Dynamic Frameworks

If you've developed any type of Apple GUI software, you've definitely used dynamic frameworks in your day-to-day development.

A dynamic framework is a bundle of code loaded into an executable at runtime, instead of at compile time. Examples in iOS include `UIKit` and the `Foundation` frameworks. Frameworks such as these contain a dynamic library and optionally assets, such as images.

There are numerous advantages in electing to use dynamic frameworks instead of static frameworks. The most obvious advantage is you can make updates to the framework without having to recompile the executable that depends on the framework.

Imagine if, for every major or minor release of iOS, Apple said, "Hey y'all, we need to update UIKit so if you could go ahead and update your app as well, that would be grrrreat." There would be blood in the streets and the only competition would be Android vs. Windows Phone!

Why dynamic frameworks?

In addition to the positives of using dynamic frameworks, the kernel can map the dynamic framework to multiple processes that depend on the framework. Take UIKit, for example: it would be stupid and a waste of disk space if each running iOS app kept a unique copy of UIKit resident in memory. Furthermore, there could be different versions of UIKit compiled into each app, making it incredibly difficult to track down bugs.

As of iOS 8, Apple decided to lift the dynamic library restriction and allow third-party dynamic libraries to be included in your app. The most obvious advantage was developers could share frameworks across different iOS extensions, such as the Today Extension and Action Extensions.

Today, all Apple platforms allow third party dynamic frameworks to be included without rejection in the ever-so-lovely Apple Review process.

With dynamic frameworks comes a very interesting aspect of learning, debugging, and reverse engineering. Since you've the ability to load the framework at runtime, you can use LLDB to explore and execute code at runtime, which is great for spelunking in both public and private frameworks.

Statically inspecting an executable's frameworks

Compiled into each executable is a list of dynamic libraries (most often, frameworks), expected to be loaded at runtime. This can be further broken down into a list of required frameworks and a list of optional frameworks. The loading of these dynamic libraries into memory is done using a piece of code called the **dynamic loader**, or dyld.

If a required framework fails to load, the dynamic library loader will kill the program. If an optional framework fails to load, everything continues as usual, but code from that library will obviously not be able to run!

You may have used the optional framework feature in the past, perhaps when your iOS or Mac app needed to use code from a library added in a newer OS version than the version targeted by your app. In such cases, you'd perform a runtime check around calls to code in the optional library to check if the library was loaded.

I spout tons of this theory stuff, but it'll make more sense if you see it for yourself.

Open Xcode and create a new iOS project, **Single View Application** named **DeleteMe**.

Yep, this project won't hang around for long, so feel free to remove it once you're done with this chapter. You'll not write a line of code within the app (but within the load commands is a different story). Make sure you choose Objective-C then click Next.

> **Note:** You're using Objective-C because there's more going on under the hood in a Swift app. At the time of writing, the Swift ABI is not finalized, so every method Swift uses to bridge Objective-C uses a dynamic framework packaged into your app to "jump the gap" to Objective-C. This means within the Swift bridging frameworks are the corresponding dependencies to the proper Objective-C Frameworks. For example, **libswiftUIKit.dylib** will have a required dependency on the UIKit framework.

Click on the Xcode project at the top of the project navigator. Then click on the **DeleteMe** target. Next, click on the **Build Phases** and open up the **Link Binary With Libraries**.

Add the **Social** and **CallKit** framework. To the right of the CallKit framework, select **Optional** from the drop-down. Ensure that the Social framework has the **Required** value set as shown below.

Build the project on the simulator using **Cmd + B**. **Do not run just yet**. Once the project has been successfully built for the simulator, open the **products** directory in the Xcode project navigator.

Right click on the produced executable, `DeleteMe`, and select **Show in Finder**.

Next, open up the `DeleteMe` IPA by right clicking the IPA and selecting **Show Package Contents**.

Next, open a new `Terminal` window and type the following but **don't press Enter**:

```
otool -L
```

Be sure to add a space at the end of the command. Next, drag the `DeleteMe` executable from the `Finder` window into the `Terminal` window. When finished, you should have a command that looks similar to the following:

```
otool -L /Users/derekselander/Library/Developer/Xcode/
DerivedData/DeleteMe-fqycokvgjilklcejwonxhuyxqlej/Build/
Products/Debug-iphonesimulator/DeleteMe.app/DeleteMe
```

Press Enter and observe the output. You'll see something similar to the following:

```
/System/Library/Frameworks/CallKit.framework/CallKit
(compatibility version 1.0.0, current version 1.0.0)
/System/Library/Frameworks/Social.framework/Social
(compatibility version 1.0.0, current version 87.0.0)
/System/Library/Frameworks/Foundation.framework/Foundation
(compatibility version 300.0.0, current version 1349.13.0)
/usr/lib/libobjc.A.dylib (compatibility version 1.0.0, current
version 228.0.0)
```

```
/usr/lib/libSystem.dylib (compatibility version 1.0.0, current
version 1238.0.0)
/System/Library/Frameworks/UIKit.framework/UIKit (compatibility
version 1.0.0, current version 3600.6.21)
```

You found the compiled binary DeleteMe and dumped out the list of dynamic frameworks it links to using the ever-so-awesome **otool**. Take note of the instructions to CallKit and the Social framework you manually added earlier. By default, the compiler automatically adds the "essential" frameworks to the iOS app, like UIKit and Foundation.

Take note of the directory path responsible for loading these frameworks;

```
/System/Library/Frameworks/
/usr/lib/
```

Remember these directories; you'll revisit them for a "eureka" moment later on.

Let's go a tad bit deeper. Remember how you optionally required the CallKit framework, and required the Social framework? You can view the results of these decisions by using otool.

In Terminal, press the up arrow to recall the previous Terminal command. Next, change the capital **L** to a lowercase **l** and press Enter. You'll get a longer list of output that shows all the **load commands** for the DeleteMe executable.

```
otool -l /Users/derekselander/Library/Developer/Xcode/
DerivedData/DeleteMe-fqycokvgjilklcejwonxhuyxqlej/Build/
Products/Debug-iphonesimulator/DeleteMe.app/DeleteMe
```

Search for load commands pertaining to CallKit by pressing **Cmd + F** and typing **CallKit**. You'll stumble across a load command similar to the following:

```
Load command 12
          cmd LC_LOAD_WEAK_DYLIB
      cmdsize 80
         name /System/Library/Frameworks/CallKit.framework/
CallKit (offset 24)
    time stamp 2 Wed Dec 31 17:00:02 1969
      current version 1.0.0
compatibility version 1.0.0
```

Next, search for the Social framework as well:

```
Load command 13
          cmd LC_LOAD_DYLIB
      cmdsize 80
         name /System/Library/Frameworks/Social.framework/Social
```

```
(offset 24)
    time stamp 2 Wed Dec 31 17:00:02 1969
        current version 87.0.0
compatibility version 1.0.0
```

Compare the **cmd** in the load commands output. In `CallKit`, the load command is `LC_LOAD_WEAK_DYLIB`, which represents an optional framework, while the `LC_LOAD_DYLIB` of the `Social` load command indicates a required framework.

This is ideal for an application that supports multiple iOS versions. For example, if you supported iOS 9 and up, you would strongly link the `Social` framework and weak link the `CallKit` framework since it's only available in iOS 10 and up.

Modifying the load commands

There's a nice little command that lets you augment and add the framework load commands named **install_name_tool**.

Open Xcode and build and run the application so the simulator is running `DeleteMe`. Once running in the LLDB `Terminal`, verify the `CallKit` framework is loaded into the `DeleteMe` address space. Pause the debugger, then type the following into LLDB:

```
(lldb) image list CallKit
```

If the `CallKit` module is correctly loaded into the process space, you'll get output similar to the following:

```
[  0] 0484D8BA-5CB8-3DD3-8136-D8A96FB7E15B 0x0000000102d10000 /
Applications/Xcode.app/Contents/Developer/Platforms/
iPhoneSimulator.platform/Developer/SDKs/iPhoneSimulator.sdk/
System/Library/Frameworks/CallKit.framework/CallKit
```

Time to hunt down where the `DeleteMe` application is running from. Open a new `Terminal` window and type the following:

```
pgrep -fl DeleteMe
```

Provided `DeleteMe` is running, this will give you the full path of `DeleteMe` under the simulator app. You'll get output similar to the following:

```
61175 /Users/derekselander/Library/Developer/CoreSimulator/
Devices/D0576CB9-42E1-494B-B626-B4DB75411700/data/Containers/
Bundle/Application/474C8786-CC4F-4615-8BB0-8447DC9F82CA/
DeleteMe.app/DeleteMe
```

You'll now modify this executable's load commands to point to a different framework.

Grab the fullpath to the `DeleteMe` executable.

Stop the execution of the `DeleteMe` executable and temporarily close Xcode. If you were to accidentally build and run the `DeleteMe` application through Xcode at a later time, it would undo any tweaks you're about to make.

In the same `Terminal` window, paste the full path you received from the output of your `pgrep` command along with the `install_name_tool` command as follows:

```
install_name_tool \
  /Users/derekselander/Library/Developer/CoreSimulator/Devices/
D0576CB9-42E1-494B-B626-B4DB75411700/data/Containers/Bundle/
Application/474C8786-CC4F-4615-8BB0-8447DC9F82CA/DeleteMe.app/
DeleteMe
```

Before you execute this command, add the change argument along with the full path to the `CallKit` framework and the new framework you want to replace it with. Just for kicks, you'll replace it with the `NotificationCenter` framework.

```
install_name_tool \
  -change \
    /System/Library/Frameworks/CallKit.framework/CallKit \
    /System/Library/Frameworks/NotificationCenter.framework/
NotificationCenter \
      /Users/derekselander/Library/Developer/CoreSimulator/
Devices/D0576CB9-42E1-494B-B626-B4DB75411700/data/Containers/
Bundle/Application/474C8786-CC4F-4615-8BB0-8447DC9F82CA/
DeleteMe.app/DeleteMe
```

Verify if your changes were actually applied:

```
otool -L /Users/derekselander/Library/Developer/CoreSimulator/
Devices/D0576CB9-42E1-494B-B626-B4DB75411700/data/Containers/
Bundle/Application/474C8786-CC4F-4615-8BB0-8447DC9F82CA/
DeleteMe.app/DeleteMe
```

If everything went smoothly, you'll notice something different about the linked frameworks now...

```
/System/Library/Frameworks/NotificationCenter.framework/
NotificationCenter (compatibility version 1.0.0, current version
1.0.0)
/System/Library/Frameworks/Social.framework/Social
(compatibility version 1.0.0, current version 87.0.0)
/System/Library/Frameworks/Foundation.framework/Foundation
(compatibility version 300.0.0, current version 1349.13.0)
/usr/lib/libobjc.A.dylib (compatibility version 1.0.0, current
```

```
version 228.0.0)
/usr/lib/libSystem.dylib (compatibility version 1.0.0, current
version 1238.0.0)
/System/Library/Frameworks/UIKit.framework/UIKit (compatibility
version 1.0.0, current version 3600.6.21)
```

Verify these changes exist at runtime.

You're in a bit of a predicament here. If you build and run a new version of DeleteMe using Xcode, it will erase these changes. Instead, launch the DeleteMe application through the simulator and then attach to it in a new LLDB Terminal window. To do this, launch DeleteMe in the simulator. Next, type the following into Terminal:

```
lldb -n DeleteMe
```

In LLDB, check if the CallKit framework is still loaded.

```
(lldb) image list CallKit
```

You'll get an error as output:

```
error: no modules found that match 'CallKit'
```

Can you guess what you'll do next? Yep! Verify the NotificationCenter framework is now loaded.

```
(lldb) image list NotificationCenter
```

Boom! You'll get output similar to the following:

```
[  0] 0FCE1DF5-7BAC-3195-94CB-C6100116FF99 0x000000010b8c7000 /
Applications/Xcode.app/Contents/Developer/Platforms/
iPhoneSimulator.platform/Developer/SDKs/iPhoneSimulator.sdk/
System/Library/Frameworks/NotificationCenter.framework/
NotificationCenter
```

Changing around frameworks (or adding them!) to an already compiled binary is cool, but that took a little bit of work to set up. Fortunately, LLDB is wonderful for loading frameworks in to a process at runtime, which is what you'll do next. Keep that LLDB Terminal session alive, because you'll learn about a much easier way to load in frameworks.

Loading frameworks at runtime

Before you get into the fun of learning how to load and explore commands at runtime, let me give you a command to help explore directories using LLDB. Start by adding the following to your ~/.lldbinit file:

```
command regex ls 's/(.+)/po @import Foundation; [[NSFileManager
defaultManager] contentsOfDirectoryAtPath:@"%1" error:nil]/'
```

This creates a command named ls, which will take the directory path you give it and dump out the contents. This command will work on the directory of the device that's being debugged. For example, since you're running on the simulator on your computer's local drive it will dump that directory. If you were to run this on an attached iOS, tvOS or other appleOS device, it would dump the directory you give it on that device, with one minor caveat which you'll learn about shortly.

Since LLDB is already running and attached to DeleteMe, you'll need to load this command into LLDB manually as well since LLDB has already read the ~/.lldbinit file. Type the following into your LLDB session:

```
(lldb) command source ~/.lldbinit
```

This simply reloads your lldbinit file.

Next, find the full path to the frameworks directory in the simulator by typing the following:

```
(lldb) image list -d UIKit
```

This will dump out the directory holding UIKit.

```
[  0] /Applications/Xcode.app/Contents/Developer/Platforms/
iPhoneSimulator.platform/Developer/SDKs/iPhoneSimulator.sdk//
System/Library/Frameworks/UIKit.framework
```

You actually want to go one level higher to the Frameworks directory. Copy that full directory path and use the new command ls that you just created, like so:

```
(lldb) ls /Applications/Xcode.app/Contents/Developer/Platforms/
iPhoneSimulator.platform/Developer/SDKs/iPhoneSimulator.sdk//
System/Library/Frameworks/
```

This will dump all the *public* frameworks available to the simulator. There are many more frameworks to be found in different directories, but you'll start here first.

From the list of frameworks, load the **Speech** framework into the `DeleteMe` process space like so:

```
(lldb) process load /Applications/Xcode.app/Contents/Developer/
Platforms/iPhoneSimulator.platform/Developer/SDKs/
iPhoneSimulator.sdk//System/Library/Frameworks/Speech.framework/
Speech
```

LLDB will give you some happy output saying the `Speech` framework was loaded into your process space. Yay!

Here's something even cooler. By default, `dyld` will search a set of directories if it can't find the location of the framework. You don't need to specify the full path to the framework, just the framework library along with the framework's name.

Try this out by loading the `MessagesUI` framework.

```
(lldb) process load MessageUI.framework/MessageUI
```

You'll get the following output:

```
Loading "MessageUI.framework/MessageUI"...ok
Image 1 loaded.
```

Sweet.

Exploring frameworks

One of the foundations of reverse engineering is exploring dynamic frameworks. Since a dynamic framework requires the code to compile the binary into a **position independent** executable, you can still query a significant amount of information in the dynamic framework — even when the compiler strips the framework of debugging symbols. The binary needs to use position-independent code because the compiler doesn't know exactly where the code will reside in memory once `dyld` has done its business.

Having solid knowledge of how an application interacts with a framework can also give you insight into how the application works itself. For example, if a stripped application is using a `UITableView`, I'll set breakpoint queries in certain methods in `UIKit` to determine what code is responsible for the `UITableViewDataSource`.

Often when I'm exploring a dynamic framework, I'll simply load it into the processes address space and start running various `image lookup` queries to see what the module holds. From there, I'll execute various interesting methods that look like they'd be fun to play around with.

If you jumped chapters and have that clueless face going on for the image lookup command, check out Chapter 7, "Image".

Here's a nice little LLDB command regex you might want to stick into your ~/.lldbinit file. It dumps Objective-C easily accessible class methods (i.e. Singletons) for exploration.

Add the following to your ~/.lldbinit file.

```
command regex dump_stuff "s/(.+)/image lookup -rn '\+\[\w+(\(\w+
\))?\ \w+\]$' %1 /"
```

This command, dump_stuff, expects a framework or frameworks as input and will dump Objective-C class methods that have zero arguments. This definitely isn't a catch-all for all Objective-C naming conventions, but is a nice, simple command to use for a quick first pass when exploring a framework.

Load this command into the active LLDB session and then give it a go with the Social framework.

```
(lldb) command source ~/.lldbinit
(lldb) dump_stuff Social
```

You might find some amusing methods to play around with in the output...

Here are some helpers to these methods that are definitely worth sticking in your ~/.lldbinit file as well:

```
command regex ivars 's/(.+)/expression -lobjc -O -- [%1
_ivarDescription]/'
```

This will dump all the ivars of a inherited NSObject instance.

```
command regex methods 's/(.+)/expression -lobjc -O -- [%1
_shortMethodDescription]/'
```

This will dump all the methods implemented by the inherited NSObject instance, or the class of the NSObject.

```
command regex lmethods 's/(.+)/expression -lobjc -O -- [%1
_methodDescription]/'
```

This will recursively dump all the methods implemented by the inherited NSObject and recursively continue on to its superclass.

For example, you might choose to inspect an instance of the SLFacebookUpload class like so:

```
(lldb) ivars [SLFacebookUpload new]
<SLFacebookUpload: 0x600000056320>:
in SLFacebookUpload:
  _uploadID (NSString*): nil
  _uploadType (long): 0
  _totalBytes (unsigned long): 0
  _transferredBytes (unsigned long): 0
in NSObject:
  isa (Class): SLFacebookUpload (isa, 0x103914078)
```

Or perhaps you're just curious about what methods this class implements:

```
(lldb) methods SLFacebookUpload
<SLFacebookUpload: 0x10f75f078>:
in SLFacebookUpload:
    Class Methods:
        + (BOOL) supportsSecureCoding; (0x10f6e3b5b)
    Properties:
        @property (retain, nonatomic) NSString* uploadID;
(@synthesize uploadID = _uploadID;)
        ...
        @property (nonatomic) unsigned long transferredBytes;
(@synthesize transferredBytes = _transferredBytes;)
    Instance Methods:
        - (id) uploadID; (0x10f6e3b63)
        ...
        - (void) setTotalBytes:(unsigned long)arg1;
(0x10f6e3bd3)
(NSObject ...)
```

Or get *all* the methods available through this class and superclasses:

```
(lldb) lmethods SLFacebookUpload
<SLFacebookUpload: 0x10f75f078>:
in SLFacebookUpload:
    Class Methods:
        + (BOOL) supportsSecureCoding; (0x10f6e3b5b)
    Properties:
        @property (retain, nonatomic) NSString* uploadID;
(@synthesize uploadID = _uploadID;)
        ...
        @property (nonatomic) unsigned long transferredBytes;
(@synthesize transferredBytes = _transferredBytes;)
    Instance Methods:
        - (id) uploadID; (0x10f6e3b63)
        ...
        - (void) setTotalBytes:(unsigned long)arg1;
(0x10f6e3bd3)
```

```
in NSObject:
    Class Methods:
        + (id) CKSQLiteClassName; (0x126ecbb5e)
        ...
        + (BOOL) isFault; (0x10fd08a6d)
    Properties:
        @property (retain, nonatomic) NSArray*
accessibilityCustomRotors;
        ...
        @property (readonly, copy) NSString* debugDescription;
    Instance Methods:
        - (id) mf_objectWithHighest:(^block)arg1; (0x126776a76)
        ...
        - (BOOL) isFault; (0x10fd08a70)
```

Note: You only explored the frameworks in the public frameworks directory **System/Library/Frameworks**. There are many other fun frameworks to explore in other subdirectories starting in **System/Library**.

Loading frameworks on an actual iOS device

If you have a valid iOS developer account, an application you've written, and a device, you can do the same thing you did on the simulator but on the device. The only difference is the location of the **System/Library** path.

If you're running an app on the simulator, the public frameworks directory will be located at the following location:

```
/Applications/Xcode.app/Contents/Developer/Platforms/
iPhoneSimulator.platform/Developer/SDKs/iPhoneSimulator.sdk/
System/Library/Frameworks/
```

But some super-observant readers might say, "Wait a second, using `otool -L` on the simulator gave us **/System/Library/Frameworks** as the absolute path, not that big long path above. What gives?"

Remember how I said `dyld` searches a specific set of directories for these frameworks? Well, there's a special simulator-specific version named `dyld_sim`, which looks up the proper simulator location. This is the correct path where these frameworks reside on an actual iOS device.

So if you're running on an actual iOS device, the frameworks path will be located at:

```
/System/Library/Frameworks/
```

But wait, I hear some others say, "What about sandboxing?"

The iOS kernel has different restrictions for different directory locations. In iOS 10 and earlier, the **/System/Library/** directory is readable by your process! This makes sense because your process needs to call the appropriate public and private frameworks from within the processes address space.

If the Sandbox restricted reading of these directories, then the app wouldn't be able to load them in and then the app would fail to launch.

You can try this out by getting Xcode up and running and attached to any one of your iOS applications. While LLDB is attached to an iOS device, try running `ls` on the root directory:

```
(lldb) ls /
```

Now try the /System/Library/ directory:

```
(lldb) ls /System/Library/
```

Some directories will fail to load. This is the kernel saying "Nope!". However, some directories can be dumped.

You have the power to look at live frameworks and dynamically load them inside your app so you can play with and explore them. There are some interesting and powerful frameworks hidden in the **/System/Library** subdirectories for you to explore on your iOS, tvOS or watchOS device.

Where to go from here?

That **/System/Library** directory is really something. You can spend a lot of time exploring the different contents in that subdirectory. If you have an iOS device, go explore it!

In this chapter you learned how to load and execute frameworks through LLDB. However, you've been left somewhat high and dry for figuring out how to develop with dynamically loaded private frameworks in code.

In the next two chapters, you'll explore loading frameworks at runtime through code using Objective-C's method swizzling, as well as function interposition, which is a more Swifty-style strategy for changing around methods at runtime.

This is especially useful if you were to pull in a private framework. I think it's one of the most exciting things about reverse engineering Apple software. :]

Chapter 15: Hooking & Executing Code with dlopen & dlsym

Using LLDB, you've seen how easy it is to create breakpoints and inspect things of interest. You've also seen how to create classes you wouldn't normally have access to. You've been unable to wield this power at development time because you can't get a public API if the framework, or any of its classes or methods, are marked as private. However, all that is about to change.

It's time to learn about the complementary skills of developing with these frameworks. In this chapter, you're going to learn about methods and strategies to "hook" into Swift and C code as well as execute methods you wouldn't normally have access to.

This is a critical skill to have when you're working with something such as a private framework and want to execute or augment existing code within your own application. To do this, you're going to call on the help of two awesome and special functions: **dlopen** and **dlsym**.

The Objective-C runtime vs. Swift & C

Objective-C, thanks to its powerful runtime, is a truly dynamic language. Even when compiled and running, not even the program knows what will happen when the next `objc_msgSend` comes up.

There are different strategies for hooking into and executing Objective-C code; you'll explore these in the next chapter. This chapter focuses on how to hook into and use these frameworks under Swift.

Swift acts a lot like C or C++. If it doesn't need the dynamic dispatch of Objective-C, the compiler doesn't have to use it. This means when you're looking at the assembly for a Swift method that doesn't need dynamic dispatch, the assembly can simply call the address containing the method. This "direct" function calling is where the `dlopen` and `dlsym` combo really shines. This is what you're going to learn about in this chapter.

Setting up your project

For this chapter, you're going to use a starter project named **Watermark**, located in the **starter** folder.

This project is very simple. All it does is display a watermarked image in a `UIImageView`.

However, there's something special about this watermarked image. The actual image displayed is hidden away in a array of bytes compiled into the program. That is, the image is not bundled as a separate file inside the application. Rather, the image is actually located within the executable itself. Clearly the author didn't want to hand out the original image, anticipating people would reverse engineer the **Assets.car** file, which typically is a common place to hold images within an application.

First, you'll explore hooking into a common C function. Once you've mastered the concepts, you'll execute a hidden function that's unavailable to you at development time thanks to the Swift compiler. Using dlopen and dlsym, you'll be able to call and execute a private method inside a framework with zero modifications to the framework's code.

Now that you've got more theory than you've ever wanted in an introduction, it's finally time to get started.

Easy mode: hooking C functions

When learning how to use the dlopen and dlsym functions, you'll be going after the getenv C function. This simple C function takes a char * (null terminated string) for input and returns the environment variable for the parameter you supply.

This function is actually called quite a bit when your executable starts up.

Open and launch the **Watermark** project in Xcode. Create a new symbolic breakpoint, putting getenv in the **Symbol** section. Next, add a custom action with the following:

```
po (char *)$rdi
```

Now, make sure the execution automatically continues after the breakpoint hits.

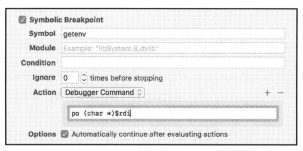

Finally, build and run the application on the iPhone Simulator then watch the console. You'll get a slew of output indicating this method is called quite frequently. It'll look similar to the following:

```
"DYLD_INSERT_LIBRARIES"
"NSZombiesEnabled"
"OBJC_DEBUG_POOL_ALLOCATION"
```

```
"MallocStackLogging"
"MallocStackLoggingNoCompact"
"OBJC_DEBUG_MISSING_POOLS"
"LIBDISPATCH_DEBUG_QUEUE_INVERSIONS"
"LIBDISPATCH_CONTINUATION_ALLOCATOR"
... etc ...
```

> **Note:** A far more elegant way to dump all environment variables available to your application is to use the DYLD_PRINT_ENV. To set this up, go to **Product\Manage Scheme**, and then add this in the Environment variables section. You can simply add the name, **DYLD_PRINT_ENV**, with no value, to dump out all environment variables at runtime.

However, an important point to note is all these calls to getenv are happening before your executable has even started. You can verify this by putting a breakpoint on getenv and looking at the stack trace. Notice main is nowhere in sight. This means you'll not be able to alter these function calls unless you declare an alternative getenv function before dyld loads the frameworks.

Since C doesn't use dynamic dispatch, hooking a function requires you to intercept the function before it's loaded. On the plus side, C functions are relatively easy to grab. All you need is the name of the C function without any parameters along with the name of the dynamic framework in which the C function is implemented.

However, since C is all-powerful and used pretty much everywhere, there are different tactics of varying complexity you can explore to hook a C function. If you want to hook a C function inside your own executable, that's not a lot of work. However, if you want to hook a function called before your main function is executed, the complexity definitely goes up a notch.

As soon as your executable loads from main, it's already imported all the dynamic frameworks specified in the load commands, as you learned in the previous chapter. The dynamic linker will recursively load frameworks in a depth-first manner. Once the linker gets an address for a particular function, it'll replace all references of a function with the actual address of this function in memory.

This means if you want to have the function hooked before your application starts up, you'll need to create a dynamic framework to put the hooking logic in so it'll be available before the main function is called. You'll explore this easy case of hooking a C function inside your own executable first.

Back to the Watermarks project!

Open **AppDelegate.swift**, and replace
`application(_:didFinishLaunchingWithOptions:)` with the following:

```
func application(_ application: UIApplication,
didFinishLaunchingWithOptions launchOptions:
[UIApplicationLaunchOptionsKey : Any]? = nil) -> Bool {
  if let cString = getenv("HOME") {
    let homeEnv = String(cString: cString)
    print("HOME env: \(homeEnv)")
  }
  return true
}
```

This creates a call to `getenv` to get the `HOME` environment variable.

Next, remove the symbolic `getenv` breakpoint you previously created and build and run the application.

The console output will look similar to the following:

```
HOME env: /Users/derekselander/Library/Developer/CoreSimulator/
Devices/D0576CB9-42E1-494B-B626-B4DB75411700/data/Containers/
Data/Application/AAC2D01C-045D-4384-B09E-1A83885D69FD
```

This is the `HOME` environment variable set for the Simulator you're running on.

Say you wanted to hook the `getenv` function to act completely normally, but return something different to the output above if and only if `HOME` is the parameter.

As mentioned earlier, you'll need to create a framework that's relied upon by the `Watermark` executable to grab that address of `getenv` and change it before it's resolved in the main executable.

In Xcode, navigate to **File\New\Target** and select **Cocoa Touch Framework**. Choose **HookingC** as the product name, and set the language to **Objective-C**.

Once this new framework is created, create a new C file. In Xcode, select **File\New\File**, then select **C file**. Name this file **getenvhook**. Uncheck the checkbox for **Also create a header file**. Save the file with the rest of the project.

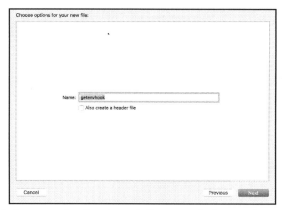

Make sure this file belongs to the **HookingC** framework that you've just created, and **not Watermark**.

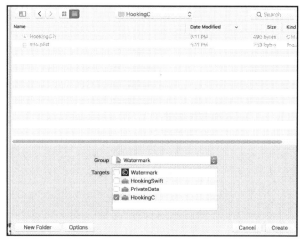

Okay... you're finally about to write some code... I swear.

Open **getenvhook.c** and replace its contents with the following:

```
#import <dlfcn.h>
#import <assert.h>
#import <stdio.h>
#import <dispatch/dispatch.h>
#import <string.h>
```

- `dlfcn.h` will be responsible for two very interesting functions: `dlopen` and `dlsym`.

- `assert.h` the assert will test the library containing the real `getenv` is correctly loaded.

- `stdio.h` will be used temporarily for a C `printf` call.

- `dispatch.h` will be used to to properly set up the logic for GCD's `dispatch_once` function.

- `string.h` will be used for the `strcmp` function, which compares two C strings.

Next, redeclare the `getenv` function with the hard-coded stub shown below:

```
char * getenv(const char *name) {
  return "YAY!";
}
```

Finally, build and run your application to see what happens. You'll get the following output:

```
HOME env: YAY!
```

Awesome! You were able to successfully replace this method with your own function. However, this isn't quite what you want. You want to call the original `getenv` function and augment the return value if `"HOME"` is supplied as input.

What would happen if you tried to call the original `getenv` function inside your `getenv` function? Try it out and see what happens. Add some temporary code so the `getenv` looks like the following:

```
char * getenv(const char *name) {
  return getenv(name);
  return "YAY!";
}
```

Your program will... sort of... run and then eventually crash. This is because you've just created a stack overflow. All references to the previously linked `getenv` have disappeared now that you've created your own `getenv` fuction.

Undo that previous line of code. That idea won't work. You're going to need a different tactic to grab the original `getenv` function.

First things first though, you need to figure out which library holds the `getenv` function. Make sure that problematic line of code is removed, and build and run the application again. Pause execution and bring up the LLDB console. Once the console pops up, enter the following:

```
(lldb) image lookup -s getenv
```

You'll get output looks similar to the following:

```
1 symbols match 'getenv' in /Users/derekselander/Library/
Developer/Xcode/DerivedData/Watermark-
frqludlofnmrzcbjnkmuhgeuogmp/Build/Products/Debug-
iphonesimulator/Watermark.app/Frameworks/HookingC.framework/
HookingC:
        Address: HookingC[0x0000000000000f60]
(HookingC.__TEXT.__text + 0)
        Summary: HookingC`getenv at getenvhook.c:16
1 symbols match 'getenv' in /Applications/Xcode.app/Contents/
Developer/Platforms/iPhoneSimulator.platform/Developer/SDKs/
iPhoneSimulator.sdk//usr/lib/system/libsystem_c.dylib:
        Address: libsystem_c.dylib[0x000000000005f1c4]
(libsystem_c.dylib.__TEXT.__text + 385956)
        Summary: libsystem_c.dylib`getenv
```

You'll get two hits. One of them will be the getenv function you created yourself. More importantly, you'll get the location of the getenv function you actually care about. It looks like this function is located in **libsystem_c.dylib**, and its full path is at /usr/lib/system/libsystem_c.dylib. Remember, the simulator prepends that big long path to these directories, but the dynamic linker is smart enough to search in the correct areas. Everything after iPhoneSimulator.sdk is where this framework is actually stored on a real iOS device.

Now you know exactly where this function is loaded, it's time to whip out the first of the amazing "dl" duo, dlopen. Its function signature looks like the following:

```
extern void * dlopen(const char * __path, int __mode);
```

dlopen expects a fullpath in the form of a char * and a second parameter, which is a mode expressed as an integer that determines how dlopen should load the module. If successful, dlopen returns an opaque handle (a void *) ,or NULL if it fails.

After dlopen (hopefully) returns a reference to the module, you'll use dlsym to get a reference to the getenv function. dlsym has the following function signature:

```
extern void * dlsym(void * __handle, const char * __symbol);
```

dlsym expects to take the reference generated by dlopen as the first parameter and the name of the function as the second parameter. If everything goes well, dlsym will return the function address for the symbol specified in the second parameter or NULL if it failed.

Replace your getenv function with the following:

```
char * getenv(const char *name) {
  void *handle = dlopen("/usr/lib/system/libsystem_c.dylib",
RTLD_NOW);
```

```
    assert(handle);
    void *real_getenv = dlsym(handle, "getenv");
    printf("Real getenv: %p\nFake getenv: %p\n", real_getenv,
getenv);
    return "YAY!";
}
```

You used the RTLD_NOW mode of dlopen to say, "Hey, don't wait or do any cute lazy loading stuff. Open this module right now." After making sure the handle is not NULL through a C assert, you call dlsym to get a handle on the "real" getenv.

Build and run the application. You'll get output similar to the following:

```
Real getenv: 0x10d2451c4
Fake getenv: 0x10a8f7de0
2016-12-19 16:51:30.650 Watermark[1035:19708] HOME env: YAY!
```

Your function pointers will be different than my output, but take note of the difference in address between the real and fake getenv.

You're starting to see how you'll go about this. However, you'll need to make a few touch-ups to the above code first. For example, you can cast function pointers to the exact type of function you expect to use. Right now, the real_getenv function pointer is void *, meaning it could be anything. You already know the function signature of getenv, so you can simply cast it to that.

Replace your getenv function one last time with the following:

```
char * getenv(const char *name) {
  static void *handle;          // 1
  static char * (*real_getenv)(const char *); // 2

  static dispatch_once_t onceToken;
  dispatch_once(&onceToken, ^{  // 3
    handle = dlopen("/usr/lib/system/libsystem_c.dylib",
RTLD_NOW);
    assert(handle);
    real_getenv = dlsym(handle, "getenv");
  });

  if (strcmp(name, "HOME") == 0) { // 4
    return "/";
  }

  return real_getenv(name); // 5
}
```

You might not be used to this amount of C code, so let's break it down:

1. This creates a static variable named `handle`. It's static so this variable will survive the scope of the function. That is, this variable will not be erased when the function exits, but you'll only be able to access it inside the `getenv` function.

2. You're doing the same thing here as you declare the `real_getenv` variable as static, but you've made other changes to the `real_getenv` function pointer. You've cast this function pointer to correctly match the signature of `getenv`. This will allow you to call the real `getenv` function through the `real_getenv` variable. Cool, right?

3. You're using GCD's `dispatch_once` because you really only need to call the setup once. This nicely complements the `static` variables you declared a couple lines above. You don't want to be doing the lookup logic every time your augmented `getenv` runs!

4. You're using C's `strcmp` to see if you're querying the `"HOME"` environment variable. If it's true, you're simply returning `"/"` to signify the root directory. Essentially, you're overriding what the `getenv` function returns.

5. If `"HOME"` is not supplied as an input parameter, then just fall back on the default `getenv`.

Find `application(_:didFinishLaunchingWithOptions:)` in **AppDelegate.swift**. Replace this method with:

```
func application(_ application: UIApplication,
didFinishLaunchingWithOptions launchOptions:
[UIApplicationLaunchOptionsKey : Any]? = nil) -> Bool {
  if let cString = getenv("HOME") {
    let homeEnv = String(cString: cString)
    print("HOME env: \(homeEnv)")
  }

  if let cString = getenv("PATH") {
    let homeEnv = String(cString: cString)
    print("PATH env: \(homeEnv)")
  }
  return true
}
```

Build and run the application. Provided everything went well, you'll get output similar to the following:

```
HOME env: /
PATH env: /Applications/Xcode.app/Contents/Developer/Platforms/
iPhoneSimulator.platform/Developer/SDKs/iPhoneSimulator.sdk/usr/
bin:/Applications/Xcode.app/Contents/Developer/Platforms/
iPhoneSimulator.platform/Developer/SDKs/iPhoneSimulator.sdk/
```

```
bin:/Applications/Xcode.app/Contents/Developer/Platforms/
iPhoneSimulator.platform/Developer/SDKs/iPhoneSimulator.sdk/usr/
sbin:/Applications/Xcode.app/Contents/Developer/Platforms/
iPhoneSimulator.platform/Developer/SDKs/iPhoneSimulator.sdk/
sbin:/Applications/Xcode.app/Contents/Developer/Platforms/
iPhoneSimulator.platform/Developer/SDKs/iPhoneSimulator.sdk/usr/
local/bin
```

As you can see, your hooked `getenv` augmented the `HOME` environment variable, but defaulted to the normal `getenv` for `PATH`.

Although annoying, it's worth driving this point home yet again. If you called a `UIKit` method, and `UIKit` calls `getenv`, your augmented `getenv` function will not get called during this time because the `getenv`'s address had already been resolved when `UIKit`'s code loaded.

Hard mode: hooking Swift methods

Going after Swift code that isn't dynamic is a lot like going after C functions. However, there are a couple of complications with this approach that make it a bit harder to hook into Swift methods.

First off, Swift often uses classes or structs in typical development. This is a unique challenge because `dlsym` will only give you a C function. You'll need to augment this function so the Swift method can reference `self` if you're grabbing an instance method, or reference the class if you're calling a class method. When accessing a method that belongs to a class, the assembly will often reference offsets of `self` or the class when performing the method. Since `dlysm` will grab you a C-type function, you'll need to creatively utilize your knowledge of assembly, parameters and registers to turn that C function into a Swift method.

The second issue you need to worry about is that Swift mangles the names of its methods. The happy, pretty name you see in your code is actually a scary long name in the module's symbol table. You'll need to find this method's correct mangled name in order to reference the Swift method through `dlysm`.

As you know, this project produces and displays a watermarked image. Here's the challenge for you: using only code, display the original image in the UIImageView. You're not allowed to use LLDB to execute the command yourself, nor are you allowed to modify any contents in memory once the program is running.

Are you up for this challenge? :] Don't worry, I'll show you how it's done!

First, open **AppDelegate.swift** and remove all the printing logic found inside `application(_:didFinishLaunchingWithOptions:)`. Next, open **CopyrightImageGenerator.swift**.

Inside this class is a `private` computed property containing the `originalImage`. In addition, there's a public computed property containing the `watermarkedImage`. It's this method that calls the `originalImage` and superimposes the watermark. It's up to you to figure out a way to call this `originalImage` method, without changing the `HookingSwift` dynamic library at all.

Open **ViewController.swift** and add the following code to the end of `viewDidLoad()`:

```
if let handle = dlopen("", RTLD_NOW) {}
```

You're using Swift this time, but you'll use the same `dlopen` & `dlsym` trick you saw earlier. You now need to get the correct location of the `HookingSwift` framework. The nice thing about `dlopen` is you can supply relative paths instead of absolute paths.

Time to find where that framework is relative to the `Watermark` executable.

In Xcode, make sure the **Project Navigator** is visible (through **Cmd + 1**). Next, open the **Products** directory and right-click the `Watermark.app`. Next, select **Show in Finder**.

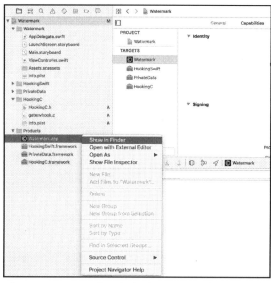

Once the Finder window pops up, right click the `Watermark` bundle and select **Show Package Contents**. It's in this directory the actual `Watermark` executable is located, so you simply need to find the location of the `HookingSwift` framework's executable relative to this `Watermark` executable.

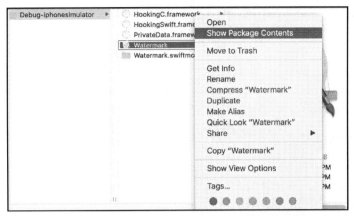

Next, select the Frameworks directory. Finally select the **HookingSwift.framework**. Within this directory, you'll come across the HookingSwift binary.

This means you've found the relative path you can supply to dlopen. Modify the dlopen function call you just added so it looks like the following:

```
if let handle = dlopen("./Frameworks/HookingSwift.framework/
HookingSwift", RTLD_NOW) {
}
```

Now to the hard part. You want to grab the name of the method responsible for the originalImage property inside the CopyrightImageGenerator class. By now, you know you can use the image lookup LLDB function to search for method name compiled into an executable.

Since you know originalImage is implemented in Swift, use a "Swift style" type of search with the image lookup command. Make sure the app is running then type the following into LLDB:

```
(lldb) image lookup -rn HookingSwift.*originalImage
```

You'll get output similar to the following:

```
1 match found in /Users/derekselander/Library/Developer/Xcode/
DerivedData/Watermark-frqludlofnmrzcbjnkmuhgeuogmp/Build/
Products/Debug-iphonesimulator/Watermark.app/Frameworks/
HookingSwift.framework/HookingSwift:
        Address: HookingSwift[0x00000000000017a0]
(HookingSwift.__TEXT.__text + 1200)
        Summary:
HookingSwift`HookingSwift.CopyrightImageGenerator.(originalImage
in _71AD57F3ABD678B113CF3AD05D01FF41).getter :
Swift.Optional<__ObjC.UIImage> at CopyrightImageGenerator.swift:
43
```

In the output, search for the line containing **Address:**
HookingSwift[0x00000000000017a0]. This is where this method is implemented
inside the HookingSwift framework. This will likely be a different address for you.

For this particular example, the function is implemented at offset 0x00000000000017a0
inside the HookingSwift framework. Copy this address and enter the following
command into LLDB:

```
(lldb) image dump symtab —m HookingSwift
```

This dumps the symbol table of the HookingSwift framework. In addition to dumping
the symbol table, you've told LLDB to show the mangled names of the Swift functions.
Search for (Cmd + F) the address you just copied.

You'll get an address that matches the address you copied:

Here's the line that interests you.

```
[    7]     21 D X Code          0x00000000000017a0
0x000000010ee207a0 0x0000000000000090 0x000f0000
_TFC12HookingSwift23CopyrightImageGeneratorgP33_71AD57F3ABD678B1
13CF3AD05D01FF4113originalImageGSqCSo7UIImage_
```

Yep, that huge angry alphanumeric chunk at the end is the Swift mangled function
name. It's this monstrosity you'll stick into dlsym to grab the address of the
originalImage getter method.

Open **ViewController.swift** and add the following code inside the if let you just
added:

```
let sym = dlsym(handle,
 "_TFC12HookingSwift23CopyrightImageGeneratorgP33_71AD57F3ABD678B
113CF3AD05D01FF4113originalImageGSqCSo7UIImage_")!
print("\(sym)")
```

You've opted for an implicitly unwrapped optional since you want the application to
crash if you got the wrong symbol name.

Build and run the application. If everything worked out, you'll get a memory address at the tail end of the console output (yours will likely be different):

```
0x0000000103105770
```

This address is the location to `CopyrightImageGeneratorg`'s `originalImage` method that `dlsym` provided. You can verify this by creating a breakpoint on this address in LLDB:

```
(lldb) b 0x0000000103105770
```

LLDB creates a breakpoint on the following function:

```
Breakpoint 1: where =
HookingSwift`HookingSwift.CopyrightImageGenerator.(originalImage
in _71AD57F3ABD678B113CF3AD05D01FF41).getter :
Swift.Optional<__ObjC.UIImage> at CopyrightImageGenerator.swift:
35, address = 0x0000000103105770
```

Great! You can bring up the address of this function at runtime, but how do you go about calling it? Thankfully, you can use the `typealias` Swift keyword to cast functions signatures.

Open **ViewController.swift**, and add the following directly under the `print` call you just added:

```
typealias privateMethodAlias = @convention(c) (Any) ->
UIImage? // 1
let originalImageFunction = unsafeBitCast(sym, to:
privateMethodAlias.self) // 2
let originalImage = originalImageFunction(imageGenerator) // 3
self.imageView.image = originalImage // 4
```

Here's what this does:

1. This declares the type of function that is syntactically equivalent to the Swift function for the `originalImage` property getter.

   There's something very important to notice here. `privateMethodAlias` is designed so it takes one parameter type of `Any`, but the actual Swift function expects no parameters. Why is this?

   It's due to the fact that by looking at the assembly to this method, the reference to `self` is expected in the RDI register.

   This means you need to supply the instance of the class as the first parameter into the function to trick this C function into thinking it's a Swift method. If you don't do this, there's a chance the application will crash!

2. Now you've made this new alias, you're casting the `sym` address to this new type and calling it `originalImageFunction`.

3. You're executing the method and supplying the instance of the class as the first and only parameter to the function. This will cause the `RDI` register to be properly set to the instance of the class. It'll return the original image without the watermark.

4. You're assigning the `UIImageView`'s image to the original image without the watermark.

With these new changes in, build and run the application. As expected, the original, watermark-free image will now be displayed in the application.

Congratulations — you've discovered two new amazing functions and how to use them properly. Grabbing the location of code at runtime is a powerful feature that lets you access hidden code the compiler normally blocks from you. In addition, it lets you hook into code so you can perform your own modifications at runtime.

Where to go from here?

You're learning how to play around with dynamic frameworks. The previous chapter showed you how to dynamically load them in LLDB. This chapter showed you how to modify or execute Swift or C code you normally wouldn't be able to. In the next chapter, you're going to play with the Objective-C runtime to dynamically load a framework and use Objective-C's dynamic dispatch to execute classes you don't have the APIs for.

This is one of the most exciting features of reverse engineering — so get prepared, and caffeinated, for your foray into the next chapter!

Chapter 16: Exploring and Method Swizzling Objective-C Frameworks

In the previous two chapters, you explored dynamic loading as well as how to use the `dlopen` and `dlsym` functions. So long as you knew the name and location of the code, it didn't matter if the compiler tried to hide it from you.

You'll cap off this round of dynamic framework exploration by digging into Objective-C frameworks using the Objective-C runtime to hook and execute methods of interest.

For this chapter, you'll *pretend* the iOS **Social** framework is a private framework, and won't use any headers or modules to help aid you in developing against the APIs found within the framework. You'll dynamically load the `Social` framework using `dlopen`, augment and execute APIs from the framework to share the original non-watermarked image of the two doggies in the `Watermark` project you started using from the previous chapter.

Loading and exploring the Social framework

Before you go off hacking around in the `Social` framework, it's best if you do some reconnaissance using LLDB, to hunt for methods and classes of importance.

Open the **Watermark** project in the starter folder. Build and run the application on the simulator.

While you were away, the interns were hard at work on the application adding a `UINavigationBar` and `UIBarButtonItem`. However, they forgot to implement the `IBAction` the share button hooks up to.

Once it's running, pause execution and use LLDB to dynamically load the `Social` framework, like so:

```
(lldb) process load /System/Library/Frameworks/Social.framework/
Social
```

Provided everything loaded correctly, you'll get the following output:

```
Loading "/Systen/Library/Frameworks/Social.framework/
Social"...ok
Image 0 loaded.
```

You now have access to all the code available to the `Social` framework in your executable, so it's time to explore what this framework has to offer. But where should you start? You could dump everything in the `Social` framwork using `image lookup -rn . Social`, but that produces too much output. Fortunately, there are more elegant ways for hunting down important code.

When you're completely stumped on where to start exploring the internals of a framework, your best bet is to research and launch the view controllers within the framework and work your way back from there.

In LLDB, type the following:

```
(lldb) image lookup -rn 'ViewController\ init' Social
```

Hmmm... there's too many view controllers in the `Social` framework that have methods that begin with `init`. Time to try a different tactic to see if there's one that stands out.

Type the following into LLDB:

```
(lldb) image lookup -rn '\+\[.*ViewController\ [a-zA-Z]+' Social
```

This one is a bit more complex. This is matching any nonprivate class methods i.e. methods that don't begin with the underscore. Scan through the output and see if any methods stand out as initialization class methods for `UIViewControllers`.

Judging from the output, three methods look promising as initializers for a view controller. I'll refrain from discussing this "private" API, so instead I'll simply note one is a public API and the other two are private. All three of these APIs begin with + [SLComposeViewController composeViewController.

This puts you in a weird position. Which of these APIs is the correct (aka public) one you should use? Remember, you're not allowed to consult the `Social` frameworks header files since this is a "private" framework, right? :]

You could try executing each one individually and pass `nil` as the one and only parameter. There's something special about one method. If you pass in `nil`, the method will spit some console output out and return `nil` instead of a valid instance.

I don't know about you, but if a class instantiation method spits out `nil` when it recieves a "bad" parameter, I'll want to explore that method more in detail. By this logic, you can deduce you'll want to explore +[SLComposeViewController composeViewControllerForServiceType:] even further.

But what should you pass in as the parameter to composeViewControllerForServiceType:? You don't even know the *type* of parameter to pass in yet. You can play around with this view controller by creating a breakpoint and "catching it" before it's deallocated.

First,you need to discover if there's any overridden `dealloc` message for a `UIViewController`.

Type the following into LLDB:

```
(lldb) image lookup -rn UIViewController.dealloc
```

You'll get one hit:

```
1 match found in /Applications/Xcode.app/Contents/Developer/
Platforms/iPhoneSimulator.platform/Developer/SDKs/
iPhoneSimulator.sdk//System/Library/Frameworks/UIKit.framework/
UIKit:
        Address: UIKit[0x00000000001c5f19] (UIKit.__TEXT.__text
+ 1850457)
        Summary: UIKit`-[UIViewController dealloc]
```

You'll need a breakpoint on this dealloc since you don't want to catch a dealloc for non-UIViewController related dealloc calls.

Type the following into LLDB:

```
(lldb) rb UIViewController.dealloc
```

Next, enter the following command into LLDB, which tells LLDB to honor any existing breakpoints you've created:

```
(lldb) expression -i0 -O -lobjc -- [SLComposeViewController
composeViewControllerForServiceType:nil]
```

After executing the above command, execution will stop on UIViewController's implementation of dealloc. If you look at the stack trace you'll see SLComposeViewController has an overriden dealloc method as well.

But that's fine. All you need is a valid instance in memory — and this class has not yet completely removed itself from memory. If you're on a different frame, make sure you're back on the head of the stack by selecting the top frame in Xcode or by typing frame select 0 in LLDB.

Now that you stopped on this breakpoint, grab the instance of this SLComposeViewController class using LLDB and your x64 register calling convention skills:

```
(lldb) po $rdi
```

This will spit out the SLComposeViewController instance you're after:

```
<SLComposeViewController: 0x7f9d796102c0>
```

Since the dealloc method hasn't jumped up the class hierarchy, a valid instance still exists. Take this instance and apply the ivar dumping command you acquired in Chapter 21, "Dynamic Frameworks".

```
(lldb) ivars 0x7f9d796102c0
```

This will dump all the ivars underlying the SLComposeViewController's properties. Search for serviceType. You'll stumble accross the type of class this ivar holds:

```
_serviceType (NSString*): nil
```

This seems to imply a string is what should be passed to composeViewControllerForServiceType:.

This means you should turn your attention to the DATA section within the Social framework to see if there are any strings hard coded within this framework that can be applied to this method.

From LLDB, dump the symbol table for the Social framework.

```
(lldb) image dump symtab Social —s address
```

This will dump the symbol table of the Social framework sorted by implementation address.

Since the framework uses the SL abbreviation and you're looking for an NSString containing serviceType, search for SLServiceType in the console output. As always, ⌘ + f is your friend.

From the output, you'll get the following hits that look to pertain to what you want.

```
[ 4297]    4297    X Data              0x00000000000a1e20
0x0000000111de1e20 0x0000000000000008 0x000f0000
SLServiceTypeTwitter
[ 4291]    4291    X Data              0x00000000000a1e28
0x0000000111de1e28 0x0000000000000008 0x000f0000
SLServiceTypeFacebook
[ 4294]    4294    X Data              0x00000000000a1e30
0x0000000111de1e30 0x0000000000000008 0x000f0000
SLServiceTypeSinaWeibo
[ 4295]    4295    X Data              0x00000000000a1e38
0x0000000111de1e38 0x0000000000000008 0x000f0000
SLServiceTypeTencentWeibo
[ 4296]    4296    X Data              0x00000000000a1e40
0x0000000111de1e40 0x0000000000000008 0x000f0000
SLServiceTypeTudou
[ 4299]    4299    X Data              0x00000000000a1e48
0x0000000111de1e48 0x0000000000000008 0x000f0000
SLServiceTypeYouku
[ 4298]    4298    X Data              0x00000000000a1e50
0x0000000111de1e50 0x0000000000000008 0x000f0000
SLServiceTypeVimeo
[ 4292]    4292    X Data              0x00000000000a1e58
0x0000000111de1e58 0x0000000000000008 0x000f0000
SLServiceTypeFlickr
[ 4293]    4293    X Data              0x00000000000a1e60
0x0000000111de1e60 0x0000000000000010 0x000f0000
SLServiceTypeLinkedIn
```

Ooh! You can play around with the SLServiceTypeTwitter hit, since every iOS developer seems to have a Twitter account.

Type the following in LLDB:

```
(lldb) po SLServiceTypeTwitter
```

You'll get the following output:

```
com.apple.social.twitter
```

Good, good — this value seems to be what we're looking for. Let's make sure it's an NSString:

```
(lldb) po [SLServiceTypeTwitter class]
```

You'll get the following output:

```
__NSCFConstantString
```

Bingo. Apply this value to the composeViewControllerForServiceType: you failed to utilize earlier:

```
(lldb) po [SLComposeViewController
composeViewControllerForServiceType:@"com.apple.social.twitter"]
<SLComposeViewController: 0x7fd030c141d0>
```

You'll get a valid address, meaning composeViewControllerForServiceType:'s input worked exactly how you'd expect it to.

Next, type the following into LLDB, replacing the address below with the address of the SLComposeViewController you created above.

```
(lldb) methods 0x7fd030c141d0
```

This dumps the methods of the class using your previously implemented methods command.

You'll see some methods in the console output like the ones highlighted below:

```
- (BOOL) setInitialText:(id)arg1; (0x11a80b7aa)
- (BOOL) addImage:(id)arg1; (0x11a80bdf4)
@property (copy, nonatomic) ^block completionHandler;
(@synthesize completionHandler = _completionHandler;)
```

As always, you'll have different load addresses for these methods, so the output will differ slightly. You've obtained enough information to instantiate this view controller and present it on the screen. You'll now implement and instantiate SLComposeViewController through code based on your previous research using LLDB.

Chapter 16: Exploring and Method Swizzling Objective-C Frameworks   223

Implementing your Social framework research

Click on the **HookingC** directory in the Xcode project directory. In Xcode, select **File\New\File\Objective-C File**. Name the file **P_SLComposeViewController**, select **Category** as the file type and select **NSObject** for the class. Then save the file.

Next, open **NSObject+P_SLComposeViewController.m** and replace its contents with:

```
#import "NSObject+P_SLComposeViewController.h"
#import <dlfcn.h>

@implementation NSObject (P_SLComposeViewController)

+ (void)load {
  dlopen("Social.framework/Social", RTLD_NOW);
}

@end
```

You're using the Objective-C `load` class method (which Swift doesn't have) to say as soon as this class loads into the runtime, use `dlopen` to load the `Social` framework. Using the usual `RTLD_NOW` indicates to not continue execution until the load has completed.

Next, open **NSObject+P_SLComposeViewController.h** and replace its contents with:

```
#import <Foundation/Foundation.h>

@interface NSObject (P_SLComposeViewController)

+ (id)composeViewControllerForServiceType:(NSString
*)serviceType;
- (BOOL)setInitialText:(id)text;
- (BOOL)addImage:(id)image;
@property (copy, nonatomic) id completionHandler;

@end
```

Finally, in the project navigator, select **NSObject+P_SLComposeViewController.h** and under **Target Membership** in the right sidebar, make sure **Public** is chosen next to **HookingC**. This ensures the header is available publicly.

Build and run the application. You'll get a couple of warnings saying the methods you've declared in the header file are not found.

Open **NSObject+P_SLComposeViewController.m** and replace everything below the header imports with the following:

```
#pragma clang diagnostic push
#pragma clang diagnostic ignored "-Wincomplete-implementation"

@implementation NSObject (P_SLComposeViewController)
@dynamic completionHandler;

+ (void)load {
    dlopen("Social.framework/Social", RTLD_NOW);
}

@end

#pragma clang diagnostic pop
```

This disables the incomplete implementation warning and adds @dynamic completionHandler to tell the compiler this property is implemented elsewhere.

This will stop the compiler's warnings about unimplemented methods as well as the nonexistent completionHandler property.

Exploring private code in Objective-C vs Swift

Although Swift is all the rage as the future of Apple development, it does add some annoyances to instantiating and exploring private code at runtime.

You've created a header file that says any **NSObject** implements the above methods. This is required because we're working with Swift.

If you were to only use Objective-C, you could use a much cleaner method by creating a protocol that implements the above methods.

For example, if you only planned to work with Objective-C, you could use the following (don't implement this, it's only for show):

```
@protocol P_SLComposeViewControllerProtocol <NSObject>

+ (id)composeViewControllerForServiceType:(NSString
*)serviceType;
- (BOOL)setInitialText:(id)text;
- (BOOL)addImage:(id)image;
@property (copy, nonatomic) id completionHandler;

@end
```

This would create an Objective-C protocol. You could then use this protocol using the following code:

```
id<P_SLComposeViewControllerProtocol> vc =
  [(id<P_SLComposeViewControllerProtocol>)
    NSClassFromString(@"SLComposeViewController")

composeViewControllerForServiceType:@"com.apple.social.twitter"]
;

[vc setInitialText:@"hello world"];
```

With Objective-C, you just declare and cast an object, telling the compiler it implements the protocol, and hence has those methods and properties. But with Swift, there are runtime checks for protocol implementation on objects so the Swift runtime gets angry and will crash your program, since the real `SLComposeViewController` definitely doesn't implement `P_SLComposeViewControllerProtocol`. This is why you have to do the ugly workaround of saying all `NSObjects` implement the above methods.

You're using Swift because it's a good exercise to see the extra headaches that come with exploring this language. However, when you're out exploring in the real world, you'll find that Objective-C is the path of least resistance when exploring and hooking into private Objective-C code.

Calling the private UIViewController

Now you've implemented the `NSObject` category in the HookingC framework, open **ViewController.swift** and add the following code to `sharingButtonTapped(_:)`:

```
guard let vcClass =
  NSClassFromString("SLComposeViewController") else { return }

let vc = vcClass.composeViewController(forServiceType:
  "com.apple.social.twitter") as! UIViewController

vc.setInitialText("Yay! Doggie Love!")
if let originalImage = imageView.image {
  vc.addImage(originalImage)
}

present(vc, animated: true)
```

Next, open **HookingC.h** and add the following at the end of the file:

```
#import "NSObject+P_SLComposeViewController.h"
```

This adds the category header to the bridging header, so it's available from Swift.

Build and run the application. Tap on the share button in the upper right corner and see what happens.

If you have a Twitter account added to your simulator, you'll get an error-free popup. However, if aren't logged in to your Twitter account on the Simulator, you'll get the following error:

Stick with this setup for a second. I'll force you to sign into your Twitter account later in the chapter.

Reverse engineering Objective-C blocks

Reverse engineering blocks are a slightly trickier game to play since you don't know what parameters should be passed in, or what the return type is. In addition, the memory layout of Swift's closures are implemented differently than Objective-C's blocks which is a gotcha you'll soon run into.

With that said, you're going to implement the completion closure for SLComposeViewController!

Open **ViewController.swift** and add the following logic inside the sharingButtonTapped(_:), right before the SLComposeViewController is presented:

```
vc.completionHandler = {
  print("SLComposeViewController completed")
}
```

Make sure you have no Twitter accounts signed into the iOS Simulator. Build and run, tap the share button, then cancel the share view controller when it appears.

Uh oh... You'll get a nice little crash.

```
24
25  import UIKit
26
27  @UIApplicationMain
28  class AppDelegate: UIResponder, UIApplicationDelegate {          Thread 1: EXC_BAD_ACCESS (code=1, address=
29      var window: UIWindow?
30
31      func application(_ application: UIApplication, didFinishLaunchingWithOptions launchOptions:
          [UIApplicationLaunchOptionsKey : Any]? = nil) -> Bool {
32          return true
33      }
34  }
35
```

Fortunately, you still have LLDB attached to the broken pieces of your once-running program. You can use LLDB to hunt for the culprit that caused this!

Jump down to the next frame using LLDB:

```
(lldb) frame select 1
```

Take a look at that assembly. The line above the red instruction pointer of death indicates a `call` instruction was made to an offset of the contents in the RDI regsiter. But what the hell is in the RDI register?

Jump back to the first frame (you can't access the RDI register from frame 1):

```
(lldb) frame select 0
```

From there, print out the `RDI` register:

```
(lldb) po $rdi
```

This will give the helpful output of (**Function**). Interesting... let's see if it's an NSObject subclass.

```
(lldb) po [$rdi class]
_SwiftValue

(lldb) po [$rdi superclass]
NSObject
```

Based on your previous findings in a previous chapter of exploring Objective-C blocks (Chapter 7, "Image"), the class should inherit from the private class, NSBlock. So the compiler (er... actually we) made an incorrect assumption to the Objective-C type the Swift closure should be cast to.

This means you need to explicitly cast the Swift closure to an Objective-C block. This is because the Swift compiler has no type information about the completionHandler, so it doesn't automatically translate it for us.

Recall in **NSObject+P_SLComposeViewController.h** you declared completionHandler as having the type id.

Open **ViewController.swift** and replace the contents of sharingButtonTapped(_:) with the following:

```
@IBAction func sharingButtonTapped(_ sender: Any) {
  guard let vcClass =
    NSClassFromString("SLComposeViewController") else { return }

  let vc = vcClass.composeViewController(forServiceType:
    "com.apple.social.twitter") as! UIViewController

  vc.setInitialText("Yay! Doggie Love!")
  if let originalImage = imageView.image {
    vc.addImage(originalImage)
  }
  typealias CompletionBlock = @convention(block) () -> Void
  vc.completionHandler = {
    print("SLComposeViewController completed")
  } as CompletionBlock

  present(vc, animated: true)
}
```

You've added a **typealias** called CompletionBlock that will cast this Swift closure to the proper Objective-C object. Build and run the application and try again.

Upon completion of presenting the SLComposeViewController, whether a success or failure, the program won't crash. Congratulations!

The unaddressed Objective-C block parameters

Now that you're an assembly pro, you should go investigate the assembly instruction just before the call to the Objective-C block.

You'll take a look at the call stack trace when your newly working Swift closure executes. In Xcode, create a GUI breakpoint on the line where the completionHandler is set.

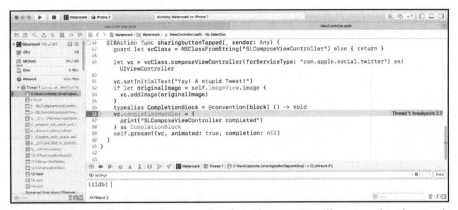

Build and run the application, then tap the share button. You'll get one breakpoint hit when setting the completionHandler. Continue through this one.

Next, tap on **Cancel** from the error alert and wait for the breakpoint to be triggered once again.

Once the breakpoint is hit, there should be a thunk method in the stack trace at frame 1. Jump down to frame 2 using LLDB:

```
(lldb) frame select 2
```

Scan the assembly for anything interesting. There it is! Do you see it?

```
     Watermark   Thread 1    5 -[SLComposeViewController completeWithResult:]
61   0x10d51fa4b <+220>: setb   r14b
62   0x10d51fa4f <+224>: jmp    0x10d51fa54              ; <+229>
63   0x10d51fa51 <+226>: xor    r14d, r14d
64   0x10d51fa54 <+229>: mov    rdi, r13
65   0x10d51fa57 <+232>: call   qword ptr [rip + 0x858ab] ; (void *)0x0000000100c5
66   0x10d51fa5d <+238>: mov    r13, qword ptr [rbp - 0x30]
67   0x10d51fa61 <+242>: mov    rdi, r12
68   0x10d51fa64 <+245>: call   qword ptr [rip + 0x8589e] ; (void *)0x0000000100c5
69   0x10d51fa6a <+251>: mov    r12, qword ptr [rip + 0xb934f] ;
     SLComposeViewController._completionHandler
70   0x10d51fa71 <+258>: mov    rdi, qword ptr [rbx + r12]
71   0x10d51fa75 <+262>: test   rdi, rdi
72   0x10d51fa78 <+265>: je     0x10d51fa92              ; <+291>
73   0x10d51fa7a <+267>: mov    rsi, r15
74   0x10d51fa7d <+270>: call   qword ptr [rdi + 0x10]
75   0x10d51fa80 <+273>: mov    rdi, qword ptr [rbx + r12]
76   0x10d51fa84 <+277>: mov    qword ptr [rbx + r12], 0x0
77   0x10d51fa8c <+285>: call   qword ptr [rip + 0x85876] ; (void *)0x0000000100c5
```

Right before the call to the Objective-C block, a parameter is being shot into the RSI register. This means the Objective-C block has got to have a parameter that is being supplied to it.

Provided the RSI register is not overwritten at the time the execution has stopped, you can dump out the contents of the RSI parameter, and since you stopped right at the beginning of the block execution, the RSI register should still be intact.

Jump back to frame 0, and print out the contents of the RSI register.

```
(lldb) frame select 0
(lldb) register read rsi
     rsi = 0x0000000000000000
```

There's nothing in there. But this tells you something. After careful study of how Apple writes their APIs you can either assume a `nil NSObject` is being passed in. Or, perhaps it's something else. In this case, perhaps it's an `enum` to signify if the view controller completed successfully or not.

There's only one way to verify this. You'll need to successfully post something (anything) to Twitter using the Simulator and observe the `RSI` register to see what, if anything, changes.

Log in to Twitter through the **Settings** application on the Simulator and then find the Twitter panel. Enter in your Twitter account information.

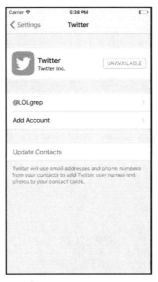

Yeah, I know you have one. This is for reverse engineering, so get over it. :]

Jump back to the `Watermark` program and bring up the `SLComposeViewController`. This time, no error alert will hinder your way. Create a new tweet to post to Twitter. Feel free to change around the content so you're not posting a picture of two very lovely, very cute doggies that the world should see... I'll get over it.

Post the content and wait for the Swift closure to hit.

Once the breakpoint triggers, inspect the RSI register again using LLDB:

```
(lldb) register read rsi
     rsi = 0x0000000000000001
```

Ahah! Its value is now 1. This suggests that the parameter passed in is an enum (or a Boolean, to be fair) which changes upon success or failure. This means you need to update the completionHandler block for the correct type.

Open **NSObject+P_SLComposeViewController.h** and rewrite the file so it looks like the following:

```
typedef enum : NSUInteger {
  P_SLComposePostFailed = 0,
  P_SLComposePostSuccess = 1
} P_SLComposePost;

@interface NSObject (P_SLComposeViewController)

+ (id)composeViewControllerForServiceType:(NSString
*)serviceType;
- (BOOL)setInitialText:(id)text;
- (BOOL)addImage:(id)image;
@property (copy, nonatomic) void (^completionHandler)
(P_SLComposePost);

@end
```

You've created an enum of type NSUInteger named P_SLComposePost. You've two values for this enum: a success and a failure.

Once you've made these changes, this will cause a build error in the completionHandler in **ViewController.swift**. Change the completionHandler logic so you're passing in the P_SLComposePost parameter, like so:

```
vc.completionHandler = { result in
  let resultString = result == P_SLComposePostFailed ?
"failed" : "success"
  print("SLComposeViewController completed with result: \
(resultString)")
}
```

Note you no longer need the typealias trick. This is because you've also changed the type of completionHandler from id to a block type. So the compiler knows the Swift closure should be treated as an Objective-C block here.

Build and run the application. This time, choose the Cancel action instead of posting to Twitter. You'll now get the correct output supplied by the result parameter you just implemented.

Good job! You've successfully explored and loaded code written by others to send a tweet (that's good, right?) without any header information or other details about the module.

Finding and executing code is just one challenge when working with frameworks. The next challenge is to augment the parameters or logic to fit your needs when working with private frameworks.

Objective-C method swizzling

Finally, on to swizzling. Took a while, but we're finally here.

There's several reasons you may want to method swizzle when reverse engineering a program or framework. One reason might be that you want to hook into a private method to figure where it's being called from and what parameters are being passed.

The next more likely reason to swizzle a method is to augment the logic of the method. For example, you can change around certain parameters being passed in, change around the return object for the method, or even disable the method entirely.

The very nice and convenient thing about Objective-C method swizzling is unlike hooking C or Swift functions, where you have to grab the address before the dynamic linker resolves the function, you can swizzle an Objective-C method anytime after the class is loaded and it'll apply to all calls to that method in any framework that calls it.

You'll augment the **setInitialText:** method for `SLComposeViewController` to change what is being said. You're going to go after an easy example, but always remember, you can do much, much more with swizzling methods.

Open **NSObject+P_SLComposeViewController.m**, and add the following import at the top of the file:

```
#import <objc/runtime.h>
```

This will let you access the APIs for the Objective-C funtime err... runtime.

Next, add the following class method:

```
+ (void)swizzleOriginalSelector:(SEL)originalSelector
withSizzledSelector:(SEL)swizzledSelector forClass:(Class)class
isClassMethod:(BOOL)isClassMethod {
  // 1
  Method originalMethod;
  Method swizzledMethod;

  // 2
  if (isClassMethod) {
```

```
    originalMethod = class_getClassMethod(class,
originalSelector);
    swizzledMethod = class_getClassMethod([self class],
swizzledSelector);
  } else {
    originalMethod = class_getInstanceMethod(class,
originalSelector);
    swizzledMethod = class_getInstanceMethod([self class],
swizzledSelector);
  }

  // 3
  NSAssert(originalMethod, @"originalMethod should not be nil");
  NSAssert(swizzledMethod, @"swizzledMethod should not be nil");

  // 4
  method_exchangeImplementations(originalMethod,
swizzledMethod);
}
```

That's a big code snippet. Let's break it down:

1. You're declaring variables of type `Method` for the original and swizzled methods that are passed in as selectors. These will eventually hold the function pointers for the two methods.

2. Next you obtain those function pointers. If it's a class method, `class_getClassMethod` is used; otherwise, it's an instance method, so `class_getInstanceMethod` is used.

3. Next, you're asserting neither item is `nil` since you want to resolve any incorrect assumptions before the program continues.

4. Finally, you exchange the implementations between the two methods.

Now you've created your method that handles all the swizzling, it's time to make the swizzled method. Add the following below the method you just added:

```
- (BOOL)p_sl_setInitialText:(id)text {
  return [self p_sl_setInitialText:[text uppercaseString]];
}
```

Here's the heart of the trick: since you're replacing a method, when you want to call the original method, you need to call the swizzled method since they have switched spots. In this case, you call the original method, replacing the parameter with the uppercased version of the string.

Finally, replace load with the following:

```
+ (void)load {
  static dispatch_once_t onceToken;
  dispatch_once(&onceToken, ^{
    dlopen("Social.framework/Social", RTLD_NOW);

    Class cls = NSClassFromString(@"SLComposeViewController");
    [self swizzleOriginalSelector:@selector(setInitialText:)
          withSizzledSelector:@selector(p_sl_setInitialText:)
                  forClass:cls
              isClassMethod:NO];
  });
}
```

Build and run the application; Tap on the share button and notice the change to ALL CAPS (aka Kayne West casing).

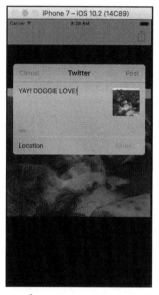

How cool is that? Now you changed your post message to show you are super duper excited about those two doggies... because they're awesome.

Where to go from here?

In this chapter, you explored a framework you pretended was private. You were able to dynamically load the framework and you were able to instantiate a view controller, setting some properties of interest. There's much more to explore in this framework, both public and private, so keep on looking if you enjoyed this chapter.

This is why reverse engineering Objective-C is so much fun, because you can hook into methods that are quietly called in private code you don't have the source for and make changes or monitor what it's doing.

Again, if I haven't made it clear enough, check out the frameworks found in `/System/Library` on your actual iOS device and see what you can dynamically load, explore and swizzle. There quite literally could be a whole book written on the explorations you can do within the subdirectories of `/System/Library/`.

Section IV: Custom LLDB Commands

You've learned the basic LLDB commands, the assembly that goes into code and the miscellaneous low-level concepts that make a program...well, a program.

Now it's time to put all that knowledge together to create some very powerful and complex debugging scripts. As you will soon see, you're only limited by your skill and imagination... and finding the correct class (or header file) to do your debugging bidding.

LLDB ships with an integrated Python module that allows you to access most parts of the debugger through Python. This lets you leverage all the power of Python (and its modules) to help uncover whatever dark secrets vex you.

Come with an open mind and experience the depths of the lldb Python module!

Chapter 17: Hello Script Bridging

Chapter 18: Debugging Script Bridging

Chapter 19: Script Bridging Classes and Hierarchy

Chapter 17: Hello Script Bridging

LLDB has several ways you can make your own customized commands. The first way is through the easy-to-use `command alias` you saw in Chapter 8, "Persisting and Customizing". This command simply creates an alias for a static command. While easy to implement, it really only allowed you to execute commands with no input.

After that came the `command regex`, which let you specify a regular expression to capture input then apply it to a command. You learned about this command in Chapter 9, "Regex Commands". This command works well when you want to feed input to an LLDB command, but it was inconvenient to execute multiline commands and you could only provide one input argument using this method.

Next up in the tradeoff between convenience and complexity is LLDB's **script bridging**. With script bridging, you can do nearly anything you like. Script bridging is a **Python** interface LLDB uses to help extend the debugger to accomplish your wildest debugging dreams.

However, there's a cost to the script bridging interface. It has a steep learning curve, and the documentation, to put it professionally, sucks. Fortunately, you've got this book in your hands to help guide you through learning script bridging. Once you've a grasp on LLDB's Python module, you can do some very cool (and very scary!) things.

Python 101

As mentioned, LLDB's script bridge is a Python interface to the debugger. This means you can load and execute Python scripts in LLDB. In those Python scripts, you include the lldb module to interface with the debugger to obtain information such as the arguments to a custom command.

Don't know Python? Don't fret. Python is one of the most friendly languages to learn. And just like the Swift Playgrounds everyone's losing their mind over, Python has an attractive REPL for learning.

> **Note**: At the time of writing, there are signs LLDB is slowly migrating over from Python version 2 to Python 3. Just like Swift, there are breaking changes in these different versions. In order to make sure you're learning the correct version of Python, you need to know which version of Python LLDB is using. At the time of writing, LLDB uses Python 2.7.10.

Let's figure out which version of Python LLDB is using. Open a Terminal window and type the following:

```
lldb
```

As expected, LLDB will start. From there, execute the following commands to find out which Python version is linked to LLDB:

```
(lldb) script import sys
(lldb) script print (sys.version)
```

The **script** command brings up the Python interpreter for LLDB. If you just typed in script without arguments, you'd be greeted with LLDB's Python REPL.

If LLDB's Python version is different than 2.7.x, freak out and complain loudly on the book's forum.

> **Note**: If the version is 2.7.x this is still valid. As long as the version you're running is not Python 3.X.Y by default your system will work as described. Your system-installed Python version does not have to match 2.7.10 exactly; bug fix releases work fine also.

Now that you know the Python version LLDB works with, ensure you have the correct version of Python symlinked to the `python` Terminal command. Open a new Terminal window and type the following:

```
python --version
```

If the Python version matches the one that LLDB has, then launch Python with no arguments in the Terminal:

```
python
```

If you have a different version of Python symlinked (i.e. 3.X.Y), you need to launch Python with the correct version number. For example, in Terminal, type `python` and press Tab. Different version(s) of Python might pop up with the correct version number. Enter the correct version number associated with the LLDB version of Python:

```
python2.7
```

Either way, ensure the LLDB version of Python matches the one you have in your Terminal:

```
>>> import sys
>>> print (sys.version)
```

Notice in the actual Python REPL there's no need to prefix any of the commands with the LLDB script command.

Playing around in Python

If you are unfamiliar with Python, this section will help you quickly get familiar with the language. If you're already knowledgeable about Python, feel free to jump to the next section.

In your Terminal session, open a Python REPL by typing the following:

```
python
```

Next, in the Python REPL, type the following:

```
>>> h = "hello world"
>>> h
```

You'll see the following output:

```
'hello world'
```

Python lets you assign variables without needing to declare the type beforehand. Unlike Swift, Python doesn't really have the notion of constants, so there's no need for a `var` or `let` declaration for a variable.

> **Note:** If you have a different version of Python, then some of the commands might have different syntax. You'll need to consult Google to figure out the correct equivalent command.

Going a step further, play around with the variable `h` and do some basic string manipulation:

```
>>> h.split(" ")
['hello', 'world']
```

This will give a Python **list**, which is somewhat like an array that can store different types of objects.

If you need your Swift fix equivalent, then imagine a list is something similar to the following Swift code:

```
var h: [Any] = []
```

You can verify this by looking up the Python's class type. In Terminal, press the up arrow to bring up the previous command and append the `.__class__` call to the end like so:

```
>>> h.split(" ").__class__
<type 'list'>
```

Note there are two underscores preceding and following the word class.

What type of class is the `h` variable?

```
>>> h.__class__
<type 'str'>
```

That's good to know; a string is called `str`. You can get help on the `str` object by typing the following:

```
>>> help (str)
```

This will dump all the info pertaining to `str`, which is too much to digest at the moment.

Exit out of this documentation by typing the q character and narrow your search by looking only for the `split` function used previously:

```
>>> help (str.split)
```

You'll get some documentation output similar to the following:

```
Help on method_descriptor:

split(...)
    S.split([sep [,maxsplit]]) -> list of strings

    Return a list of the words in the string S, using sep as the
    delimiter string.  If maxsplit is given, at most maxsplit
    splits are done. If sep is not specified or is None, any
    whitespace string is a separator and empty strings are
    removed from the result.
```

Reading the above documentation, you can see the first optional argument expects a string, and an optional second argument to indicate the maximum upper limit to split the string.

What do you think will happen when you try to execute the following command? Try your best to figure it out before executing it.

```
>>> h.split(" ", 0)
```

Now to turn your attention towards functions. Python uses indentation to define scope, instead of the braces that many other languages use, including Swift and Objective-C. This is a nice feature of Python, since it forces developers to not be lazy slobs with their code indentation.

Declare a function in the REPL:

```
>>> def test(a):
...
```

You'll get an ellipsis as output, which indicates you have started creating a function. Type two spaces and then enter the code. If you don't have a consistent indentation, the python function will produce an error.

```
...     print(a + " world!")
```

Press Enter again to exit out of the function. Now, test out your newly created `test` function:

```
>>> test("hello")
```

You'll get the expected `hello world!` printed out.

Now that you can "truthfully" put three years of Python experience on your resume, it's time to create an LLDB Python script.

Creating your first LLDB Python script

From here on out, you'll be creating all your LLDB Python scripts in the `~/lldb` directory. If you want to have them in a different directory, everytime I say `~/lldb`, you need to invoke your "mental symlink" to whatever directory you've decided to use.

In Terminal, create the ~/lldb directory:

```
mkdir ~/lldb
```

In your favorite ASCII text editor, create a new file named **helloworld.py** in your newly created `~/lldb` directory. For this particular example, I'll use the my-editor-is-better-neutral-argument, `nano`.

```
nano ~/lldb/helloworld.py
```

Add the following code to the file:

```
def your_first_command(debugger, command, result,
internal_dict):
  print ("hello world!")
```

Make sure you indent the `print ("hello world")` line (ideally with two spaces) or else it won't be included as part of the function!

For now, ignore the parameters passed into the function. Remember when you learned about your `hello_world.c` or `hello_world.java`, and the instructor (or the internet) said to just ignore the params in main for now? Yeah, same thing here. These params are the defined way that LLDB interacts with your Python code. You'll explore them in upcoming chapters.

Save the file. If you're using `nano`, `Ctrl + O` will write to disk.

Create a new tab in Terminal and launch a new LLDB session:

```
lldb
```

This will launch a blank, unattached LLDB session.

In this new LLDB session, import the script you created:

```
(lldb) command script import ~/lldb/helloworld.py
```

If the script is imported successfully, there will be no output.

But how do you execute the command? The only thing the above command did was bring the helloworld (yes, named after the file) module's path in as a candidate to use for Python.

If you plan to use this function in Python, you'll need to import the module if you want to use any of the functions. Type the following into LLDB:

```
(lldb) script import helloworld
```

You can verify you have successfully imported the module by dumping all the methods in the helloworld python module:

```
(lldb) script dir(helloworld)
```

The dir function will dump the contents of the module. If you successfully imported the module, you'll see the following output:

```
['__builtins__', '__doc__', '__file__', '__name__',
'__package__', 'your_first_command']
```

Take note of the function you created earlier: your_first_command is listed in the output.

Although the above two commands weren't necessary to set up the command, it does show you how this script bridging works. You imported the helloworld module into the Python context of LLDB, but when you execute normal commands, you aren't executing in a Python context (although the command logic underneath could be using Python).

So how do you make your command available only through LLDB, and not through the Python context of LLDB?

Head back to LLDB and type the following:

```
(lldb) command script add -f helloworld.your_first_command yay
```

This adds a command to LLDB, which is implemented in the helloworld Python module with the function your_first_command. This scripted function is assigned to the LLDB command **yay**.

Execute the yay command now:

```
(lldb) yay
```

Provided everything worked, you'll get the expected hello world! output.

Setting up commands efficiently

Once the high of creating a custom function in script bridging has worn off, you'll come to realize you don't want to type this stuff each time you start LLDB. You want those commands to be there ready for you as soon as LLDB starts.

Fortunately, LLDB has a lovely function named **__lldb_init_module**, which is a hook function called as soon as your module loads into LLDB.

This means you can stick your logic for creating the LLDB command in this function, eliminating the need to manually set up your LLDB function once LLDB starts!

Open the helloworld.py class you created and add the following function below your_first_command's definition:

```
def __lldb_init_module(debugger, internal_dict):
    debugger.HandleCommand('command script add -f
helloworld.your_first_command yay')
```

Here you're using a parameter passed into the function named debugger. With this object, an instance of SBDebugger, you're using a method available to it called HandleCommand. Calling debugger.HandleCommand is pretty much equivalent to typing something into LLDB.

For example, if you typed: po "hello world", the equivalent command would be debugger.HandleCommand('po "hello world"')

Remember the python help command you used earlier? You can get help documentation from this command by typing:

```
(lldb) script help(lldb.SBDebugger.HandleCommand)
```

At the time of writing, you'll get a rather disappointing amount of help documentation:

```
HandleCommand(self, *args) unbound lldb.SBDebugger method
    HandleCommand(self, str command)
```

That's why there's such a steep learning curve to this stuff, and the reason not many people venture into learning about script bridging. That's why you picked up this book, right?

Save your **helloworld.py** file and open up your ~/.lldbinit file in your favorite editor.

You're now going to specify you want the helloworld module to load at startup every time LLDB loads up.

At the end of the file, add the following line:

```
command script import ~/lldb/helloworld.py
```

Save and close the file.

Open Terminal and start up another tab with LLDB in it like so:

```
lldb
```

Since you specified to have the helloworld module imported into LLDB upon startup, and you also specified to create the yay function as soon as the helloworld python module loads through the __lldb_init_module module, the yay LLDB command will be available immediately to you.

Try it out now:

```
(lldb) yay
```

If everything went well you'll see the following output:

```
hello world!
```

Awesome! You now have a foundation for building some very complex scripts into LLDB. In the following chapters, you'll explore more of how to use this incredibly powerful tool.

For now, close all those Terminal tabs and give yourself a pat on the back.

Where to go from here?

If you don't feel comfortable with Python, now is the time to start brushing up on it. If you have past development experience, you'll find Python to be a fun and friendly language to learn. It's a great language for quickly building other tools to help with everyday programming tasks.

Chapter 18: Debugging Script Bridging

You've learned the basics of LLDB's Python script bridging. Now you're about to embark on the frustrating yet exhilarating world of making full LLDB Python scripts.

As you learn about the classes and methods in the Python lldb module, you're bound to make false assumptions or simply type incorrect code. *In short, you're going to screw up.* Depending on the error, sometimes these scripts fail silently, or they may blow up with an angry `stderr`.

You need a methodical way to figure out what went wrong in your LLDB script so you don't pull your hair out. In this chapter, you'll explore how to inspect your LLDB Python scripts using the Python `pdb` module, which is used for debugging Python scripts.

Although it might not seem like it at first, this is the **most important** chapter in the LLDB Python section, since it'll teach you how to explore and debug methods when you're learning this new Python module. I would have (figuratively) killed for a chapter like this when I was first learning script bridging.

Debugging your debugging scripts with pdb

Included in the Python distribution on your system is a Python module named pdb. This is a module used to set breakpoints in a Python script, just like you do with LLDB itself! In addition, pdb has other debugging essential features that let you step into, out of, and over code to inspect potential areas of interest.

You're going to continue using the helloworld.py script in ~/lldb from the previous chapter. If you haven't read that chapter yet, copy the helloworld.py from the **starter** directory into a directory named **lldb** inside your home directory.

Either way, you should now have a file at ~/lldb/helloworld.py.

Now open up helloworld.py and navigate to the your_first_command function, replacing it with the following:

```python
def your_first_command(debugger, command, result,
internal_dict):
    import pdb; pdb.set_trace()
    print ("hello world")
```

> **Note:** It's worth pointing out that pdb will not work when debugging Python scripts in Xcode. The Xcode console window will hang once pdb is tracing a script so you'll need to do all Python script debugging in a Terminal window.

Save your changes and open a Terminal window to create a new LLDB session. In Terminal, type:

```
lldb
```

Next, execute the yay command (which is defined in helloworld.py, remember?) like so:

```
(lldb) yay woot
```

Execution will stop and you'll get output similar to the following:

```
> /Users/derekselander/lldb/helloworld.py(3)your_first_command()
-> print ("hello world")
(Pdb)
```

The LLDB script gave way to pdb. The Python debugger has stopped execution on the print line of code within helloworld.py inside the function your_first_command.

When creating an LLDB command using Python, there's specific parameters expected in the defining Python function. You'll now explore these parameters, namely the **debugger**, **command**, and **result** parameters.

Explore the command argument first, by typing the following into your pdb session:

```
(Pdb) command
```

This will dump out the commands you supplied to the yay command. This will always come in the form of a str, even if you've multiple arguments or integers as input. Since there's no logic to handle any commands, the yay command will silently ignore all input. If you typed in yay woot as indicated earlier, only woot would be spat out as the command.

Next up on the parameter exploration list is the result parameter. Type the following into pdb:

```
(Pdb) result
```

This will dump out something similar to the following:

```
<lldb.SBCommandReturnObject; proxy of <Swig Object of type
'lldb::SBCommandReturnObject *' at 0x110323060> >
```

This is an instance of SBCommandReturnObject, which is a class the lldb module uses to let you indicate if the execution of an LLDB command was successful. In addition, you can append messages that will be displayed when your command finishes.

Type the following into pdb:

```
(Pdb) result.AppendMessage("2nd hello world!")
```

This appends a message which will be shown by LLDB when this command finishes. In this case, once your command finishes executing, 2nd hello world! will be displayed. However, your script is still frozen in time thanks to pdb.

Once your LLDB scripts get more complicated, the SBCommandReturnObject will come into play, but for simple LLDB scripts, it's not really needed. You'll explore the SBCommandReturnObject command more later in this chapter.

Finally, onto the debugger parameter. Type the following into pdb:

```
(Pdb) debugger
```

This will dump out another object of class SBDebugger, similar to the following:

```
<lldb.SBDebugger; proxy of <Swig Object of type
'lldb::SBDebugger *' at 0x110067180> >
```

You explored this class briefly in the previous chapter to help create the LLDB yay command. You've already learned one of the most useful commands in SBDebugger: HandleCommand.

Resume execution in pdb. Like LLDB, it has logic to handle a c or continue to resume execution.

Type the following into pdb:

```
(Pdb) c
```

You'll get the following output:

```
hello world!
2nd hello world!
```

pdb is great when you need to pause execution in a certain spot to figure out what's going wrong. For example, you could have some complicated setup code, and pause in an area where the logic doesn't seem to be correct.

This is a much more attractive solution than constantly typing script in LLDB to execute one line of Python code at a time.

pdb's post mortem debugging

Now that you've a basic understanding of the process of debugging your scripts, it's time to throw you into the deep end with an actual LLDB script and see if you can fix it using pdb's post mortem debugging features.

Depending on the type of error, pdb has an attractive option that lets you explore the problematic stack trace in the event the code you're running threw an exception. This type of debugging methodology will only work if Python threw an exception; this method will *not* work if you receive unexpected output but your code executed without errors.

However, if your code has error handling (and as your scripts get more complex, they really should; more on that in a later chapter), you can easily hunt down potential errors while building your scripts.

Find the **starter** folder of the resources for this chapter. Next, copy the `findclass.py` file over to your default `~/lldb` directory. Remember, if you're stubborn and decided to go with a different directory location, you'll need to adjust accordingly.

Don't even look at what this code does yet. It's not going to finish executing as-is, and you'll use `pdb` to inspect it after you view the error.

Once the script has been copied to the correct directory, open a Terminal window and launch and attach LLDB to any program which contains Objective-C. You could choose a macOS application or something on the iOS Simulator, or maybe even a watchOS application.

For this example, I'll attach to the macOS `Photos` application, but you're strongly encouraged to attach to a different application. Hey, that's part of being an explorer!

Make sure the application is alive and running and attach LLDB to it:

```
lldb -n Photos
```

Once the process has attached, import the new script into LLDB:

```
(lldb) command script import ~/lldb/findclass.py
```

Provided you placed the script in the correct directory, you should get no output. The script will install quietly.

Figure out what this command does by looking at the documentation, since you haven't even looked at the source code for it yet. Type the following into LLDB:

```
(lldb) help findclass
```

You'll get output similar to the following:

```
Syntax: findclass

The findclass command will dump all the Objective-C runtime
classes it knows about. Alternatively, if you supply an argument
for it, it will do a case sensitive search looking only for the
classes which contain the input.

Usage: findclass  # All Classes
Usage: findclass UIViewController # Only classes that contain
UIViewController in name
```

Cool! Lets try this command. Try dumping out all classes the Objective-C runtime knows about.

```
(lldb) findclass
```

You'll get a rather annoying error assertion similar to the following:

```
Traceback (most recent call last):
  File "/Users/derekselander/lldb/findclass.py", line 40, in
findclass
    raise AssertionError("Uhoh... something went wrong, can you
figure it out? :]")
AssertionError: Uhoh... something went wrong, can you figure it
out? :]
```

It's clear the author of this script is horrible at providing decent information into what happened in the AssertionError. Fortunately, it raised an error! You can use `pdb` to inspect the stack trace at the time the error was thrown.

In LLDB, type the following:

```
(lldb) script import pdb
(lldb) findclass
(lldb) script pdb.pm()
```

This imports `pdb` into LLDB's Python context, runs `findclass` again, then asks `pdb` to perform a "post mortem".

LLDB will change to the pdb interface and jump to the line that threw the error.

```
> /Users/derekselander/lldb/findclass.py(40)findclass()
-> raise AssertionError("Uhoh... something went wrong, can you
figure it out? :]")
(Pdb)
```

From here, you can use `pdb` as your new BFF to help explore what's happening.

Speaking of what's happening, you haven't even looked at the source code yet! Lets change that. Type the following into `pdb`:

```
(Pdb) l 1, 50
```

This will list lines 1, 50 of the `findclass.py` script.

You've the typical function signature which handles the majority of the logic in these commands:

```
def findclass(debugger, command, result, internal_dict):
```

Next up in interesting tidbits is a big long string named **codeString**, which starts its definition on line 18. It's a Python multi-line string, which starts with three quotes and finishes with three quotes on line 35. This string is where the meat of this command's logic lives.

In your **pdb** session, type the following:

```
(Pdb) codeString
```

You'll get some not-so-pretty output, since dumping a Python string includes all newlines.

```
'\n    @import Foundation;\n    int numClasses;\n    Class *
classes = NULL;\n    classes = NULL;\n    numClasses =
objc_getClassList(NULL, 0);\n    NSMutableString *returnString =
[NSMutableString string];\n    classes = (__unsafe_unretained
Class *)malloc(sizeof(Class) * numClasses);\n    numClasses =
objc_getClassList(classes, numClasses);\n\n    for (int i = 0; i
< numClasses; i++) {\n        Class c = classes[i];\n
[returnString appendFormat:@"%s,", class_getName(c)];\n        }\n
free(classes);\n    \n    returnString;\n    '
```

Let's try that again. Use **pdb** to print out a pretty version of the the codeString variable.

```
(Pdb) print codeString
```

Much better, right?!

```
@import Foundation;
int numClasses;
Class * classes = NULL;
classes = NULL;
numClasses = objc_getClassList(NULL, 0);
NSMutableString *returnString = [NSMutableString string];
classes = (__unsafe_unretained Class *)malloc(sizeof(Class) *
numClasses);
numClasses = objc_getClassList(classes, numClasses);

for (int i = 0; i < numClasses; i++) {
    Class c = classes[i];
    [returnString appendFormat:@"%s,", class_getName(c)];
}
free(classes);

returnString;
```

This **codeString** contains Objective-C code which uses the Objective-C runtime to get all the classes it knows about. The final line of this code, **returnString**, essentially lets you return the value of **returnString** back to the Python script. More on that shortly.

Scan for the next interesting part. On line 40, the debugger is currently at a **raise** call. This is also the line that provided the annoyingly vague message you received from LLDB.

```
37    res = lldb.SBCommandReturnObject()
38    debugger.GetCommandInterpreter().HandleCommand("po " ...
39    if res.GetError():
40 ->      raise AssertionError("Uhoh... something went wron...
41    elif not res.HasResult():
42        raise AssertionError("There's no result. Womp wom...
```

Note the -> on line 40. This indicates where pdb is currently paused.

But wait, res.GetError() looks interesting. Since everything is fair game to explore while pdb has the stack trace, why don't you explore this error to see if you can actually get some useful info out of this?

```
(Pdb) print res.GetError()
```

There you go! Depending whether you decided to break on a macOS, iOS, watchOS, or tvOS app, you might get a slightly different count of error messages, but the idea is the same.

```
error: warning: got name from symbols: classes
error: 'objc_getClassList' has unknown return type; cast the
call to its declared return type
error: 'objc_getClassList' has unknown return type; cast the
call to its declared return type
error: 'class_getName' has unknown return type; cast the call to
its declared return type
```

The problem here is the code within codeString is causing LLDB some confusion. This sort of error is very common in LLDB. You often need to tell LLDB the return type of a function, because it doesn't know what it is. In this case, both objc_getClassList and class_getName have unknown return types.

A quick consultation with Google tells us the two problematic methods in question have the following signatures:

```
int objc_getClassList(Class *buffer, int bufferCount);
const char * class_getName(Class cls);
```

All you need to do is cast the return type to the correct value in the codeString code.

Open up ~/lldb/findclass.py and replace the definition of codeString with the following:

```
codeString = """
@import Foundation;
int numClasses;
Class * classes = NULL;
classes = NULL;
```

```
numClasses = (int)objc_getClassList(NULL, 0);
NSMutableString *returnString = [NSMutableString string];
classes = (__unsafe_unretained Class *)malloc(sizeof(Class) *
numClasses);
numClasses = (int)objc_getClassList(classes, numClasses);

for (int i = 0; i < numClasses; i++) {
  Class c = classes[i];
    [returnString appendFormat:@"%s,", (char *)class_getName(c)];
}
free(classes);

returnString;
"""
```

Save your work and jump back to your LLDB Terminal window. You'll still be inside **pdb**, so type `Ctrl + D` to exit. Next, type the following:

```
(lldb) command script import ~/lldb/findclass.py
```

This will reload the script into LLDB with the new changes in the source code. This is required if you make any changes to the source code and you want to test out the command again.

Try your luck again and dump all of the Objective-C classes available in your process.

```
(lldb) findclass
```

Boom! You'll get a slew of output containing all the Objective-C classes in your program. From your app, from `Foundation`, from `CoreFoundation`, and so on. Heh... there's more than you thought there would be, right?

Try limiting your query to something slightly more manageable. Search for all classes containing the word `ViewController`:

```
(lldb) findclass ViewController
```

Depending on the process you've attached to, you'll get a different amount of classes containing the name ViewController.

When developing commands using the Python script bridging, **pdb** is a superb tool to keep in your toolbox to help you understand what is happening. It works great for inspecting complicated sections and breaking on problematic areas.

Where to go from here?

There's a lot more you can do with **pdb** than what I described here. Jump over to https://docs.python.org/2.7/library/pdb.html and check out the other cool features of **pdb**. Be sure to remember the version of **pdb** must match the version of Python that LLDB is using.

While you're at it, now's the time to start exploring some other Python modules and see what other cool features they have. Not only do you have the lldb Python module, but the full power of Python itself is an amazing tool to have when creating advanced debugging scripts.

Chapter 19: Script Bridging Classes and Hierarchy

You've learned the essentials of working with LLDB's Python module, as well as how to correct any errors using Python's PDB debugging module. Now you'll explore the main players within the lldb Python module for a good overview of the main parts.

You'll be building a complex LLDB Python script as you learn about these classes. You'll create a regex breakpoint that only stops after the scope in which the breakpoint hit has finished executing. This is useful when exploring initialization and accessor type methods and you want to examine the object that is being returned.

In this chapter, you'll add some arguments to this script and deal with some annoying edge cases, such handling commands differently between Objective-C and Swift.

The essential classes

Within the lldb module, there are several major classes of importance:

- **lldb.SBDebugger**: The "bottleneck" class you'll use to access instances of other classes inside your custom debugging script.

  There will always be one reference to an instance of this class passed in as a function parameter to your script. This class is responsible for handling input commands into LLDB, and can control where and how it displays the output.

- **lldb.SBTarget**: Responsible for the executable being debugged in memory, the debug files, and the physical file for the executable resident on disk.

  In a typical debugging session, you'll use the instance of SBDebugger to get the selected SBTarget. From there, you'll be able to access the majority of other classes through SBTarget.

- **lldb.SBProcess**: SBTarget has a to-many relationship to SBProcess: SBTarget manages 1 or multiple SBProcess instances. SBProcess handles memory access (reading/writing) as well as the multiple threads within the process.

- **lldb.SBThread**: SBThread manages the stack frames (SBFrames) within that particular thread, and also manages control logic for stepping.

- **lldb.SBFrame**: SBFrame manages local variables (given through debugging information) as well as any registers frozen at that particular frame.

- **lldb.SBModule**: Represents a particular executable. You've learned about modules when exploring dynamic libraries; a module can include the main executable or any dynamically loaded code.

  You can obtain a complete list of the modules loaded into your executable using the `image list` command.

- **lldb.SBFunction**: This represents a generic function — the code — that is loaded into memory. This class has a one-to-one relationship with the SBFrame class.

Got it? No? Don't worry about it! Once you see how these classes interact with each other, you'll have a better understanding of their place inside your program.

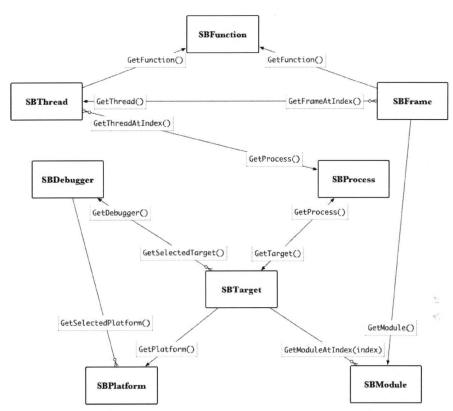

This diagram is a simplified version of how the major LLDB Python classes interact with each other. If there's no direct path from one class to another, you can still get to a class by accessing other variables, not shown in the diagram, that point to an instance (or all instances) of a class (many of which are not shown in the diagram).

That being said, the entry-point into the majority of these objects will be through an instance of SBDebugger, passed in as debugger in your scripts. From there, you'll likely go after the SBTarget through GetSelectedTarget() to access all the other instances.

Exploring the lldb module through... LLDB

Since you'll be incrementally building a reasonably complex script over the next two chapters, I would strongly recommend creating an LLDB command alias for reloading the ~/.lldbinit script while running LLDB.

Append the following to your ~/.lldbinit file:

```
command alias reload_script command source ~/.lldbinit
```

This adds a command called reload_script which reloads the ~/.lldbinit file. Now whenever you save your work, you can simply reload the updated contents without having to restart LLDB.

In addition, this is a useful command to ensure everything inside your ~/.lldbinit file is still valid. Typically, errors in your ~/.lldbinit will go unnoticed since you're never notified of them. However, reloading while LLDB is alive and active will dump any syntax errors in your scripts right to the LLDB console.

While you're building out this new script, you'll create a one-time-use burner project to explore these LLDB Python APIs. To mix things up, you'll create a **tvOS** project this time.

Open Xcode. Select **File\New\Project...** . Choose **tvOS\Single View Application**. Call this new project **Meh** (because I am out of creative names to use! :]). Make sure the language is set to **Swift**. Then save the project wherever you want.

Once the project has been created, open **ViewController.swift** and add a GUI breakpoint to the beginning of viewDidLoad().

Build, run and wait for the breakpoint to be triggered. Jump over to the LLDB console.

Next, type the following into LLDB:

```
(lldb) script lldb.debugger
```

You'll get output similar to the following:

```
<lldb.SBDebugger; proxy of <Swig Object of type
'lldb::SBDebugger *' at 0x113f2f990> >
```

LLDB has a few easily accessible global variables that map to some of the classes described above:

- lldb.SBDebugger -> lldb.debugger

- `lldb.SBTarget -> lldb.target`

- `lldb.SBProcess -> lldb.process`

- `lldb.SBThread -> lldb.thread`

- `lldb.SBFrame -> lldb.frame`

You've just explored the global variable `lldb.debugger`. Now it's time to explore the other variables.

Type the following into LLDB:

```
(lldb) script lldb.target
```

You'll get output similar to the following:

```
<lldb.SBTarget; proxy of <Swig Object of type 'lldb::SBTarget *'
at 0x1142daae0> >
```

This probably doesn't mean much to you at the moment because it's only displaying the instance of the class, and not the context of what it does, nor what it represents.

This is why the `print` command might be more useful when you're starting to explore these classes.

```
(lldb) script print lldb.target
```

This will give you some intelligible output to provide some context:

```
Meh
```

Using the `print` command is a useful trick when you want to get a summary of an instance, just like how calling `po` on an object gives you an `NSObject`'s `description` method in Objective-C. If you didn't use the `print` command, you'd have to hone in on properties and attributes of `SBTarget` to figure out the name of the target.

> **Note:** It's fine that you're playing with global Python variables in one-line scripts. However, it's important you don't use these global variables in your actual Python scripts since you can modify the state (i.e step out of a function), and these global variables will not update until your script has finished.
>
> The correct way to reference these instances is to start from `SBDebugger`, which is passed into your script function, and drill down to the appropriate variable from there.

Go through the remainder of the major global variables and print them out. Start with the following:

```
(lldb) script print lldb.process
SBProcess: pid = 47294, state = stopped, threads = 7, executable
= Meh
```

This will print out the process being run. As always, your data might differ (pid, state, thread etc...).

Next, type the following into LLDB:

```
(lldb) script print lldb.thread
thread #1: tid = 0x13a921, 0x000000010fc69ab0
Meh`ViewController.viewDidLoad(self=0x00007fa8c5b015f0) -> () at
ViewController.swift:13, queue = 'com.apple.main-thread', stop
reason = breakpoint 1.1
```

This will get the thread that triggered the breakpoint.

Next, try the frame variable:

```
(lldb) script print lldb.frame
frame #0: 0x000000010fc69ab0
Meh`ViewController.viewDidLoad(self=0x00007fa8c5b015f0) -> () at
ViewController.swift:13
```

This will get you the specific frame where the debugger is paused. You could, of course, access other frames in other threads. These global variables are merely convenience getters for you. I would strongly recommend using these global LLDB variables when you're playing with and learning about these classes.

Check out http://lldb.llvm.org/python_reference/index.html to learn about which methods these classes implement.

Alternatively, you can use Python's help function to get the docstrings for a particular class. For example, if you were in the Xcode debugging console, and you wanted info on the active SBTarget, you could do this:

```
(lldb) script help(lldb.target)
```

Don't be afraid to ask for help from the help function. I use it all the time when I'm figuring out my plan of attack through the lldb module. :]

Creating the BreakAfterRegex command

It's time to create the command you were promised you'd build at the beginning of this chapter!

How would you design a command to stop immediately after a function, print out the return value, then continue? Take a bit of happy thinking time for yourself, and try to figure out how you'd go about creating this script.

I'm serious — stop reading until you've given this an honest attempt. I'll wait.

...

Good. What did you come up with?

When writing these types of scripts, it's always good practice to envision what you want to achieve, and work your way back from there.

You'll name your command script **BreakAfterRegex.py**. The steps the command needs to take are as follows:

- First, use LLDB to create a regex breakpoint.

- Next, add a breakpoint action to **step-out** of execution (remember that from Chapter 6, "Thread, Frame & Stepping Around"?) until the program counter has finished executing the current frame.

- Finally, you'll use your knowledge of registers from Section 2 to print out the correct register that holds the return value.

Since you're now a debugging expert, you'll add some logic to handle parsing and custom parameters also.

Using your favorite text editor, create **BreakAfterRegex.py** in your **~/lldb** directory.

Once the file is created, open it and add the following:

```python
import lldb

def __lldb_init_module(debugger, internal_dict):
  debugger.HandleCommand('command script add -f
BreakAfterRegex.breakAfterRegex bar')

def breakAfterRegex(debugger, command, result, internal_dict):
  print ("yay. basic script setup with input:
{}".format(command))
```

You should know what this is doing by now — but in case you forgot, `__lldb_init_module` is a callback function called by LLDB after your script has finished loading into LLDB Python address space.

From there, it references an `SBDebugger` instance passed in as `debugger` to execute the following line of code:

```
command script add -f BreakAfterRegex.breakAfterRegex bar
```

This will add a command named `bar` which is implemented by `breakAfterRegex` within the module `BreakAfterRegex` (named after the file, naturally). If you gave a silly command like `wootwoot` instead of `bar`, your LLDB command would be named that instead.

Open your `~/.lldbinit` file and append the following line:

```
command script import ~/lldb/BreakAfterRegex.py
```

Save the file. Open Xcode, which should still be paused on `viewDidLoad()`. In the LLDB console, reload the script using your newly created convenience command:

```
(lldb) reload_script
```

You'll get a variable amount of output, as LLDB will display all the scripts it's loading. This will reload the contents in your `lldbinit` file and make the `bar` command functional.

Let's try out the `bar` command. In LLDB, type the following:

```
(lldb) bar UIViewController test -a -b
```

The output in your new LLDB script will echo back the parameters you've supplied to it.

Look back at what you typed into ~/lldb/BreakAfterRegex.py to see why it does that.

You've got the basic skeleton up and working. It's time to write the code to create a breakpoint based upon your input. You'll start with creating input designed solely for handling the regular expression, and then at the end of the chapter you'll provide logic to handle the parsing and logic of options.

Back in def breakAfterRegex(debugger, command, result, internal_dict):, remove the print statement and replace it with the following logic:

```
def breakAfterRegex(debugger, command, result, internal_dict):
  # 1
  target = debugger.GetSelectedTarget()
  breakpoint = target.BreakpointCreateByRegex(command)

  # 2
  if not breakpoint.IsValid() or breakpoint.num_locations == 0:
    result.AppendWarning("Breakpoint isn't valid or hasn't found
any hits")
  else:
    result.AppendMessage("{}".format(breakpoint))

  # 3

breakpoint.SetScriptCallbackFunction("BreakAfterRegex.breakpoint
Handler")
```

Here's what you're doing:

1. Create a breakpoint using the regex input from the supplied parameter. The breakpoint object will be of type SBBreakpoint.

2. If breakpoint creation is unsuccessful, the script will warn you it couldn't find anything to break on. If successful, the breakpoint object is printed out.

3. Finally, the breakpoint is set up so the function breakpointHandler is called whenever the breakpoint hits.

What's that I hear you say? What's an SBBreakpoint? Well, you can look it up through LLDB! :]

```
(lldb) script help(lldb.SBBreakpoint)
```

OK — back on the main road after that little sightseeing trip. Where were we? Oh right — you haven't created the handler function that will be called when the breakpoint is hit. You'll do that now.

Right below **breakAfterRegex**, add the following function:

```
def breakpointHandler(frame, bp_loc, dict):
  function_name = frame.GetFunctionName()
  print("stopped in: {}".format(function_name))
  return True
```

This function is called whenever any of the breakpoints you created using your new command are hit, and will then print out the function name. Notice the return of True at the end of the function. Returning True will result in your program stopping execution. Returning False, or even omitting a return statement, which in Python means return None, will result in the program continuing to run after this method executes.

This is a subtle but important point, so pay attention. When creating callback functions for breakpoints, you have a different method signature to implement. This consists of a SBFrame, SBBreakpointLocation, and a Python dictionary. The SBFrame, as already mentioned, represents the frame you've stopped in. The SBBreakpointLocation is an instance of one of your breakpoints found in SBBreakpoint.

This makes sense because you could have many hits for a single breakpoint, especially if you try to break on a frequently implemented function, such as main, or if you use a well-matched regular expression.

Here's another diagram that showcases the simplified interaction of classes when you've stopped on a particular function:

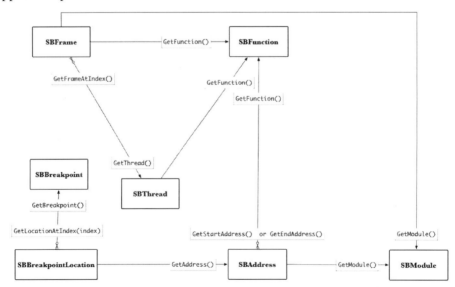

As you (might have?) noticed, SBFrame, and SBBreakpointLocation are your lifelines to the majority of important lldb classes. Using the previous diagram, you can get to all the major class instances through SBFrame or through SBFrame's reference to SBModule.

Remember, you should never use lldb.frame or other global variables inside your scripts since they could hold a stale state while being executed in a script, so you must traverse the variables starting with the frame, or bc_loc to get to the instance of the class you want.

If you accidentally make a typo, or don't understand some code, simply insert a breakpoint in the script using the Python pdb module and work your way back from there. You learned about PDB in Chapter 31, "Debugging Script Bridging".

This script is starting to get complicated — looks like a good time to reload and test it out. Open the Xcode console window and reload your script:

```
(lldb) reload_script
```

Go through the motions of executing some commands again to test it out:

```
(lldb) bar
somereallylongmethodthatapplehopefullydidntwritesomewhere
```

You'll get output similar to the following:

```
warning: Breakpoint isn't valid or hasn't found any hits
```

Ok, good. Time to try out an actual breakpoint. Let's go after a rather frequently executed method.

In the LLDB console type the following:

```
(lldb) bar NSObject.init\]
```

You'll see something similar to the following:

```
SBBreakpoint: id = 3, regex = 'NSObject.init\]', locations = 2
```

Continue execution and use the Simulator remote to click around the tvOS Simulator to trigger the breakpoint. If you're having trouble tripping the breakpoint, one surefire way is to navigate to the simulator's home screen. From the simulator, **Hardware\Home** (or more easily, ⌘ + **Shift** + **H**).

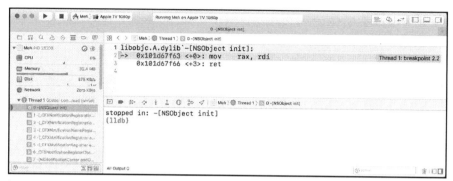

Cool. You've successfully added a Python action for a regex breapoint you created through your Python script. That's pretty darn neat-o.

Right now, you've stopped on one of NSObject's init methods, which could be a class or an instance method. This is very likely a subclass of NSObject. You'll manually replicate the actions you're about to implement in the Python script using LLDB.

Using the LLDB console, finish executing this method:

```
(lldb) finish
```

Remember your register calling conventions? Since you're working on the tvOS Simulator and this architecture is x64, you'll want to use the **RAX** register. Print out the return value of NSObject's init in LLDB.

```
(lldb) po $rax
```

Depending on where and how you were playing with the Simulator, you'll see a different object. I received the following output:

```
<_CFXNotificationNameWildcardObjectRegistration: 0x61000006e8c0>
```

If curiosity gets the better of you, feel free to explore the properties and methods within the class you just stumbled across using the strategies discussed in Chapter 23, "Exploring and Method Swizzling Objective-C Frameworks".

Stepping out and printing is the exact logic you'll implement now in your custom script callback function.

Open **BreakAfterRegex.py** and revisit the **breakpointHandler** function. Modify it to look like the following:

```
def breakpointHandler(frame, bp_loc, dict):
  # 1
    '''The function called when the regular
```

```
    expression breakpoint gets triggered
    '''

    # 2
    thread = frame.GetThread()
    process = thread.GetProcess()
    debugger = process.GetTarget().GetDebugger()

    # 3
    function_name = frame.GetFunctionName()

    # 4
    debugger.SetAsync(False)

    # 5
    thread.StepOut()

    # 6
    output = evaluateReturnedObject(debugger,
                                    thread,
                                    function_name)
    if output is not None:
      print(output)

    return False
```

B-B-B-B-B-Breakdown time!

1. Yep, if you're building a full-on Python command script, you've got to add some docstrings. You'll thank yourself later. Trust me.

2. You're climbing the hierarchical reference chain to grab the instance of SBDebugger and SBThread. Your starting point is through SBFrame.

3. This grabs the name of the parent function. Since you're about to step out of this current SBFrame, it's about to get invalidated, so grab any stack references you can before the stepping-out occurs.

4. SetAsync is an interesting function to use when tampering with control flow while scripting in a program. The debugger will run asynchronously while executing, so you need to tell it to synchronously wait until stepOut completes its execution before handing control back to the Python script.

   A good programmer will clean up the state to the async's previous value, but that becomes a little complicated, as you could run into threading issues when this callback function triggers if multiple breakpoints were to hit this callback function. This is not a noticeable setting change when you're debugging, so it's fine to leave it off.

5. You then step out of the method. After this line executes, you'll no longer be in the frame you previously stopped in.

6. You're calling a soon-to-be implemented method **evaluateReturnedObject** that takes the appropriate information and generates an output message. This message will contain the frame you stopped in, the return object, and the frame the breakpoint stepped out to.

You're all done with that Python function! Now you need to implement evaluateReturnedObject. Add it below the previous function:

```python
def evaluateReturnedObject(debugger, thread, function_name):
    '''Grabs the reference from the return register
    and returns a string from the evaluated value.
    TODO ObjC only
    '''

    # 1
    res = lldb.SBCommandReturnObject()
    interpreter = debugger.GetCommandInterpreter()
    target = debugger.GetSelectedTarget()
    frame = thread.GetSelectedFrame()
    parent_function_name = frame.GetFunctionName()

    # 2
    expression = 'expression -lobjc -O -- {}'.format(
        getRegisterString(target))

    # 3
    interpreter.HandleCommand(expression, res)

    # 4
    if res.HasResult():
        # 5
        output = '{}\nbreakpoint: '\
        '{}\nobject: {}\nstopped: {}'.format(
            '*' * 80,
            function_name,
            res.GetOutput().replace('\n', ''),
            parent_function_name)
        return output
    else:
        # 6
        return None
```

Here's what that does:

1. You first instantiate a new **SBCommandReturnObject**. You've seen this class already in your primary functions as the result parameter. However, you're creating your own here because you'll use this instance to evaluate and modify an expression. A typical po "something" will produce output, including two newlines, straight to

the console. You need to grab this output before it goes to the console and remove those newlines... because you're fancy like that.

2. Here you create the expression to be executed that prints out the return value. The **getRegisterString** is yet another unimplemented function you'll implement in just a moment — I promise this will be the last time I do that to you! This function will return the syntax needed to get access to the register which holds the return value.

   This is required because you can't know if this script is running on a watchOS, iOS, tvOS, or macOS device, so you'll need to augment the register name depending upon the architecture. Remember also you need to use the Objective-C context, since Swift hides the registers from you!

3. Finally, you execute the expression through the debugger's command interpreter, **SBCommandInterpreter**. This class interprets your commands but allows you to control where the output goes, instead of immediately piping it to stderr or stdout.

4. Once the **HandleCommand** has executed, the output of the expression should now reside in the SBCommandReturnObject instance. However, it's good practice to ensure the return object really has any output to give to us.

5. If everything worked correctly, you format the old, stepped-out function along with the object and currently stopped function into a string and return that.

6. However, if there was no input to print from the SBCommandReturnObject, you return **None**.

One more method, and then you're (sort of) done! Implement getRegisterString at the bottom of your Python script:

```
def getRegisterString(target):
    triple_name = target.GetTriple()
    if "x86_64" in triple_name:
        return "$rax"
    elif "i386" in triple_name:
        return "$eax"
    elif "arm64" in triple_name:
        return "$x0"
    elif "arm" in triple_name:
        return "$r0"
    raise Exception('Unknown hardware. Womp womp')
```

You're using the SBTarget instance to call **GetTriple**, which returns a description of the hardware the executable is designed to run on. Next, you determine which syntax you need to access the register responsible for the return value based on your architecture. If it's an unknown architecture, then raise an exception.

You've done it! Save your work, open Xcode and reload the script with your trusty reload_script command.

Next, before you get started with the full-blown command, remove all previous breakpoints like so:

```
(lldb) br del
About to delete all breakpoints, do you want to do that?: [Y/n]
Y
All breakpoints removed. (1 breakpoint)
```

It's time to take this beauty for a spin!

Type the following into LLDB:

```
(lldb) bar NSObject.init\]
```

This time your script will execute your completed command's script when it hits the breakpoint.

Do whatever you need to do through the tvOS Simulator to trigger the init breakpoint; closing the application will work (⌘ + Shift + H), as will bringing up the Apple TV Remote (found in the **Hardware** menu) and tapping on the remote.

Once hit, you'll get some beautiful output which showcases the method you've stopped on (in this case –[NSObject init]), the object that is being created, and the calling method as well.

Since you've created a breakpoint on a frequently-called method, you'll soon hit the same breakpoint again.

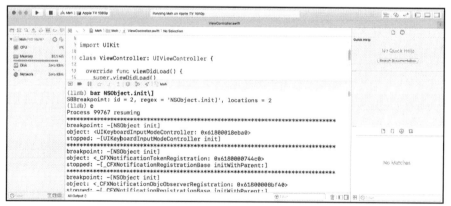

This is a fun tool to have at your disposal. You could, for instance, create a well-crafted regex breakpoint to trigger everytime an NSURL request is created within any application... owned by you or not.

For example, you could try:

```
(lldb) bar NSURL(\(\w+\))?\ init
```

The "weird" syntax is needed because a lot of the initialization methods for NSURL are in categories. Alternatively, you could use this script on a problematic getter method of a Core Data object that is returning unusal values.

You've got the required functionality. It's time to start adding complexity to this script through optional parameters.

Adding script arguments

The lovely thing about LLDB Python scripts is you have all the power of Python — and its modules — at your disposal.

There's three notable modules that ship with Python that are worth looking into when parsing arguments: **getopt**, **optparse**, and **argparse**.

getopt is kind of low level and optparse is on its way out since it's deprecated after Python 2.7. Unforunately argparse is mostly designed to work with Python's sys.argv — which is not available to your scripts. This means optparse will be your go-to option.

Jump to the top of **BreakAfterRegex.py** and add the following import statements:

```
import optparse
import shlex
```

The **shlex** module has a nice little command that conveniently splits up the arguments supplied to your command on your behalf while keeping string arguments intact. optparse will be used to interpret these commands; i.e., what they should do when entered and if they're correct or not.

Head to the very bottom of the **BreakAfterRegex.py** and create the **generateOptionParser** method:

```
def generateOptionParser():
    parser = optparse.OptionParser()
    parser.add_option("-m", "--module",
                      action="store",
                      type="string",
                      dest="module",
                      help="constrain regex to module")
    return parser
```

This simple method generates a parser that allows only one option: -m or --module, followed by a string of input. If present, this option will be stored under the name module (given by the dest option) in a tuple return object that parses the options as a dictionary and the arguments into a separate list.

Jump back to the beginning of breakAfterRegex function and augment it to look like the following:

```
def breakAfterRegex(debugger, command, result, internal_dict):
    '''Creates a regular expression breakpoint and adds it.
    Once the breakpoint is hit, control will step out of the
    current function and print the return value. Useful for
    stopping on getter/accessor/initialization methods
    '''

    # 1
    command_args = shlex.split(command)

    # 2
    parser = generateOptionParser()

    # 3
    try:
        # 4
        (options, args) = parser.parse_args(command_args)
    except:
        result.SetError("option parsing failed")
        return

    target = debugger.GetSelectedTarget()

    # 5
    breakpoint = target.BreakpointCreateByRegex(
    ' '.join(args), options.module)
    # The rest remains unchanged
```

Here's the final code explanation for this chapter!

1. Grab the command function parameter, which is a string, and turn it into a Python list. In addition, the shlex.split method is smart enough to parse arguments whether in single quotes or double quotes.

2. Using the newly created generateOptionParser function, you create a parser to handle the command's input.

3. Parsing input can be error-prone. Python's usual approach to error handling is throwing exceptions. It's no surprise then optparse throws if it finds an error. If you don't catch exceptions in your scripts, LLDB will go down! Therefore, the parsing is contained in a try-except block to prevent LLDB from dying due to bad input.

4. The `OptionParser` class has a **parse_args** method. You're passing in your `command_args` variable, and will receive a tuple in return. This consists of two values: **options**, which consists of all option arguments (i.e. only the `module` argument if present) and **args** which consists of any other input.

   You'll use the `args` list variable, turn it back into a string and apply this command string in `BreakpointCreateByRegex`.

5. You turn the `args` list back into a string. In addition, you add a second parameter. `BreakpointCreateByRegex` has a default parameter of type string, which specifies the module name to constrain your regular expression breakpoint search.

   By default, this parameter is set to **None**, so you can supply the `options.module` variable to the second parameter regardless, since the `options.module` parameter will either be a `string` or **None**, thanks to `OptionParser` doing its job.

Enough code. Reload this thing and see what it does.

Back in Xcode, kill off any previous breakpoints and reload the script.

```
(lldb) break del -f
All breakpoints removed. (1 breakpoint)
(lldb) reload_script
```

Give the `bar` command different permutations of input to see how it handles the logic. Your `bar` command should "blend in" with the other commands available to LLDB.

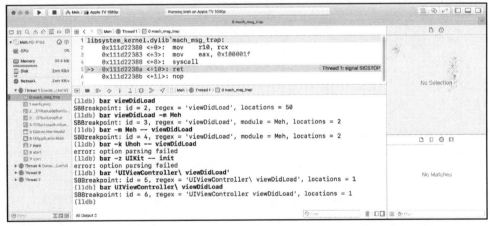

Beautiful. You are on your way to creating some very complex Python scripts!

Where to go from here?

You've begun your quest to create Python LLDB scripts of real-world complexity. In the next chapter, you'll take this script even further and add some cool options.

But for now, have fun and play around with this `bar` script! Attach LLDB to some applications running in the simulator and play around with the command. Try the already mentioned `NSURL` initialization (or `NSURLRequest` initialization) breakpoints.

Once you get bored of that, see what objects are using Core Data by inspecting the return value of `-[NSManagedObject valueForKey:]` or check out all the items that are being created from a nib or storyboard by breaking on an `initWithCoder:` method.

Appendix A: LLDB Cheatsheet

Derek Selander

A cheatsheet for commands and ideas on how to use LLDB.

Getting help

```
(lldb) help
```

List all commands and aliases.

```
(lldb) help po
```

Get help documentation for po (expression) command.

```
(lldb) help break set
```

Get help documentation for breakpoint set.

```
(lldb) apropos step-in
```

Search through help documentation containing step-in.

Finding code

```
(lldb) image lookup -rn UIAlertController
```

Look up all code containing `UIAlertController` that's compiled or loaded into an executable.

```
(lldb) image lookup -rn (?i)hosturl
```

Case insensitive search for any code that contains `"hosturl"`.

```
(lldb) image lookup -rn 'UIViewController\ set\w+:\]'
```

Look up all setter property methods `UIViewController` implements or overrides.

```
(lldb) image lookup -rn . Security
```

Look up all code located within the `Security` module.

```
(lldb) image lookup -a 0x10518a720
```

Look up code based upon address `0x10518a720`.

```
(lldb) image lookup -s mmap
```

Look up code for the symbol named `mmap`.

Breakpoints

```
(lldb) b viewDidLoad
```

Creates a breakpoint on all methods named `viewDidLoad` for both Swift and Objective-C.

```
(lldb) b setAlpha:
```

Creates a breakpoint on either the `setAlpha:` Objective-C method or the setter of the Objective-C `alpha` property.

```
(lldb) b -[CustomViewControllerSubclass viewDidLoad]
```

Creates a breakpoint on the Objective-C method [CustomViewControllerSubclass viewDidLoad].

```
(lldb) rbreak CustomViewControllerSubclass.viewDidLoad
```

Creates a regex breakpoint to match either an Objective-C or Swift class CustomViewControllerSubclass which contains viewDidLoad. Could be Objective-C -[CustomViewControllerSubclass viewDidLoad] or could be Swift ModuleName.CustomViewControllerSubclass.viewDidLoad () -> ().

```
(lldb) breakpoint delete
```

Deletes all breakpoints.

```
(lldb) breakpoint delete 2
```

Deletes breakpoint ID 2.

```
(lldb) breakpoint list
```

List all breakpoints and their IDs.

```
(lldb) rbreak viewDid
```

Creates a regex breakpoint on .*viewDid.*.

```
(lldb) rbreak viewDid -s SwiftRadio
```

Creates a breakpoint on .*viewDid.*, but restricts the breakpoint(s) to the SwiftRadio module.

```
(lldb) rbreak viewDid(Appear|Disappear) -s SwiftHN
```

Creates a breakpoint on viewDidAppear or viewDidDisappear inside the SwiftHN module.

```
(lldb) rb "\-\[UIViewController\ set" -s UIKit
```

Creates a breakpoint on any Objective-C style breakpoints containing -[UIViewController set within the UIKit module.

```
(lldb) rb . -s SwiftHN -o
```

Create a breakpoint on every function in the SwiftHN module, but remove all breakpoints once the breakpoint is hit.

```
(lldb) rb . -f ViewController.m
```

Create a breakpoint on every function found in ViewController.m.

Expressions

```
(lldb) po "hello, debugger"
```

Prints "hello, debugger" regardless of the debugging context.

```
(lldb) expression -lobjc -O -- [UIApplication sharedApplication]
```

Print the shared UIApplication instance in an Objective-C context.

```
(lldb) expression -lswift -O -- UIApplication.shared
```

Print the shared UIApplication instance in a Swift context.

```
(lldb) b getenv
(lldb) expression -i0 -- getenv("HOME")
```

Creates a breakpoint on getenv, executes the getenv function, and stops at the beginning of the getenv function.

```
(lldb) expression -u0 -O -- [UIApplication test]
```

Don't let LLDB unwind the stack if you're executing a method that will cause the program to crash.

```
(lldb) expression -p -- NSString *globalString = [NSString
stringWithUTF8String: "Hello, Debugger"];
(lldb) po globalString
Hello, Debugger
```

Declares a global NSString* called globalString.

```
(lldb) expression -g -O -lobjc -- [NSObject new]
```

Debug the debugger that's parsing the [NSObject new] Objective-C expression.

Stepping

```
(lldb) thread return false
```

Return early from code with `false`.

```
(lldb) thread step-in
(lldb) s
```

Step in.

```
(lldb) thread step-over
(lldb) n
```

Step over.

```
(lldb) thread step-out
(lldb) finish
```

Step out of a function.

```
(lldb) thread step-inst
(lldb) ni
```

Step in if about to execute a function. Step an assembly instruction otherwise.

GDB formatting

```
(lldb) p/x 128
```

Print value in hexadecimal.

```
(lldb) p/d 128
```

Print value in decimal.

```
(lldb) p/t 128
```

Print value in binary.

```
(lldb) p/a 128
```

Print value as address.

```
(lldb) x/gx 0x000000010fff6c40
```

Get the value pointed at by `0x000000010fff6c40` and display in 8 bytes.

```
(lldb) x/wx 0x000000010fff6c40
```

Get the value pointed at by `0x000000010fff6c40` and display in 4 bytes.

Memory

```
(lldb) memory read 0x000000010fff6c40
```

Read memory at address `0x000000010fff6c40`.

```
(lldb) po id $d = [NSData dataWithContentsOfFile:@"..."]
(lldb) mem read `(uintptr_t)[$d bytes]` `(uintptr_t)[$d bytes] +
(uintptr_t)[$d length]` -r -b -o /tmp/file
```

Grab an instance of a remote file and write it to `/tmp/file` on your computer.

Registers & assembly

```
(lldb) register read -a
```

Display all registers on the system.

```
(lldb) register read rdi rsi
```

Read the `RSI` and the `RDI` register in x64 assembly.

```
(lldb) register write rsi 0x0
```

Set the `RSI` register to 0x0 in x64 assembly.

```
(lldb) register write rflags `$rflags ^ 64`
```

Toggle the zero flag in x64 assembly (augment if condition logic).

```
(lldb) register write rflags `$rflags | 64`
```

Set the zero flag (set to 1) in x64 assembly (augment if condition logic).

```
(lldb) register write rflags `$rflags & ~64`
```

Clear the zero flag (set to 0) in x64 assembly (augment if condition logic).

```
(lldb) register write pc `$pc+4`
```

Increments the program counter by 4.

```
(lldb) disassemble
```

Display assembly for function in which you're currently stopped.

```
(lldb) disassemble -p
```

Disassemble around current location; useful if in the middle of a function.

```
(lldb) disassemble -b
```

Disassemble function while showing opcodes; useful for learning what is responsible for what.

```
(lldb) disassemble -n '-[UIViewController setTitle:]'
```

Disassemble the Objective-C –[UIViewController setTitle:] method.

```
(lldb) disassemble -a 0x000000010b8d972d
```

Disassemble the function that contains the address 0x000000010b8d972d.

Modules

```
(lldb) image list
```

List all modules loaded into the executable's process space.

```
(lldb) image list -b
```

Get the names of all the modules loaded into the executable's process space.

```
(lldb) process load /Path/To/Module.framework/Module
```

Load the module located at path into the executable's process space.

Appendix B: Python Environment Setup

Derek Selander

It's not my place to force an IDE on you for Python development. However, if you're actively looking for a Python editor for the Python related chapters — then we should have a little chat. :]

Getting Python

Good news: if you have a Mac, it automatically ships (at the time of writing) with Python version 2.7. This is the same version LLDB uses.

If, for some weird reason, you like to `rm` random things in Terminal and you need to reinstall Python, you can download Python here: https://www.python.org/downloads/. Make sure to download the version of Python that matches the version packaged with LLDB. If you're not sure which version to get, you can get the LLDB Python version through Terminal:

```
lldb
(lldb) script import sys; print sys.version
```

Don't worry about the final part of the version number. If you have 2.7.12 and LLDB quotes 2.7.10, that will work just fine.

Python text editors

A list of Python editors can be found here: https://wiki.python.org/moin/PythonEditors.

For the small, quick Python scripts you'll write in this book, I would recommend using **Sublime Text**. Sublime Text can be found at https://www.sublimetext.com/; although it's a paid application, it's free to try with no time limit.

Both this book, as well as all my LLDB Python scripts, were written (and debugged) through Sublime Text 3.

You'll likely want to install a couple of additional components to Sublime Text to make developing and debugging LLDB Python scripts easier.

The easiest way to install these additional components is to use the Sublime Text Package Control, which is an excellent package manager for Sublime Text. You can find instructions on how to install the Package Control at https://packagecontrol.io/installation;

Once installed, you'll be able to easily search for new components designed for Sublime Text by pressing ⌘ + **Shift** + **P** and typing **install**. A selection item of **Package Control: Install Package** will appear. Select this option.

After the package manager has been installed, you can search for packages that will help you in Python development. Here's a few packages I would recommend using if you're developing in Python:

- **AutoPep8**: Automatically formats Python code to conform to the PEP 8 style guide using `autopep8` and `pep8` modules. https://packagecontrol.io/packages/AutoPEP8

- **PythonBreakpoints**: A Sublime Text plugin to quickly set Python breakpoints by injecting the `set_trace()` call of `pdb` or another debugger of your choice. https://packagecontrol.io/packages/Python%20Breakpoints

- **Anaconda**: Anaconda turns your Sublime Text 3 into a fully featured Python development IDE including autocompletion, code linting, `autopep8` formatting, `McCabe` complexity checker `Vagrant` and `Docker` support for Sublime Text 3 using `Jedi`, `PyFlakes`, `pep8`, `MyPy`, `PyLint`, `pep257` — and `McCabe` will never freeze your Sublime Text 3. https://packagecontrol.io/packages/Anaconda

Working with the LLDB Python module

When working with Python, you'll often import modules to execute code or classes within that module. When working with LLDB's Python module, you'll sometimes come across an `import lldb` somewhere in the script, usually right at the top.

By default, Xcode will launch a version of Python that's bundled within Xcode. When Xcode launches this bundled version of Python, the path to where the lldb module is located is set up automatically. However, in your normal Python development, you won't have access to this module if you were to execute your script through Sublime Text. As a result, you'll need to modify your **PYTHONPATH** environment variable to include the appropriate directory where the lldb Python module lives.

In Terminal, ensure your **~/.bash_profile** exists:

```
touch ~/.bash_profile
```

Open `.bash_profile` file in your favorite text editor (like Sublime!) and add the following line of code:

```
export PYTHONPATH=/Applications/Xcode.app/Contents/
SharedFrameworks/LLDB.framework/Versions/A/Resources/Python:
$PYTHONPATH
```

> **Note**: This assumes your Xcode is located at `/Applications/Xcode.app`. If it isn't, because you particularly like being different, then you'll need to change the path.

Save and close the file. You'll be able to access the lldb module from any Python session on your computer.

Doing this gives you the advantage of checking for syntax errors in Sublime Text (or equivalent) during debugging time — instead of finding a syntax error when your script is loaded into LLDB.

Conclusion

Wow! You've made it all the way to this conclusion! You either must have jumped straight to this page or you're way more masochistic than what I could have anticipated.

This stuff is hard, but if you've made it this far, there's not much stopping you. After a while, the challenge shifts away from technical to mental. That is, the challenge changes from being a question of whether you can figure something out, to a question of how much time can you allocate to understanding a process until you need to move on.

If you have any questions or comments about the projects or concepts in this book, or have any stories to tell from your own debugging adventures, please stop by our forums at http://www.raywenderlich.com/forums.

From here, you have a few paths to explore depending on what you found most interesting in this book.

- If exploring code in Python to make better debugging scripts interests you, then you might want to see what other modules exist in Python 2.7 (or the equivalent Python version LLDB has) to see how far down the rabbit hole you can go. You can find the list of modules in Python 2.7 here: https://docs.python.org/2/py-modindex.html or hunt down one of the many books on Amazon about Python.

- If reverse engineering Apple internals interests you, I would strongly recommend you check out **Jonathan Levin**'s work on anything related to Apple, namely his updated books like **MacOS and iOS Internals, Volume III: Security & Insecurity** at https://goo.gl/23hC3t.

- If more generic reverse engineering/hacking interests you, then you might be interested in **Hacking: The Art of Exploitation, 2nd Edition** by **Jon Erickson** at https://goo.gl/3JNwK8.

- If you want the equivalent of an LLDB newsletter, I would recommend to (nicely!) stalk **Jim Ingram**'s activity on Stack Overflow http://stackoverflow.com/users/2465073/jim-ingham. He works on LLDB at Apple, and combing through his responses on StackOverflow will give you a tremendous amount of insight into LLDB.

Thanks for purchasing this book. If it wasn't for you, I wouldn't be able to make car payments.

Oh, right — and your continued support is what makes the books, tutorials, videos and other things we do at raywenderlich.com possible. We truly appreciate it!

– Derek, Darren, Matt and Chris

The *Advanced Apple Debugging & Reverse Engineering* team

61860071R00162

Made in the USA
Lexington, KY
23 March 2017